"If you're interested   s a must-read."

—b **Berkowitz**
author, *His Secret Life: Male Sexual Fantasy*
commentator, ABC's *The View*
former host, CNBC's *Real Personal*

"*Hot & Heavy* is long overdue; female overeaters have been understudied, ignored and, thereby, deprived of their repressed sexuality. Judi Hollis is bold enough to finally give them a voice with which to demand whatever they want or need."

—**Susan Willard**
director, Eating Disorders Program
Tulane University Medical Center

"Provocative . . . best book on soul food and a view into the private world of the juiciest females."

—**Pat Love**
author, *Hot Monogamy*

"Dr. Hollis shows the connection between feelings of deprivation with food, money or sex. Spiritual fulfillment stops the hungers."

—**Paula Nelson**
author, *The Joy of Money*
commentator, CNN

"Sexy and fun, but grounded in spirit . . . all you need to know about internal grounding to achieve heights of passion and intimacy. . . ."

—**George Viddler**
author, *The Principles of Seduction*

Hot & HEAVY

Finding Your *Soul* Through Food and Sex

JUDI HOLLIS, Ph.D.

Health Communications, Inc.
Deerfield Beach, Florida

www.hci-online.com

Library of Congress Cataloging-in-Publication Data

Hollis, Judi.
  Hot & heavy : finding your soul through food and sex / Judi Hollis.
    p.   cm.
  Includes bibliographical references and index.
  ISBN 1-55874-633-1
    1. Eating disorders—Psychological aspects. 2. Sex (Biology)—Nutritional
aspects. 3. Psychosexual disorders. 4. Women—Mental health. 5. Compulsive
eaters—Rehabilitation. 6. Self-help techniques. I. Title. II. Title: Hot and heavy.
  RC552.E18H65 1998   98-40749
  616.85'26—dc21   CIP

©1998 Judi Hollis

ISBN 1-55874-633-1

Publisher: Health Communications, Inc.
            3201 S.W. 15th Street
            Deerfield Beach, FL 33442-8190

Cover design by Lawna Patterson Oldfield
Cover illustration ©1998 SuperStock, Inc.

*To all the men
I've loved before . . .*

Love is no use unless it's wise and kind and undramatic,
Something steady and sweet to smooth out your nerves when you're tired
Something tremendously cozy and unflurried by scenes and jealousies.
That's what I want, what I've always wanted really.
Oh, my dear, I do hope it's not going to be dull for you.

—Noel Coward
Private Lives

Contents

Author's Invitation and Disclaimer

The names, experiences, writings and statements of patients, clients, listeners or workshop attendees used in this work are thoroughly disguised so there should be no way to identify any specific person.

In my last book, *Fat & Furious,* when I addressed the mother-daughter wound, men complained, "What about us? What about the mother-son thing?" I answered, "My experience is with a predominantly female clientele and I, myself, am female. I wouldn't demean you guys by pretending to be an expert in your experience. Write *your own* books." Some felt validated, appreciated and motivated.

Now in this book about eating and sexuality, I have chosen to focus solely on sex between men and women. Even though I know there are many meaningful, sensual connections within the homosexual community, and that their relationship struggles mirror others, I don't have enough experience with these issues to write about them. I do hope the readers involved can make their own connections. I again invite those who can to find their own voice and write.

Furthermore, the *in-your-face* style of this book is used so that you see a juicy, straight-talkin' woman who can also have a spiritual consciousness. At first, it may offend you to read words describing heaven and spirit alongside those describing bodily functions and copulation. Any feelings of discomfort can signal—for you and for us all—just how strongly our society alienates the body from the soul. This book is an attempt to heal the split caused by that alienation.

Acknowledgments

Writing wrenches my soul and whets my appetite. It's a lot like love. Penetrating the hearts of my readers is a form of intercourse. Sometimes it's predictable, but often it's a surprise. It's always a call to awakening. Some days, I write in a state of amazing grace, and other days I'm doomed to struggle. Thank you for witnessing all sides of this blessing and inspiring me to write difficult truths. I have maintained a faithful readership for over a decade, and I appreciate all the comments and enthusiasm. This book was encouraged and birthed by women around the country who clamored for an honest exploration of food, sex and intimacy. The subject is so personal, it's difficult to stay open. Just as I was finishing rewrites for this book, I led a retreat at the Omega Institute in Rhinebeck, New York. The women assembled there and my co-leader, Terry Nathanson, joined to solidify these ideas. We reached such "over the top" spiritual heights just by attending, witnessing, focusing, dancing and playing. Thanks to them and all my clients for the tremendous privilege and opportunity to bear fair "witness."

I most especially thank the agents and editors who resoundingly rejected this book. Their criticisms helped me improve the manuscript, and their lack of understanding forced me to simplify. They taught me tenacity and faith in my own projects and my own voice. Their fears fueled my courage. I will be ever grateful, as I developed an authentic adult message.

In the final months of working on this manuscript, Yves Bolomet, editor of my first book and adviser to this one, was killed on a motorcycle. He challenged me to stay true to the depth of this message. I've met his challenge and I thank him.

I must thank my parents, Gilbert and Rebecca Stockman, as well as Kris Konold for early encouragement and for alerting me about the difficulties with such a topic.

My dear friend Beverly Rubenstein is a model of courageous womanhood who warns as well as inspires that no matter how hard we're working at this growth thing, it still gets harder! She is a welcome reminder that there is no relief from the authentic life. Nancy Murray has continued as a fervent, loyal supporter who believed so strongly in my work, organized retreats and workshops, and contributed by sharing her own wondrous life. She, along with friends like Helene Robbins, Gail Dubov, Barbara Greene-Ruskin and especially the artist-actress Elizabeth Stephenson, gave me safe harbor for deeply heartfelt discussions. They helped me flesh out my message. My cousin, Carol Schaye-Viegener, and my brother, David Stockman, are two of my favorite soul mates. No matter what the topic, we always open to the same page. What a gift! I've also been blessed with men friends like Bruce James, whose joy-filled spirit has helped launch the "Hollis Hollow" retreats, and Herb Rhodes, who in our friendship and his quiet passing has modeled pure, true love. Dr. Barry Diskant and Dan Gutman are friends who keep teaching me so well the art of fine dining and the sport of intelligent conversation. Hallock Hoffman in Palm Springs and Dave Elders in New York rescued me from so many computer crashes and panics. Jamie Allen transferred copy and was ever eager to revise. My editor, Lisa Drucker, was so enthusiastic throughout the project, "getting it" right away and making the statement ever clearer.

And then there is my "Oh, Henry!" Dr. Henry Kaplan has awakened me to higher vibrations as I grow into a permeable, resonating, spiritual adult.

I was an oak. Now I'm a willow. Now I can bend. . . .

Preface

"The truth is, I am still looking for a man who can excite me as much as a baked potato." My actress friend Savannah Boucher wrote and delivered that line in the Henry Jaglom film *Eating*.

Doesn't food serve best to soothe the savage beast? You're totally in control. And food asks little of you. Men can be such trouble at times, and eating is often more intimate. A lot of women choose the immediate and transitory comfort of food over the more demanding and often less satisfying comfort of sexual couplings. Eating is oh-so-intimate. There is nothing *more* intimate. You actually use your own juices to digest the food you eat. Then, miracle of miracles, the digested food builds new cells—new parts of *you!* Food does an awful lot and quickly. Sex can do a lot, too, but more slowly. Let's explore how and why it's worth the wait.

Over the past thirty years, in public seminars and private therapy sessions, I realized I was leading women toward recognizing a painful reality. A great neediness was brimming. It was more than the need for excess food. It was a growing sexual energy, a longing to connect. I specialized as an addictionologist and eating disorders therapist, but I saw a vital link between curbing excess food intake and listening to that awakening sexual energy. There was a danger that if overeaters gave up excess food, they'd face other important longings: longings to touch and be touched. Sexual energy builds up in ballooning bodies.

An early patient reported a vital tool she'd used. "Once I lost ninety pounds. I subdued *my* compulsion to eat by masturbating up to six times a day! But I felt like a freak, and I had no one with whom to share my feelings. I went back to the food." She needed physical stimulation, as well as true contact and intimacy.

It's time to face up to that sexual/spiritual longing. I won't write this out on a prescription pad for you, but conscious, connected sex *can* curb appetite. It helps along with any diet plan or aerobic workout. Like many others, I didn't know how to address the sexual component, so I left the connection between sex and weight unexplored and unmentioned. After all, I was a psychologist, not a sex therapist. I was also afraid to address women's appetites for sex, as I'd be subject to those old locker-room jokes: "She just needs to get laid."

Instead of addressing sexual yearnings, I continued teaching behavior modification, family dynamics and spiritual integrity. I started the first eating disorder unit, wrote books, trained counselors, appeared on television, hosted my own radio show and avoided the sex thing. Now, after over two decades of maintaining my own eighty-pound weight loss and treating countless compulsive eaters, I am ready to deal with the crux of the matter, the nitty-gritty . . . *the sex thing.*

For a long time, I was content to remain mute. Every time I'd mention the connections between eating and sex, friends giggled and made the inevitable banana jokes. They didn't want to address a hunger that was briefly sated by foraging in kitchens, but left unsatisfied and ravenous in bedrooms. Women were on the prowl, but no one wanted to talk about what they were actually "stalking about."

No wonder. They all were eating instead! Everywhere around me, I saw women acting more sexually liberated—but ultimately feeling less satisfied. There was a lot of bed hopping, but little connection. Nothing is more disappointing than an unfulfilled quest for connection. Marilyn French, in *The Women's Room*, wrote, "Loneliness is not a longing for company, but a longing for kind." To connect with "our kind of people," my clients and I found that we first have to find out who *we* are, and then know clearly when the connection is (or isn't) made. Our bodies are perfect sensors for that, but if overstuffed, they can't resonate or indicate. We had to learn to tolerate the emptiness first, so we could sense with more clarity.

I remember flying in the cockpit with my ex and hearing the controller in the tower say: "United Heavy 426 for runway one niner left." That meant United Airlines' wide-bodied jumbo jet, flight number 426, was landing on the left runway #19. I always liked it when they said "heavy." These jets were given special respect and due consideration *because* they were heavy. Everyone knew they had special needs, but also special qualities and capabilities. They could land in extreme conditions. They had what it takes. They had *power!* Maybe "women of substance," women with heavy bodies, women who sense well, have special powers. They have to be dealt with differently.

I've dedicated my life to listening to the messages from those women's bodies. Not all my patients are fat, but they are all blessed with supersensitivity. In order to curb their appetites, they must pay attention to themselves. I believe those of us blessed with these "heavy" bodies are also the people who, in street lingo, are "heavy, man." We've got something to say. We need connection with partners to take us home to our own internal messenger.

I can understand if you'd rather go back to counting calories instead of attending to your sexy body. I certainly wanted to avoid this dilemma. It seemed safer. Then Penny showed up—or rather, she didn't. She'd made an appointment to see me in my New York office but couldn't make it in. She broke three separate appointments before I finally took action. I called her at home in New Jersey, two hours before the scheduled time. She'd already left me a message saying that she would mail a check for the canceled session. I called anyway and encouraged her to jump in the car and come to the city. "If you are paying anyway, why not use your time wisely?"

"But I don't really think I'm ready. I don't really know what I'll talk about," she replied. Many women felt as Penny did. They'd read *Fat & Furious* and had been awakened; they wanted consciousness, but they were also terrified.

I answered gently, "You *are* ready or you wouldn't have made the call. You don't have to know in advance what to talk about. Let's just sit and see."

"Okay, I'll be there!" she shouted hurriedly, as I heard the receiver *click*.

She arrived not one minute late and proceeded at once.

"I know it's about sex, and that's why I didn't want to come. My husband and I haven't slept together for fifteen years. He just started getting tired. I didn't want to bother. We just stopped. It all seemed like too much trouble. There was something missing. We didn't know what, but I guess because of my supersensitivity, I just knew it wasn't authentic. It just didn't seem worth doing."

Worth doing!

There it was: the reason this book had to be written. What else in all of life is more worth doing? Because conscious sexual connection is *so* important, it is also the most disowned, avoided and secret part of our lives.

I discovered that back in 1985 with the publication of my first bestseller, *Fat Is a Family Affair*. As I lectured throughout the country, people approached enthusiastically. They recounted many benefits the book had brought to their lives. They'd cite the concepts of *addiction* and the *family dynamics*, or the *behavior modification* suggestions.

There was one hidden line they never mentioned. It was an important point about paying attention and staying focused while making love. I encouraged readers to avoid disengaged sex. Most of us had experienced getting into bed, becoming sexually aroused and involved, and then losing it. Our thoughts strayed to the grocery list or problems at work, but we kept on pumping and pretending. Most of us pretend we are still there even though we've left the room.

When I mentioned briefly the emptiness of uninvolved and unconscious sex, I pointed out that surely our partners knew they'd been abandoned, and that we'd abandoned a crucial part of ourselves. I argued that such abandonment and unconsciousness in bed would lead us to binge in the kitchen.

In my second book, *Fat & Furious*, I explained how women's supersensitive bodies made us so aware that we needed a lot of comforting. We just didn't know how to listen to ourselves. Excess food served to stifle a voice crying to be heard. We had to learn how to listen to the wisdom of the body. Women's bodies are built for aware entry, and we ache in an almost audible way.

Still, few people came to see me initially talking about their sex lives. They were afraid. So was Penny. Penny knew she'd made a certain accommodation in her marriage; she'd made a decision to just let her sexual life fall away. It left her ravenous, fat and furious, hot and heavy. Penny began a journey that day that took her out of the kitchen, back to her bedroom and into her life. Since you started this book, you are up for the same journey. It is a journey back to your animal and spiritual self.

Bon Voyage!

---

*I don't see much of Alfred anymore
now that he is writing that
book about sex.*

—Mrs. Alfred Kinsey

Introduction

---

*If one wished to be perfectly sincere,
one would have to admit there are
two kinds of love—well-fed and ill-fed.
The rest is pure fiction.*

—COLETTE

New York magazine restaurant critic Gael Greene said, "Great food is like great sex—the more you have the more you want."

It's often difficult to describe a great meal. There's trouble sometimes saying exactly how something tasted. Somehow everything new and exotic tastes "a little like chicken."

Well, great sex is like that, too. You may not be able to describe it, but you surely know when it's good and when it's not. In the final analysis, you *do* know when sex works for you and when it doesn't. You know when "enough is enough," and you know when "more is better." Now think about your two very natural, organic, driving forces—your hunger for food and your hunger for sex.

To eat or love well, you must pay full *attention* to the
details and be truly alive in the moment. To fully enjoy your
meal, you must be aware of every nuance—smell, taste, texture and aftertaste. The same is true of sex. There is a direct
link between food consciousness and sex consciousness.
Eating and copulating are our two animal acts. As you eat or
live consciously, you create a unity of body and mind, and of
animal and spirit. Alienation of your animal and spiritual
selves is what caused your addictions. Carl Jung said that
addicts suffered "a hole in the soul." In this book, we will fill
that hole.

You can find your soul by changing how you take in either
food or sex. By practicing "mindfulness," paying attention in
both the bedroom and the dining room, you will slow down to
hear the vibrations of your inner essence. You will discover
your own true nature, a quiet but powerful voice you've
muffled with excess. Your soulful Self has been waiting,
watching you career between starvation and indulgence, and
now she waits in the center of your being. You will find that
voice centered where body and soul unite. Paying attention to
what you are doing in both eating and loving will keep you
out of excess and into more natural choices. The natural body
seeks homeostasis, equilibrium, the middle path. A content
natural spirit seeks equanimity, a still state, the middle path.
Excesses leave you in an unsteady state, out of sorts, seeking,
grabbing, unfulfilled.

It's not what you do, but how you do it. Think about it!
Haven't some bouts in bed left you satisfied for days while
others sent you straight to the refrigerator? You ask, "Why do
I feel this way?" What happens that makes each experience so
different? You already know it's not about orgasms alone.

Satisfaction is about whether *you* showed up consciously or not, whether at the table or in bed.

Paying conscious attention to how you eat can help you stay equally conscious in your bedroom. The opposite is also true. Consciousness in bed will change what you do in the kitchen. You'll learn to go deeper, to have the soulful experience of taking the outside environment into the temple of your body. Your struggles with food are about owning both your physical and spiritual natures. Once those two are united and integrated, your bedroom will be your cathedral and a brownie will never taste the same.

I invite you now to try on a new way of thinking about sexuality. This is a frank discussion of some new *possibilities* to help you heal. It's an erotic path to your soulful Self. If you've been turning to excess food, you need to find other forms of eroticism. You long for thoughtful connection, release, orgasm and sensation. But, along with physical pleasure, you can use sex to actually transcend the body. Then you'll deal with surrendering ego, acceptance and other spiritual concerns. You've tried countless other ways to lose weight. Now let's try conscious sex. It's time to birth yourself into your life. Let's get back to bed instead of out to lunch.

Some of us are insatiable when it comes to eating, no matter how many diets we briefly master. This insatiability is often a wonder to medical science. Doctors don't understand bypass patients who regain hundreds of pounds. Why do we eat so ravenously? Recently researchers disclosed they had isolated the gene that controls "appetite." They conjecture that in a few years, they'll have a pill to control satiety levels. We won't feel hungry. Then, in theory, we won't want to eat. Really? Can you honestly say that you're eating because of physical hunger? How much? Unfortunately, our appetites have little to do with hunger or satiety. We are responding to a deep urge, and we've been mistakenly using food to satisfy it. It's sex we need instead. Is there a pill for that appetite?

Maybe PMS—Pretty Miserable Sex—causes your overeating. The sex is miserable because it feels so unconnected. To answer your need for connection, you'll have to learn to take more time in the bedroom, as well as in the kitchen. Slowing down in the bedroom will slim your body and awaken your spirit, too.

I first saw the need for writing this book while leading a retreat in Kailua, Hawaii. As is often the case, I found an audience perfectly in tune and working with me, as I discussed the society's subjugation of women, our needs to own power and so on. My ideas were validated by countless nodding heads. Then I mentioned the scarcity of sexual men who could keep up with a healthy woman's appetites. The audience clammed up. Some got hungry, even though we'd just had lunch.

As I approached the sex talk, I presented one of my standard lectures about the *terrible too*s: how women are "too much" and how we're instructed to pare ourselves down to size so that we won't threaten anyone. I spoke to the group about how powerful women are called "castrating"—their assuming power automatically means taking something away from men. Ever since Sigmund Freud, men have been trying to convince us of how much we want to seize and rule their genitals. I promoted a discussion of this problem by asking anyone to describe her feelings of penis envy.

No woman could describe such a feeling. Women couldn't care less about owning a phallus—erect or flaccid. Most expressed consternation about imagined troubles living with an external dangling organ: "How do they walk with those things?"

Obviously, the whole concept of penis envy is something men suffer. It is something they visit on each other in high school locker rooms. Freud's theory claimed it was something about power. Supposedly, we want to capture male power as symbolized by the phallus. But if we are truly in touch with our own power, our burgeoning sexual energies, why would we want someone else's?

Anyway, there I was, railing on to a roomful of overweight women who thought they were in for nothing more than a diet talk. I told them that no word comparable to *castration* exists to describe the act of a man taking away a woman's sexual energy. Women weren't complaining that men were stealing their "femininity." Our sexuality was safely harbored within, not dangling without. I suggested that maybe the men coveted our wombs instead. Maybe we don't have words because the idea that man wants woman's sexual energy is such a powerful truth that we can't even speak its name.

I was on a roll. On and on I went, sneaking looks all the while at a stunning native woman who had caught my eye earlier because she seemed so disinterested in my lecture. She was a beautiful, large wahine who sat quietly, looking into her lap. I couldn't get a read on her involvement, identification or even interest. Was she bored? She wasn't taking notes; she just sat there, head bent, staring at the matted straw carpet.

I continued with my presentation, challenging my audience to find a word comparable to "castration" that describes a man *de-sexing* a woman. I railed, "There is no such word!"

She raised her head and shouted, "Yes there is— MARRIAGE!"

We all broke into laughter, loud and long. I sought her out at a coffee break the next day and opened with, "When you spoke yesterday we all laughed, but it really isn't funny. In fact, it's very profound."

She looked me dead on. "It's also very true . . ." she began haltingly. "I married two of them. They turn you into their mothers, and then they won't sleep with you." She started to cry. So did I. We held each other. We knew that women worked doubly hard at nurturing, supporting and excusing. We can copy what we saw our mothers giving as love, but it may serve to turn our men away. Even if we can give "good mother," our eating problems are better healed if we learn to be good lovers.

Mothering activity is wasted on most men. It infantilizes them and keeps them childlike. That "good mother" role is best left out of the bedroom. But it is the role we trained for all our lives. We watched our mothers by day. Once we were older, no one taught us how to sleep with our men at night.

We've disowned and sublimated the "lover" part of ourselves: our spiritually aware, sensual, "natural woman." It was safer to be in control as a "mom" rather than be at risk as a true sexual partner.

It is time to move on to greater intimacy. Start this next stage of the journey while still fat, so when the weight comes off, you'll be up for it. If you keep living in that "when I get thin" dress rehearsal for life, then you'll be ill prepared when life shows up. Begin at once and do your best.

We'll now embark on a journey to love and eat consciously. Loving consciously will be even harder than eating consciously. New questions will emerge. How will you maintain your separateness while staying open and vulnerable? How will you be penetrated? How do you penetrate another? You know how much you long for and fear penetration. It's a new frontier. Your body was made for it. That fully rounded, voluptuous, female body was built for comfort . . . not for speed.

This next adventure is meant to comfort as well as take you higher. It involves reclaiming all your disowned parts, becoming a fully integrated, conscious adult. All this from just a little sex? Yes! There is a lot of personal growth riding on our sexual backs. In the following pages, you will find ways to get back to your inner Self in bed. It is an almost religious experience. Sex connects you to the spirit world. Conscious lovemaking is like dying in order to be reborn. The French refer to orgasm as *la petite mort*—the little death. You will shed your old self and birth the new. Surrendering to your highest Self is what you were sent here to do. Listen to the passionate, poignant sounds of ecstatic gospel singers. Their rounded torsos vibrate toward heaven while they rock with feet planted firmly on the ground. A reviewer said of Aretha Franklin, "She makes salvation sound erotic and the erotic sound like salvation."

In chapter 1, you'll see how our culture's unrealistic body standards have kept you focused on the wrong subjects, to the point of making sex dirty, addictive and a medical malady rather than a source of joy, spirit and power. You'll see how you have been culturally programmed into self-hate instead of self-love.

In chapter 2, you'll learn to question all the psychobabble explanations that have kept you at the refrigerator instead of in bed! Some see sex as the "problem." I see it as the "solution." Sex is something we're "supposed" to do if we want to stay grounded in nature and true to our spirits.

Chapter 3 explains why it's time to start *dating*. You'll meet some models of truly sexual, frolicking, fornicating women. Why are more women choosing to remain single? Do they understand better what sex is all about? If not for snaring a mate, why, and whither, and with whom?

Chapter 4 teaches the value of holding out, being mindful of what kind of sex you want. Examining aspects of visibility and permeability in your sex life will help you pursue more spiritual satisfactions. You'll hold out for the right person, time and space.

In chapter 5, you will pay exquisite attention to all personal entries, whether at mealtime or bedtime. You'll learn to savor and suck every morsel of pleasure from food and mates. You will practice the "Divine Dine," to focus eating toward both spirituality and eroticism.

In chapter 6, you'll get closer to the bone and your own personal home. Eastern religions tell us that "the vulva is gateway to the soul." I will be asking you to keep a "vulva vigil," paying conscious attention to any penetrations of your body and psyche. This is very serious business. You will see how proper "conscious coitus" opens us to a new level of personal insight. You'll eat as you love and love as you eat.

BON APPETIT!

One

Conscious Coitus

A healthy person will resist having to choose between food and sexuality.

—Virginia Woolf

Why even think of having to choose between food and love? Aren't they the same thing? Some say, "Eating is good girls' sex." What's the connection? We actually eat the sexuality of plants in their fruits and seeds. There's food and sex everywhere. Why have to choose between food and sex? If you understand completely why this is a crucial and essential question, then this book is for you. If you don't quite get the connection, then this book is also for you. If you've suffered with weight problems and/or unsatisfying sex, then this book is definitely for you. As you read, you'll see that you really have no choice: Whether eating or loving, if you want to lose weight and keep it off, you must remain conscious. Doing so will enable you to eat and love well. If you eat well, you will love well and vice versa, because you are reprogramming your innermost self to walk with dignity, integrity and consciousness. You won't take your body anywhere your soul can't follow.

Think about what made some sexual encounters unsatisfying and why you mistakenly turn to food instead. Conscious, focused, almost mystical sex is a transformative experience. You might have resisted this potential for change and hidden in excess food. Both eating and making love are physical experiences, and your body must be respected and satisfied. You are a physical organism as well as a spiritual presence. Virginia Woolf noted, "One cannot think well, sleep well, love well if one has not dined well." Our ability to consciously savor the sensual experiences of eating and loving will keep our bodies and psyches aligned.

In this chapter, you will investigate cultural programming that taught you to demean body wisdom, and, instead, to focus on grooming your body for barter or sale. You need to walk softly toward the middle path of listening to your body and paying attention to your womanly wisdom. You will sing along with Saffire and the Uppity Blues Women, "Wild Women Don't Worry, Wild Women Never Get the Blues." If you are wild as well as wise, you'll birth yourself as a blending of total woman.

Ultimately, health involves moderation in all things. With sex, how do you find moderation? What is too much or not enough sex? Is the answer necessarily dependent on a partner? Can you use sex to keep from eating? Do you starve in the bedroom as well as the dining room? Have you become a gourmand with sex, or do you just keep your taste buds primed for food? Eating has been your most satisfying sensual experience. To lessen its importance, you must develop other sensual pleasures; satisfying sex is one of them. Don't binge in the kitchen and don't rush in the bedroom.

You will develop sensuous pleasures by *conscious coitus*, loving consciously. In conscious coitus, you'll increase your ability to pay attention each and every moment. You'll stop focusing on beauty and learn to emphasize "booty," the gift of your resonant body. Sugar- and fat-free, that sensitive instrument can take a lovely experience to a higher level.

You eat and confirm your existence. It is something so primitive and primordial, it gets you down to basics and up to the cosmos. It is so intimate. You take in the outside world, pick it up and on your own, by yourself, put it in your mouth, thus crossing your own boundaries. Thus you bring the world into your temple. You taste and chew it and ultimately swallow it, and thus know you are truly alive. It is a ritual that is sensually satisfying, and also reassuring that you are still on the planet and part of the ongoing drama. It has a certain security about it, coupled with a bit of surprise. It fills vacant time. There is an immediacy about food and a rhythm in how you take it in. It's sometimes heavenly.

Conscious coitus can be the same way. With the addition of a partner who is truly there, alive, pulsating and conscious, it can be even better. Problem is, it can also be quite scary. It often feels safer to reach for a donut. But donuts are much less satisfying. They don't fill the hole in the soul.

Even though conscious sexuality is often more satisfying than eating, it is fraught with paradox. You will go further into the body in order to transcend and leave the body. When you have conscious, connected lovemaking, you'll leave the planet and enter the cosmos. You've got to believe in that potential. It won't happen every time, but you've got to know it's possible. If copulation has no higher meaning, then we are doomed. You were given this life in order to work on your spiritual and physical connections. If you're not in it for spirit's sake, but instead just in it for spreading seed or getting off, then to paraphrase popular folk wisdom, "A stiff man has no conscience, and a moist woman rules the world." As that moist woman, you must use your power responsibly. You'll have to first face major fears of the power of your sexuality.

If you've grown up in this society, you probably have many conflicts about sexuality and food. With either the gift of eating or of sexuality, we must negotiate the gap between feelings of fullness and emptiness. Both food and sex can have low and high meanings. We vacillate from spent and drained to exuberant and almost mystical. You can have both high-class and low-down experiences. You can travel from down and dirty, primitive and guzzling, to spiritual and cosmic; instead of falling, you can rise in love.

Do you fear the power of all that juicy, moist womanhood? Naomi Wolf, in *The Beauty Myth*, tells us that in higher primates, females are the sexual initiators. In many goddess-worshiping cultures, goddesses had many lovers. Some other religions feared the power of "insatiable" females. They saw these women as capable of continual and varied orgasms. Women's capacity for pleasure is inexhaustible.

Women who like to eat have the potential for soulful connection. Food writer M. F. K. Fisher felt that eating was basically a brutish, physical function, like breathing or defecating.

Yet, in her writing, she elevates eating to a *high level* of appreciation. She found that food could bring pleasure in more ways than just alleviating hunger. The same is true of sex. Fisher did not elevate the quality of the food, but rather the *eater* and the eater's consciousness. Food was not elevated in dignity and power, but the person was. That person's eating was an entrée to higher consciousness. Conscious coitus is also. Through seeing the similarities between eating and loving, you increase your enjoyment of both and will transcend yourself.

So, in seeking sex, you are responding to a higher calling. You were given the rare power of discernment regarding sex in order to treat it more reverently. Only one other species has this gift: dolphins. Humans and dolphins are the only two species whose females are available for year-round mating. All other species have cycles and seasons of "heat." They desire sex only when fertile. We are fertile for only a few days each month, but we are always available for sex. We are in daily heat. We and our dolphin sisters are both considered highly intelligent life forms. Why are we both blessed with this gift of choice? Other animals only desire sex to propagate the species. We decide each time whether we do or don't want sex. We don't have to rush headlong into anything, because we have 364 more days to mate. While other species act purely on instinct, we can use sex as an invitation to something else. This makes the effort more meaningful.

Why else were we given this gift? We've certainly populated the planet, but have we elevated it? In approaching the millennium, it is our destiny and our duty to educate ourselves and our partners to go higher with sexuality. Presidential escapades make headline news, cybersex chat rooms provide anonymity and continuous scandals of preacher predilections abound while Americans continue to grow fatter. It falls to those of us suffering food cravings to bring consciousness into our kitchens and bedrooms. As you read countless self-help and diet books, you'll see that eating disorders have become our nation's major epidemic. We have a very acquisitive, consumptive society gobbling up both the earth and its food. Even so, women are hungry to reclaim their sensual selves.

Malling America

You've been programmed to avoid sex by shopping. Instead of "getting down," you get dressed up. A consumer society certainly keeps you needy and searching: It develops ever more interesting styles and widgets and then convinces you that you need them. Advertisers want you discontent and out of bed shopping. Spirituality is the last thing they would market, because there is nothing to sell. Marketing is geared to get you out buying cars to impress your friends, costumes to dress your doll self and new sofas to park on when you come home tired. When the shops close, you are ravenous. The spirit lies within and you need nothing to find it other than focused attention. If too content, you'd just stay home in bed, so the market economy debases spirituality and erotic love.

If you have been buying the popular women's magazines and following their advice—their "rules"—then you are right on schedule to get and stay fat. Why? First of all, the magazines are funded by advertisers—the same people who want you out shopping. They are instructing you to feel bad about yourself. They don't teach you about developing *you*, but more about packaging yourself.

I am inviting you to focus in on yourself as a product of nature. You are here to live, not to be evaluated. Oysters produce pearls as a by-product of trying to rid themselves of irritation. Beauty is an afterthought, not the goal. For modern women physical beauty has become a goal. It must instead become a by-product. Both weight loss and sex have to be approached the same way. You can want whatever goals you want, but pay attention to the journey. As a woman seeking conscious coitus, your journey may take longer than that of other women who are willing to settle. You have to decide which kind of woman you are.

It falls to women to reclaim our sensual, animal natures. Remember how long our country existed before women gained the right to vote? At the very time that the women's suffrage movement was flowering, Carl Jung visited our shores in 1912. At that time, he was making his break from the mechanistic sexuality of Sigmund Freud. Jung wrote that if America could, ". . . eliminate prudery, it may become the greatest country the world has ever known." As it was, he felt, "America is the most tragic country in the world today. American wives throw themselves into social activism because they are not happy with their husbands." Modern women now buy memberships at stainless-steel workout gyms. These new sweat shops harbor the angst of the diet revolution.

It's time to trade sweating for petting. As an overeater, you love and need sensuous, soulful sex. You can't play coy games about it. Looks mean nothing here. There is a big difference between packaging yourself for barter and preparing yourself for soulful connection. This book is not about sex for fat ladies. It's for all women of the past four generations, raised in the United States, who hate *feeling* fat.

Fat and thin women want to claim their own souls with their men. You must learn to be huntress for the soul. Give yourself permission to be a sexual predator. You may have been trained to believe that your body is a stimulant and attractant, there for *him*, not for you. If so, you want to be looked at to be turned on. You don't know how to feed your own sensuality; instead, you look for *him* to feed it. You must turn from being a sex object to become a sex subject. You don't wait for someone to take you and tell you what you want. Instead, identify your own wants. You might be afraid of who you will become. Women with eating disorders especially have great fears of seeming selfish and sensually voracious. Amy Bloom, in *New Woman* magazine, asks us to consider: "What will happen if we pay more attention to sensuality than to ripples in our thighs? We might set our standards so high that indifferent sex and empty connections become intolerable. We might know and love our core, most private selves, and we might expect nothing less from our lovers."

A Call to Awakening

You can't escape how much you *need* this soulful connection, and you must listen to that call. With the "graying of America," we'll all be paying more attention to conscious couplings than to quickies. As you grow older, you'll be more in tune with what you like. Most older women give up some of the focus on body image. They are more accepting of their imperfections, and many are tired of suffering. They crave connection as much as affection. They also give themselves permission to acknowledge lusty thoughts and the need for sex. The American Menopause Foundation recommends that for hot flashes, night sweats, insomnia, vaginal changes and the general malaise of menopause, more and better sex is an acceptable treatment. By the time they reach menopause, women are more discerning and more capable of conscious coitus. They want to be caressed, not mauled. They might ask for things they wouldn't dare mention at twenty. They know longevity and well-being are at stake. One woman told me, "I've got my body figured and my mate trained. Lovemaking isn't at all silent hoping and frantic squirming anymore."

Menopausal women can be helped tremendously by trading food for sex. Lovemaking triggers the release of the hormone oxytocin, which sharpens intellect, intuition and creativity. It is responsible for the *afterglow*, as well as the heightened awareness many experience during pregnancy, breast-feeding and menstruation. This afterglow from orgasm can relieve the pain from headaches and PMS, fight heart disease and keep estrogen levels up, thereby maintaining bone density and supple skin. Not only that, it boosts immunity, and the act itself burns calories!

It's also good for what ages you. Beatrice Wood, a potter who worked in her studio every day until she died at age 105, romanced writer Henri-Pierre Roche, thus inspiring the François Truffaut *ménage à trois* film, *Jules et Jim*. She attributed her staying power to "chocolates and young men— I'm enthusiastic about both." She maintained a lifelong abhorrence of alcohol, stating emphatically, "I wanted to be sober when I was seduced."

Does sober seduction get your attention? I want to whet your appetite for conscious coitus soul travel. I want you to consider "using" your partner to take yourself home to soul. You need connection to the cosmos in order to stop clamoring for excess food. Watching your connection when getting into the rhythm of making love is fascinating. That's a much more involving task than ordering out for Chinese food or following the *New York Times* recipe of the week. It involves discarding a focus on packaging for a focus on soulful vibrations.

Body as Spiritual Conduit or Prize

When we stay conscious of packaging but unconscious of vibration, we are diverted from the deeper work of attention to penetration, vulnerability and connection. It is easier to stay focused on unrealistic body images. In the United States, we want women's bodies to resemble those of twelve-year-old boys. If you have enough leisure time, you can abuse yourself into such a form. Fat or lean becomes a social class issue. Rosie O'Donnell appeals to the fat Kmart shopper but Jackie Collins graces pages of *Gourmet* and *Architectural Digest* magazines. In America, we followed thin-as-a-rail socialites like Lee Radziwill, and worldwide we worshiped Princess Di, who publicly acknowledged her struggles with bulimia. Whatever methods they use to get there, thin is high class.

For those aspiring to these social classes, you can truly never be too rich or too thin. Any roundness is suspect. I treated the owner of a fashionable, expensive Arizona health spa who pampered beautiful women from worldwide locations. Though attractive and of medium build, she could not accept her slightly rounded body. She was obsessed with attaining the boardlike body of a twelve-year-old boy. Although voted a popular magazine's Woman of the Year, she died on an operating table during intestinal bypass surgery.

Acquiring status through thinness is a relatively modern phenomenon. The ancients admired the more rotund. Ancient cultures were more attuned to fat as a sexy thing. Goddesses were full figured. They were abundant. Our modern anorexics stop menses and have no juices flowing. They've reduced the life force. They can't receive and can't give, and their vibrancy slows down measurably. They've bought into and acted out a cultural expectation to keep wild women's impulses in check. Those skeletal forms become an impenetrable wall of resistance, making those around them feel inadequate. Notice if you found this talk of "juicy women" offensive. Do you think it gross? Do you find anything gross about skeletal models who grace fashion magazines, looking vacant, lifeless and beaten? Which is truly gross?

We saw such emaciated bodies as World War II ended. When the Allies liberated prisoners from concentration camps, the results of man's inhumanity to man appalled us. Yet, today, we applaud a woman who imposes the same starvation upon herself. In America, after the war, powerful women returned from munitions factories back to homes with well-stocked Amana freezers. They mended, ironed, pushed themselves into pointy bras and then became dinosaurs who couldn't adapt. At that time, we wanted hourglass figures with rounded bodies, sexy like Marilyn Monroe. Soon Twiggy appeared as the antiwoman. Even though *she* hated the look, the culture loved it. It forced us to focus on unrealistic body size and limited female power. In 1929, the first Miss America was 5 feet, 4 inches tall and weighed 135 pounds. Today's average Miss America is 5 feet, 8 inches tall and weighs 116 pounds. In the 1960s, the average fashion model was fifteen pounds lighter than the average American woman. In the 1990s, she is thirty-five pounds lighter and four inches taller. Only 2 percent of America's females will achieve a fashion model's body without vomiting.

Today, we make a lot more money but spend a lot more of it on weight loss and treatment programs. All this because we can't really tolerate the idea of sexually powerful women. A woman liking sex is a bit too demanding. A self-loving woman who admits she likes sex may initially be attractive to a man, but the attraction often wanes. A woman looking a man directly in the eye, full frontal, delivers a message that she likes herself and she likes sex. That may be hard to take. Can she look him in the eye and have her orgasm too?

In order to avoid our sexual natures, we allow competitive cultural standards to divert us and turn us into objects of worship. We forget that life is in session. This is really and truly your one and only life. When your body quits, your life is over. Your body is your vehicle for enjoying this planet. When you objectify yourself, your body loses meaning as a life-giving organism. *You* become owned by the culture. Some say that those of us with eating disorders, whether fat or emaciated, are launching a protest vote against all this. Eating was our solution to the struggle. The solution now brings serious problems. If you hide in body-image struggles, you never have to truly develop the person within the cage to have grown-up sex.

No wonder we bought into this way of seeing ourselves. It's much easier to have an objective numerical standard than to accept yourself as a pulsating, changeable being. It also lessens your own personal responsibility if someone outside yourself makes the decisions about you being mateable or not. When others' standards rule, then you are off the hook. You won't learn anything though. Perfect bodies, 36-24-36, are easily recognizable. Appreciating something different requires more explanation to self and others. It requires owning one's own personal preferences and quirks. It involves living as a truly authentic being.

When you stop attending to others' standards and spend more time on your own evaluations, you will find it's not so

great *just* to be chosen. You'll have to ponder more meaningful questions. Sharon, a newly slim overeater, asked her new
beau, "How and when did you know you wanted to sleep with
me?" She was flattered at being so readily and easily desired,
but she was also confused. Maybe if she hadn't just lost so
much weight, she'd know more about this adventure. They'd
waited three months and now were contemplating doing *it*.

"About a half hour after I met you," he replied with a chuckle.

"But how did you know I was the one? Why me?"

"Because I'm a man, that's why."

That alone was not enough for her. Because she's a woman.
. . . *That's why*.

Her concerns and considerations about the act go much
deeper and penetrate to the soul of her being. Like many
women, she'd love to be swept away. She'd been titillated in
the 1960s by Erica Jong and others writing about quick and
easy sex, but if the truth were known, she was more calculat-
ing about it, especially this first time with a new man and
after such a long time. She had shaved her legs, perfumed,
powdered and prepared for entry. She was fully conscious and
alive and had no intention of leaving the scene.

She was concerned to keep her partner there as well. She
needed a partner who could show up and be fully present.
Though flattered and definitely interested, her agenda went
far beyond "being chosen." As she'd been losing the hundred
pounds, she'd found her fill of "choice, chosen, choosing." She'd
been raised for packaging and was flattered to be a tomato,
chick, doll or fox. Any object would do. It was nice to be mar-
ketable. However, without the excess weight, she received
signals from her body that had to do with connection and
nuances of vibration. Her sugar- and fat-free body was like a

sonar signaling that the ship was ready to dock. She couldn't make that connection unless all systems were go. Many men had come and gone without the patience or interest to go to the places she had in mind.

This one had stayed and waited. His voice was what first attracted her. It was so resonant. She responded on the level of vibration. She'd heard him before she saw him. His soft, somewhat raspy tone had sent a warming pulse to her. She'd almost melted then, and as they spent time together, their similar interests and sensibilities united them on other levels. Ultimately, she did sleep with this man when all systems were go. The "vibes" were right. She could trust the vibes because they resonated in her slightly less full, a bit hollow body. The ability to listen and attend to those signals is the "booty" of what her sensitive body had to offer and it far transcended the "beauty" of her new slimness.

She came in to see me while contemplating the deed. "I've discussed this with him a lot. I hope he doesn't get too impatient with me, but I just can't sleep with him until it feels really, really right. He says that sex isn't that important to him, that the company and good times are most important. He's saying the things gals usually say, and I feel like a pervert because I long for him so much! I know he likes me, but I'm not sure how much. I guess it's just too soon to know.

"I think I'm wrong in what I'm after; I'm looking for a man who can have the same experience I have. Do I want a man who's wired like a woman? I've had some of that. Those kinds of men eventually resent themselves. Ultimately, they then resent me. No matter how much they might fake it, no matter how sensitive or new agey they try to act, in their hearts, they are men. That means they are looking for a safe harbor to spread seed. They aren't out to go to the cosmos. What a cosmic joke for God to make women like me and men like that."

"Well," I had to respond philosophically, "we aren't really that much different. We're all somehow wounded, men a little more because they were forced to leave the nest and totally change themselves into split-off people. They grew up afraid of being called 'sissies.' They are terribly afraid of being lured into safety and warmth and then rewounded, kicked out again. They don't want to ache. They don't want to feel so deeply. With new sex, there is always an element of masturbation where no one really gets in. You usually have to know someone a while. The benefit and curse of all your efforts in therapy all these years is that you have become extremely sensitized and aware. A man will be attracted to you for that reason and long to connect with you, but will also be cautious and hold back. Even worse than that, you have the courage to confront and talk about what is really going on. A scared man will run for the hills. You ask a lot."

I later went on to ask her about what *she* was getting. Why did she pick this particular man? She'd known many others for one or many nights. Why this one now? Here is her answer: "Once you meet a man who truly senses what is going on with sex, it is hard to settle. It's not about gymnastics, aerobics or acrobatics. It's not a treasure hunt for the G-spot. It's about being there and loving the experience, moment by moment. If he's not there, I feel despair. When he shows up fully, the memory lingers on."

I commented, "It's like chef Alexander Lee of Manhattan's restaurant *Daniel* says: 'Love is like food. A great meal or someone you're really attracted to can stay on your palate forever.'"

Distrust of the Body

When, like Sharon, you have spent a lifetime demeaning and judging your body because its shape doesn't suit you, you develop a pattern of self-loathing and judgment. You might feel your body is not your own, that it is a separate being that controls you. You see no direct connection between your behavior and its effects. This has come about because weight losses and gains have not been as immediate as you imagined. For example, when you binge and then immediately jump on the scale and see you haven't gained as much as you thought, you think you beat the system and got away with something. When you diet and don't lose as much or as quickly as you'd like, you develop resentment and feel the world is out to get you and life isn't fair. You have been worshiping the scale god. The worst aspect of this is that you tend to distrust your body. You don't see it as a resource to signal vital messages to help you get on with life. Just as you are unable to recognize internal satiety and hunger cues, you distrust the body in all its rumblings. To stop overeating involves reowning self-trust and body-trust.

Can you love having a rounded, voluptuous, pulsating woman's body? You don't have to be large, but you have to be *responsive*. Your body is a vessel for entry and ecstasy. It's the vehicle to take you home. The issue is not about body image, but about connection, ecstasy, losing one's mind to the senses. As mentioned earlier, the French emphasize female orgasm as *la petite mort*—the little death. They say that women, more than men, actually die away and melt into orgasm. For many of us, orgasm feels like flipping out and leaving the planet. It feels like your head has been blown off, your eyes tingle and can't focus. A euphoric haze sets in, along with such a phenomenal sense of openness that you could drive a Mack truck through all boundaries. No wonder we have trepidation! No wonder we are more mindful of who we take to our beds and breasts.

To become more mindful, we must find a way to talk directly with other women. We must overcome embarrassment, set aside "political correctness" and really talk. You may already feel offended by this discussion, but please understand that I am just asking you to *think* a little differently. You don't have to *do* anything. We can't blame the constriction and avoidance of female sexuality on the men. Women have been doing it to themselves. It is women who are afraid to really talk about sex. We must stop blaming men as the source of our body image problems.

Some men can help us talk openly and accept our roundness. According to researcher April Fallon, psychologist at the Medical College of Pennsylvania, who asked 291 men and women to rate sketches of women's bodies, women predicted that men would want thinner bodies. However, men were more likely to prefer pictures of women twenty pounds heavier. They preferred the roundness and softness of a slightly heavier woman. They reported that it was a turnoff when a woman had a poor body image and an air of negativity. They felt the sexiest thing about any woman is *confidence*. They want to be our playmates, not our shrinks.

That means we have to stop asking men what they like and start paying more attention to what we like. When we appreciate our bodies, the men will even more. Evaluating our bodies is too heavy a burden to put on men. It is our work to do. They all have various preferences anyway. You are always at home with yourself. You're the one to please.

Modern young women are never asked to decide what they

like about their bodies but are taught early what they *shouldn't* like. According to a 1994 study at the University of Arizona, "90 percent of white girls questioned expressed dissatisfaction with their bodies." Black females liked their bodies a little more. That same year, the valedictorian of a high school in Suffolk County, New York, said "80 percent of the girls I know have experienced an eating disorder. Goals are changed from academic success to physical appearance. I would classify it as an epidemic of either anorexia or bulimia."

These young women are living out for us a strong cultural bias against large women. Even teams of professional nurses and psychotherapists were judgmental about overweight patients, believing them slovenly, slow witted and weak willed. Professionals and the lay public alike are afraid of fat people. Fat is our worst nightmare. Some believe that showing too much compassion will encourage all of us down the weight-gain path. After all, everyone overeats from time to time. In reality, most people who suffer obesity are *dieting* all the time. I know I was. I had long periods of firm resolve, many days eating less than seven hundred calories! Then I would binge and get fatter. Many obese people can even be diagnosed with anorexia, starving for long periods, even losing menses and developing lanugo, downlike body hair that wards off hypothermia. In a study of eight-year-old girls, 30 percent said they were fat. They began dieting at age eight and by age ten had moved to obesity.

Differentiate or Masticate!

Young girls are victims of our culture's pursuit of sameness. Sameness thinking helped marketers teach us what we liked, but it further caged the sensual woman's unique attention to her own preferences. Trained to know which car or dress to buy, we fashion our bodies in the same way. We don't attend to function, only form. I've always loved older, large American cars. Throughout many years living in southern California, I've had my share of big-boat Cadillac, Oldsmobile and Chrysler convertibles. These large bombs each bring a unique presence and style to the quiet streets of my desert retreat in Palm Springs. They are remembered for their character. You should be, too.

Today, body-type designers have transferred around within many companies so that every car's body style is virtually indistinguishable from any other. They want themselves and their cars to remain interchangeable. I fear we're doing the same thing with our women. What has happened to women's bodies, and how have we all decided to look as if cut from the same mold? I still crave the uniqueness of '57 Chevys, Corvettes and T-Birds.

A very buxom woman adorns the cover of Ken Mayer's book *Real Women Don't Diet!* Mayer prefers the larger frame and is not afraid to advertise it. He agrees with Kim Chernin, who wrote *The Obsession*, that men who need small women are trying to reduce the ominous larger presence of their mothers from when they were tots. They fear engulfment. Ken told svelte TV interviewer Tawny Little that he could appreciate her as a person, but not as a woman. She was "scrawny Tawny" to him.

Most of us don't think the way Ken does. Most decide who we want to be by watching picture shows. Unfortunately, many of the stars we emulate just aren't who we think they are. Directors employ body doubles to photograph the parts that just don't measure up. Julia Roberts's bony face photographs well, but her legs were too thin for the sexy prostitute she played in *Pretty Woman*.

Enter a "part model" for some shots. Singers also use body doubles in their videos. So, we are actually trying to mimic a conglomeration of many interesting combinations, like cut-up parts of cadavers.

The body design we seek isn't *normal*. In fact, it isn't even real. Will the real body please stand up? A plastic doll might be easier to copy. . . . Enter Barbie. . . .

The Barbie Burden

The "Barbie Burden" requires big hair, no waist and only slightly rounded hips. In 1996, Barbie had her thirty-sixth birthday and *Cosmopolitan* magazine turned thirty-five. Barbie was birthed while Betty Friedan wrote *The Feminine Mystique* and Simone de Beauvoir published *The Second Sex*. One climate was liberating female consciousness while another was constricting her body. Even with great lip service to freedom, the body was caged. In 1993, the Barbie franchise exceeded $1 billion in worldwide sales. A typical American girl owns an average of eight Barbies in her lifetime, and the doll is sold in 140 countries. If all current Barbie dolls in existence were placed head to toe, they would circle the globe six times. The human equivalent of a life-size Barbie doll would be 5 feet, 10 inches and weigh 110 pounds. She'd measure 36-18-33 and wear size 4 or 6. In reality, the average American woman is 5 feet, 4 inches tall, weighs 142 pounds and wears a size 12. Store mannequins have been replaced in the women's departments at a cost of $700 each. They are all wearing size 4 or 7. Size-12 mannequins are today used in the large-size department.

The following facts have "made the rounds" on the Internet:

- If shop mannequins were real women, they'd be too thin to menstruate.
- There are 3 billion women who don't look like super-models—and eight who do.
- Twenty years ago, models weighed 8 percent less than the average woman. Today, they weigh 23 percent less.
- Marilyn Monroe wore between a size 12 and a size 16.
- If Barbie were a real woman, she'd have to walk on all fours due to her proportions.
- One out of every four college-aged women has an eating disorder.
- The models in magazines are airbrushed—they are not perfect!
- A psychological study in 1995 found that three minutes spent looking at models in a fashion magazine caused 70 percent of women to feel depressed, guilty and shameful.

In 1991, a woman named Cathy Meredig created the "Happy to Be Me" doll for girls to name by themselves. The doll was almost like a real woman at size 12. Her human equivalent measurements were 36-27-38. The doll didn't sell and "went bust." At one location where Cathy tried to get distribution, she was advised, "Our corporate president's secretary resembles Barbie."

I became personally interested in the tragedy of this Barbie burden after appearing on a popular TV show featuring plastic-surgery makeovers. Beamed via satellite from a continent away was a prominent surgeon seated beside his wife, whose face he'd just lifted. With me in the studio was a woman who'd just happily spent her $80,000 inheritance on twenty separate surgeries to recreate herself in the image of Barbie. She indeed had long blond hair, a tiny waist, full lips and big breasts. She and the surgeon argued that she had the right to do whatever she liked with herself. I had no problem with that, but was asking both to take a look at when or *if* the orientation might become excessive and used as an alternative to developing other talents. How much time did it take? Did obsessional thinking take over at the first surgery, the third, the ninth?

I was most pained on the way to the airport when the Barbie look-alike informed me she ran a plastic surgery hotline where she provided counseling and referrals for women seeking enhancement surgeries. She boasted being a member of MENSA, an organization for genius-level intellects. Though I had no right to judge her choices, I did secretly wish that she had channeled that zeal and intelligence into something more interesting and more beneficial. She was no bimbette. She was just obsessed with looking like Barbie.

Passion's Price

Scrutinizing your body diverts your attention and keeps you busy marketing yourself. This may divert you from recognizing the part of you that truly savors sex. You'll make deals about your sexuality, "buff the bod" and forget your own longings. Many establish a price for others to experience their bodies without ever finding what it's worth, to themselves.

Most honest is the *prostitute* who clearly and deliberately decides what she has to sell, surveys the marketplace and establishes a going rate based on supply, demand and her own unique qualities in the situation. Although you can surely recall stories of drug addiction and battering among prostitutes, there are other stories that report prostitutes who like their work, who put themselves through college and appreciate their felt "freedom" and power in the situation. The activity is clear cut and honestly negotiated. She is attuned to the market.

More devious and ambiguous is the *trophy collector* or marriage-minded holdout, who feels from every cell of her being that the time, person and place are correct and aligned but who fears she will not land the catch if she gives up the bait. She focuses on negotiation and barter. She may grow to truly hate sex.

The woman I am addressing is the *priestess* who monitors her own body signals to determine when contact is made. She seeks higher meanings for her earthly couplings. She provides for herself and her partner a knowing gauge for spiritual connection. She finds her answers in the senses.

Madonna-Whore

Instead of trusting the senses, many women who like sex stay mute and fat. In a society polarized into Madonna-whore attitudes about female sexuality, women receive little permission to frankly discuss their loving to love and needing to love well. Instead they eat. We have a medical establishment that clinically diagnoses sex-loving women as nymphomaniacs. Full-bodied, sexually powerful women feel dangerous because, as bountiful beauties, they actually show society the brimming neediness and hunger awakening in all females. Instead of foraging through supermarket aisles, they long for other powers. This is not a desire to make more money, wear shoulder pads in the corporate boardroom or make the first call to a guy. It is a hunger for spiritual, soulful connection with a loving partner. This is not the same as "the mating game," where women seek an acceptable living situation. This is a hunger for meaningful, even if impermanent, connection.

In many cases, you may find that you are sleeping with your mother's old ideas. Often the best mothers could offer was something about waiting for marriage or love, and above all else, "Don't let yourself be used." Remember, "No one buys a cow who can get the milk for free!" But what if *you* want the milk? What if *you* are the user? What if you are consummating sex to stoke your own engine? Why should you feel depleted, left, abandoned? You are the one who *takes*. You take sperm, you take energy, you engulf and envelop his most sensitive self. You are given a gift. It is to be savored as much as chocolate pudding.

Vulva Vigil

If you admit to liking sex, then you have to practice "conscious coitus" by keeping a "vulva vigil." The idea of "holding out" to manipulate a certain outcome from *him* may be quite passé. As you develop a body consciousness and a hunger for spiritual connection, you will ask your vulva for direction. The body doesn't lie. Passage across the gateway to your heaven has to be congruent with everything else going on in your life. Your decision for conscious coitus will come from your own attentive vulva vigil. If you hold out for religious reasons, you are still not operating from the spiritual principles I have in mind.

Your spirit and senses can signal when copulation is right for you. Trusting the senses involves great personal confidence. Lessons learned about love can't be passed on. Each of us has to individually experience the fine nuances of how we respond in intimate situations. Each man and each time will have its variations. Perhaps you'd rather learn the way from a self-help book. You might find it easier to diagnose yourself with seduction dysfunction. Would you feel safer bringing out statistics, graphs and charts to follow a step-by-step program? Would you like to learn techniques to do it like the experts in a short thirty days?

You might ask, "Who has thirty days?" I offer here an invitation to the woman who *does* want to "waste" the time. . . . better here than going to "waist." Why learn someone else's movie script? You must play the starring role in your own life.

Entering the natural realm of the senses takes time. You have to take the time to lose your mind to come to your senses. Nature and sensitive women are allies defending against the unnatural, cancerous growth of modern society. Perhaps career-minded women have taken on men's compulsiveness and, consequently, their disowned sensuality. It is no accident that our modern world is producing so many diagnoses of infertility and inhibited sexual desire (ISD). Experts estimate one in five people experience some form of this problem. Even without such a diagnosis, some couples who report a "good" sex life when quizzed further report they haven't had sex in years. In eating-disorder treatment, we're told that it is the weight that keeps both partners turned off, he for lack of physical attraction, she due to embarrassment. When both are questioned further, we often learn they resort to self-stimulation. They settle for the physical release rather than mounting the arduous emotional work of reconnecting with a partner. They are thus deprived of the spiritual contact, and the hungry soul keeps eating way past when the body is satisfied.

Talking of our sexuality as "inhibited sexual desire" is the same as saying "I'm hungry" to describe every human emotion. It is too general, and it avoids attending to energies and chemistries. Worst of all, it doesn't pay attention to the higher spiritual calling, the call of the cosmos. Sexual desire turns you on to a more primitive, unwieldy place. You may feel safer in your head than in the pulsating wild ground of your body.

As a natural woman, you need time. It takes time to grow. It takes time to allow for vibration. As culmination of all the weeks a seed takes to germinate under the soil, there is an exquisite moment when that first shoot breaks through the soil and sees the light of day. Your sexuality has to be nurtured just as tenderly. You must have faith that with proper watering and nutrition, your bud will bloom also. Waiting for yourself to blossom requires faith and patience. It also requires focusing on the here and now rather than the culmination. Each forkful of food and each entry of love must be taken on its own terms. You can't try at all to repeat past performance. What made you swoon yesterday may leave you empty today. Yesterday was slow and steady. Today there's urgency. You just may be a woman full of conflicting, ever-changing messages. To understand and follow your vibrations requires such soulful presence and concentration that it can be likened to meditation. Just like meditation, it requires being fully here while at the same time letting go. Forcing it or faking it makes you leave the scene.

This ability to stay focused and mindful of your sensual experience, grounded in the body, is the gift of your femininity. As modern culture has pushed you to move faster, your attention to sexuality has been processed and repressed. This repression of the female can be likened to ecologists' concerns about destruction of the planet. Both women and the natural resources of the planet are seen as objects to be owned. Both are unpredictable and therefore feared. They are often uncontrollable and therefore hated. Both are manipulated to fit the needs of advancing technology, and they are often seen as vessels to use and discard.

As we approach the turn of the century, the campaign for more rights for women is colliding with an increasingly hedonistic pursuit of pleasure. This battle is being fought in the ground of a woman's rounded body. Feminist Adrienne Rich wrote, "The repossession by women of our bodies will bring far more essential change to human society than the seizing of the means of production by workers." The industrial revolution changed the power base for workers, and the women's movement followed with *economic* power for women. Now is the time to focus on a vulva connection to reclaim *sexual* power.

I am not saying that the solution to all our problems is sex. I am speaking to the "manner," not the act. Even though we have countless 900-number hotlines for telephone sex chats and we have cybersex at the keyboard, we are very naive about female sexuality. One way we keep it under wraps is by limiting, sanitizing and anesthetizing powerful bodies. Larger-hipped, fully juicy women are more threatening than emaciated, skeletal, amenorrheic girls. The more women focus on constricting their bodies, the less they focus on this blossoming, spiritual energy.

As Naomi Wolf suggested in *Promiscuities*, it would be better if we converted our self-conscious spotlight *on* the body to a self-confidence about light radiating *from* the body. Changing focus to this consciousness takes more than looking at calorie charts and pulse rates. It involves attending to our own souls. It comes closer to touching who you really are. As Deepak Chopra,

Marianne Williamson, Wayne Dyer and Andrew Weil carry us further into the New Age, those of us limiting food intake may have even higher spiritual messages to report. We are developing more resonance in that hollow place of the body, attending to our personal vibrations, leaving food alone, finding sensual pleasures elsewhere. Our bodies are becoming tuning forks, transmitting profound spiritual signals. You need a vibrating, slightly empty vessel and clarity to listen to those signals. You'll develop your body more for function and less for form.

Wide-Bodies Function

The function at this junction is *sex!* There is no question that we want sex desperately and fear it immensely. Pay close attention to how you negotiate that neediness. Ken Mayer reports that "Many amply-proportioned confident females exude power with their size and sexuality by their nature. They can choose to appear as feminine as they desire. While many men may be intimidated by this, I find such women quite impressive. And the more they get in touch with this power that seems to unnerve many people around them, the more pressure will be placed upon society to align itself to this new power base."

I saw this sexuality awakening as I brought women into treatment centers and curbed their eating. One group of women even made up a song for our open-mike entertainment night. They clapped hands and danced joyously to their made-up tune, "We're crackin' up for lack of shackin' up." In treatment centers, we found that fatter women like sex more than their thin counterparts. The earliest research into sexual behavior of obese women was reported in 1976 by Arthur Crisp, in the *English Journal of Psychosomatic Research*. He interviewed fat and thin women soon after Kinsey's original sex research. He asked about masturbation, petting, coitus and orgasms. It seemed obese women had a higher percentage of orgasms. In 1979, both Henry Jordan and Kelly Brownell at the University of Pennsylvania found that obese women were just as satisfied as normal-weight subjects regarding enjoyment and satisfaction but wanted more frequency than their partners and *more, more, more* of all love had to offer.

We know that fat regulates reproduction and *desire*. Fat women really enjoy sex. In ancient times, they were allowed to. Researchers at Michael Reese Hospital in Chicago report that plumper women desire sex more often than thinner women. On scales of erotic excitability and readiness, they outscored thin women two to one. Instead of celebrating the more erotic, plump body, our society favors the anorexic look. We know anorexics stop menstruating, but did you know some even stop masturbating? If you think about it, it's only natural. Starve any animal and, with dietary deprivation, sexual interest dissipates. A hungry, undernourished animal is interested in survival more than pleasure or spirit.

But is there any permission for heavier women to celebrate this gift? How can a woman who feels fat and negatively judges her body talk about how much she wants sex? Can we talk about truly sexual, sensual women who aren't here to be evaluated or objectified, but instead to have a good time? "Liberated" women are allowed to *do* it, but they are not allowed to talk about it.

Women who *do* try to promote dialogue are often seen by other women as promiscuous, sex-crazed, sex-starved or, worse, "bragging." Those who aren't reveling in their sexuality secretly begrudge those who are. Militant feminist Andrea Dworkin noted that women who'd made standard and "normal" choices had usually opted for a boring sex life. She described what she felt were "right-wing women" who had bought into a trade-off of "the promise of safety for obedience, respectability in return for self-respect and freedom." She felt these women would always resent the women living more dangerously and more on the edge. They have kept the wilder side of women relatively quiet and thus kept us all in the fat Dark Ages.

How can you actually talk out loud about lusting? Women aren't supposed to feel such things. I've found "modern" women extremely reluctant to talk about their sexuality. They like to hear *me* talk while they stare wide-eyed and frozen. Most of the literature is dominated by male writers, and most revelations reside in the medical/scientific or confessional/pornographic realm. When I spoke to these issues at a recent conference for Adult Children of Alcoholics, two women approached me offstage, warning that I "must have been incested but don't know it yet." Why so? Because I dare to say I like sex? In our society, having sex does not make you a slut. Talking about it does.

Why are we called names when we speak these truths? Talking openly does not mean you are promiscuous. It means you feel deserving. You appreciate and want to savor and heighten peak experiences. After reading here and reaching further, you may not crave *more*, but instead *better*. It may herald an even more discerning perspective. Your discernment is what causes the real trouble. What happens when you discern? Will you be punished or encouraged? Will you be indulgent, ravenous, demanding? There is a strong correlation between your attitudes toward food and sex. It goes to issues of constriction, denial, repression. In your mother's day, deprivation was about sex, today it's about food. In either case, the theme is "a controlled girl is a good girl."

So, constricting one side of our sensuality leads us to indulge another. Food is often a comforting substitute for love. We didn't get what we wanted *when* we wanted it, and now "mother's milk to the adult is never sweet." So our mournful cry ends up in the plate. Fat women wear their sadness and their badness like a badge. Those of us who admit to liking sex are real risk-takers. Some women are saying yes to sex as forcefully as we were raised to say no. To be politically correct, it seems acceptable to talk about sexuality from a victim or hostile position, but not as a celebrant. Some spend their sexual explorations focused totally on abuses from men, rather than on their own pleasures.

Some can only think of women's sexuality in terms of childbirth. What does that do for the women who choose *not* to have babies or who postpone childbirth? What if some women really don't want babies? According to Mardy S. Ireland in *Reconceiving Women: Separating Motherhood from Female Identity,* "We think of childless women in terms of absence rather than something absent in how we think of women." She takes issue with what she sees as male demands for us to reproduce and offers examples of women who lived very fulfilling lives though remaining childless. They lived unwedded bliss with very full lives as opposed to mothers who stayed home. If becoming a mature woman is just about reproducing, then consciousness is irrelevant.

Women have been schooled to keep quiet about sex, so it stays obligatory. When you speak out, sister, you make it instead a spiritual calling. Your voice might upset many and might make you public domain. Sallie Tisdale, author of *Talk*

Dirty to Me, taught me about how threatening it really is to write of such matters. She reported that since her book came out, "everyone thinks I have no boundaries, that they can touch me at will, hug me, say anything to me." If we admit to liking sex, that doesn't make us welcome mats or open invitations. In truth, you can talk about it without doing it. You can talk openly about sex and still get shy and embarrassed. You can have both openness and boundaries at the same time. Your sexuality can remain personal and you can hold out for your very best. In both *Joy of Sex* and *Joy of Cooking*, we are encouraged to wait for the best thing. We want to hold out to orchestrate it just right. Did you ever notice that when bingeing, it's usually on junk food? Why? Because you don't take the time to be discriminating. When you take that time with both dining and partnering, you can't take either entry casually.

Attention to Vibration

As diet books sell off the shelves, the weight-loss industry takes in more than $33 billion a year. It is second only to the arms race, another meaningless battle taking no prisoners. It's not a battle to be won, but a vibration to tune in to. You must become more attentive to vibration, the call of the wild. If stuffed, you can't feel the vibration.

When you listen to your own vibrations, you become available for a peak sexual experience. Most peak experiences are solitary, but not so with sex. With sex, you are more connected to yourself as well as to your partner. There is the sense that we are frozen in time as well as timeless. We live and die in the eternal now. Somehow fear and passion can freeze us. It's similar to being in a car accident where everything slows down so that you see every nanosecond of impact and watch each particle of glass splinter. That heightening of excitement must relate to losing oneself, letting go, dying to be reborn.

This can happen with concentration and paying attention. Metaphorically, you risk letting go into death as well as feeling a newborn sense of just beginning life. You will be totally engrossed, paying rapt attention. You'll probably seem more positive and more open to all kinds of experience. This will happen for you naturally and organically if you can wrestle free of the self-consciousness of the diet mentality. Do you want to achieve high rating as an art object, or would you rather be a sensual projector of your Self and your bountiful energy?

So, what can happen when all this attention is paid? Communications occur on a pulsating, cellular level. It's beyond consciousness and it happens whether your brain believes it or not. In the early 1970s at an auto plant in Hawthorne, California, efficiency experts watched workers and found that there was a reciprocity, a responsiveness that occurred between the observers and the observed. They named this "the Hawthorne Effect." In medical tests as well, researchers found that "when two individual muscle cells from two different hearts are observed under microscopes, each pulses with its own separate rhythm. When moved closer, they begin to pulse together, perfectly synchronized." Teams of women workers move to coordinated ovulation cycles.

Synchronicity happens even with machinery. As early as 1665, the Dutch scientist Christian Huygens noticed that if you put two oscillators close together, they start pulsing in the same rhythm. They show a tendency to "lock in." He surmised that nature tries to use the least amount of energy. In human affairs as well, it takes less energy to pulse in sync than in opposition. Your nature seeks such stasis. When you feed your body less food, you can trust its reverberations. It will seek a more loving, easier resonance. A half-full body can resonate like a tuning fork to ring out your true vibrations.

So, if you can believe with me now how important it is to make the proper soulful and vibratory connections, you will hold out with, "My sexuality is too special to be treated casually. I must keep a 'vulva vigil.' I will watch closely and listen intently." This is a courageous statement that will encourage you to embrace your own life. There is a risk involved.

To Lose the Fat Risk, You Must Be at Risk

As you learn to accept yourself as a tuning fork, transmitter of energy, you'll have to forgive yourself for initially continuing to be sexually attracted to the same type of struggle that existed in your family. It is hard to break tradition. Who you choose will help you see how far along the path you are. Patterns are woven into every cell of your being on a vibratory level. It takes time to respond to your own new rhythm.

The novelist Morris West addressed this saying, "It costs so much to be a full human being that there are few who have the love and courage to pay the price. One has to abandon altogether the search for security and reach out to the risk of living with both arms. One has to embrace life like a lover."

What I've been inviting you to is a by-product of getting in touch with your own true self. Once connected, you can't go back to lack of connection. You'll have to take your time, pay rapt attention to the quality of your inner life, look with innocent, baby-like eyes drawn to the ever-changing light. Taste as if it's all new—all for the first time. You will love with a spark of divinity. Decide if you are willing to live an unpredictable life.

Are you willing to honestly *choose* your life and your power? True life is hard. Circumstances come and go, but you can choose your attitude toward events. Pain is inevitable; suffering is optional.

He's Got the Headaches

The cooperation needed to effectively accomplish the event of lovemaking is a true melding in a relationship. He knows some things and so do you. Sometimes, you might have to become more of the teacher. Your sexual encounters will prove more exciting and grounded as you seek different things from sex. It will be your opportunity to own your body, your psyche and, ultimately, the cosmos. At the same time, with the right partner, it will be a chance to ooze into your sensuality and give from your storehouse of heat and love. More important, it can also help recharge your batteries, a function that food only fulfills halfway. You may fear that curbing food intake will send you raping and pillaging through the streets. It *may!*

The raping and pillaging fantasies are sometimes realistic. After losing a lot of weight, some women do initially become promiscuous. Many married women I have counseled fear that, as a result of their weight loss, they will want to leave their husbands. These women instead play it safe and actually stay "chained" in fat.

Just like with food, it's either feast or famine. Sometimes compulsive spending or gambling, decorating or charity organizing can help divert the sexual energies for a while. Ultimately though, the body will seek its just deserts. I believe it should be a requirement of eating disorder treatments that we help patients accept their body's needs for such stimulation and teach masturbation as an alternative to chowing down. We must face our realistic bodily needs. Naomi Wolf in *The Beauty Myth* reports that four wives in ten want sex more than husbands. According to the Sex Therapy Clinic at the State University of New York at Stony Brook, from 1974 to 1976, 30 percent of "low desire" cases occurred among men. In 1983, it rose to 55 percent.

For most species of mammals, the male's primary function is injecting sperm. The lioness takes care of all business for the king of beasts while he stretches and yawns and lounges. Have you found men only around for the hunt and conquest, but napping for the long haul of developing sensual and spiritual closeness? You need a man who shows up and pays attention. What if, instead, *he's* got the headaches? There's been little discussion of this ostensibly modern phenomenon. Most of the explanations for sex life diminishing after marriage are: changing social roles, fear of closeness, overwork, stress and no time. According to Joan Avna and Diana Waltz in their book *Celibate Wives*, when the sex life diminishes, women often blame themselves. Heavy women blame their weight gains. When men were asked if they'd want more sex if their wives got thinner, 23 percent said yes, while 77 percent said no.

It may be your desire for *better* sex that turns some men off. You want connection as well as sensation. Anorexics and vomiters are bingeing, starving or exercising to get endorphin highs. That can also be achieved through soulful, conscious sex. If necessary, reach for yourself instead of the shelf.

Women are denying a sexual hunger that men aren't even owning. Dr. Janet Wolfe, executive director of the Institute for Rational Emotive Therapy in New York City, first dispels the ubiquitous sexual-abuse argument for why women get fat, by stating that it is rarely trauma that turns a person off. Then she notes that sexual turn-off is often with the man, not the woman. At her clinic, four wives in ten want sex more than their husbands. Though liberated from "doing it for God and country," they now can't even do it for themselves. Dalma Heyn's book *The Erotic Silence of the American Wife* recounts so many women choosing adulterous affairs, not because their marriages are bad, but because they want more and better sex. In it, she notes that although male adulterers' transgressions are excused as born of physical cravings, we find it difficult to think the same way for women. For women, it must be emotional. For "Dalma's dolls" it isn't. It's functional. It brings color and clarity to their lives. Instead of celebrating the colorful hues, we diagnose it as problematic behavior.

Many eating-disordered women found that their appetites proved too much for their men. According to Barbara Ehrenreich in *Re-Making Love: The Feminization of Sex,* "The sexual revolution benefited women as they had more sex, but also 'on their own terms,' enjoying it as enthusiastically as men used to."

We've granted women economic power, but not powers of the flesh. We know how insatiable women can be. Even though you can now march up the corporate ladder, you can't bring sexuality to the conference table along with your briefcase. That might just be too much to take! Maybe with multiple orgasms and safely protected internal organs, you're already too far ahead. The legendary ancient Greek seer, Tiresias, was said to be both man and woman. When asked about pleasure, he said that women enjoy sex nine times more than men! Awareness of your own blossoming sexuality carries with it tremendous danger. No wonder we eat and drink! Feeling fat allows some to avoid sex, while it allows others to lapse into alcoholism and drug abuse so they can sleep around and pretend "the spirits made me do it."

In non-Western cultures, the female's greater desire and capacity for sex is heralded highly. In Chinese, Sanskrit, Zuni and Tantric texts, women's desire is stronger and her orgasms more sustaining than men's. The West is catching up! In the 1970s, we jumped off our pedestals, ready to let our inhibitions run wild.

Women were ready. . . .

Men weren't. . . .

No one taught any of us how to cope with the pulsating sexuality that had heretofore been kept under wraps. We are still reeling from the tremendous discharge of power unleashed by this sexuality, and no one is talking about how to negotiate new relationships attending to new hungers. Women eat while men run away. The world has changed and the power has shifted and no one says a word. What could I say to the husband of a curvaceous 120-pound wife when he explained, "If she just didn't have such a rounded belly, I'd be more sexually interested"? Another woman married when she weighed 95 pounds and with pregnancy went up to 110. Now her husband won't sleep with her. He thinks she's fat. You know how mortifying it is if you feel fat and he's turned off. Most of us just got fatter to forget the whole thing.

What then do you do if you want more sex? Diagnostic manuals developed mostly by men, and thin men at that, describe shy young women demurring about body changes and developing eating disorders in adolescence. In treatment centers, we learned that eating disorders are still classified as "diseases of childhood." The professional literature still addresses these problems as prepubescent struggles with maturation. Theorists explain this as the daughter's fear of growing up to live a life like her mother's. This is not totally true. Not mentioned is her fear of something she may not even see in her mother—sexuality. Her voracious appetite for food or sex may not relate to mother at all.

If you have no model, you may judge yourself excessive and label yourself "too demanding." During three decades of counseling addictive families, I found only two couples where the husband wanted more sex than the wife. In all other instances, the wife wanted more sex. These women were alive and aware and listening to themselves and their own vibrations. If you tune in to the voice of your body, it may cause new problems in your relationships. It involves power negotiations. You have to live honestly. You can't play the same old games. So many report waiting and waiting for sex, keeping their mouths shut in bed, but open at the table. They thought addressing their increased sexual desires would castrate their men. They walked on eggshells and remained married but celibate. You may have found you lost weight previously, hoping he'd jump your bones, and instead found him just as turned off. It wasn't the body, it was the booty, the prize. Are you a cherished treasure or an afterthought? You can't open your legs for that kind of penetration. You can't be with a lukewarm guy. You've got too much to give. You're too hot to drink tepid milk. You knew that was the case and in some ways regained the weight to avoid that issue. In other words, it is easier to blame it on the bod than to really attend to what is missing between the two of you.

That's why you may have stayed connected to an unlikely partner. You long to be penetrated, but fear it immensely. You probably settled for the self-stimulation of food. One client gained great insight when she insisted upon her nightly cookie and brushed her husband's hand away from her stomach. She noted a clear choice she'd made for food over sex. In 1991, *Self* magazine published a study that showed 86 percent of Americans snack between meals and 10 percent report eating late at night. They reported that they'd "rather nibble than have sex." The study conducted by Continental Baking Company found that one-third of the respondents felt guilty about noshing. They felt more guilty than when lying about weight, age or tax deductions. The reason they felt guilty about eating was that they used food to avoid sex with their partners. They were, in effect, masturbating in the plate. To stay out of the plate, reach for a mate.

Never Sated?

If you have a voracious, even excessive appetite for food, what might you find out about your desire for sex? You may not have been able to admit to yourself how truly hungry you are. You might have pretended that it wasn't important. You might have been programmed to believe that being feminine meant you were disinterested in sex. Gloria Steinem said, "We were all trained to be female impersonators. Usually faceless, demure virgins disinterested in the pleasures of the body." In the hit Broadway play, *M. Butterfly*, the lead male character who masquerades as a geisha girl tells us that "only a man can play a woman well." I propose that if modern women seek to continue that charade, they'll get fatter. Many already have. Most don't feel they have permission to like sex. It's okay if love is involved, so they exaggerate good sex into "love." Unable to accept their lustful selves, fat women work especially hard to deny their sexuality. They are fearful of the power sex has over them. Let's face it, that fat apron extending down to the knees is definitely covering a forest of unresolved problems. Try not to become squeamish here. If you can stay in open dialogue, with a frank and respectful discussion, you won't have to run back to the safety of excess weight to focus on diets instead of connections.

Women's insatiable appetites are cause for concern. Water ends thirst and food ends hunger . . . but does sex end arousal? No. Great sex generates interest in more. You may feel it's dangerous to start up the engines. You are going to become fully and truthfully who you are. Truth and wholeness touch your soul as well as your cosmic vulva. Remember, as a woman, you are equipped with a clitoris, for which there is only one known use—your pleasure!

Matters of Life and Death

While fat, I was married to an alcoholic. Approximately 30 percent of the wives of alcoholics are obese. They make a deal to avoid and deny a large and painful reality about their lives together. They live with a mutual suicide pact. He says, "Don't say anything about my drinking, and I won't say anything about your eating." This suicide pact sublimates the life force. With this pact, such couples unconsciously decide to ignore internal feelings of deadness. They shut down. No one mentions the interrelationship of the problems. There is a direct connection between denial of sexual energies and lack of spiritual connection. The suicide pact, as well as their sex life, explodes when either partner enters recovery. When the alcoholic spouse gets sober, he is then more shy and, often in early recovery, even impotent. If his wife goes untreated, she eats more to assuage the unsatisfied sexual feelings or divorces him *after* sobriety. Everyone wondered why she stayed during all the "bad times" but left soon after things got "better." Though ostensibly things seemed better, in actuality, the sobriety now brought into sharper focus the dead zone between them. Maybe when drunk and overeating, unconscious sex was tolerable. In recovery, however, truth must reign. When not responding to chaotic situations or arguing over control of substances, there may be little to keep them together.

"Chubby Chasers"

Maybe when your husband was drinking, he was called a "chubby chaser," a man who prefers fat women. I haven't heard any derogatory name for men who want emaciated women. There are special organizations and clubs for men to meet fat women. Some men report having much more meaningful sexual experiences with heavier women. When I interview men who like large women, their comments are usually highly favorable, and they are happy to share what they know. They say that large women often are more open to meeting a man, talk to anyone and don't turn people away. They describe these women as "sensual" and "open." One man found fat women more willing to go along with experimentation and to play out fantasies. Sometimes obese couples have to be really intimate and talk in order to work out some of their logistical positioning problems. They are treading on territory no one has before. This makes them feel more like pioneers and thus somewhat on the fringe.

According to Andrew, who invited me to my first "Large Encounters" dance, he feels more "real" there. I went to see what he was talking about. Upon entering a dark dance hall, I saw very large women in flashy outfits bumping and grinding to pounding, gyrating music. There were also sad women sitting quietly on a couch in the corner, scared to death.

I met two soft-spoken, well-coiffed young women as hoagies were served. They were exquisitely made up and wore polyester overblouses hiding large hips in tight slacks. Twenty-two-year-old Arnette from Long Island was that night on her very first venture *ever* into Manhattan. "My father is very protective." Like Andrew, she felt this was a place she could be "real." She felt she could relax there. Both she and her friend, Elizabeth, felt they were with their own kind of people and no one would judge them. In the usual singles bars, they didn't feel permission to be sexual. In restaurants, "normals" stare at fat people, secretly asking, "How can she eat like that?" This is equally true about dancing, flirting or sexing. "How can she?" Why shouldn't she?

This concerned Arnette. She'd heard that some men came to these events with the idea that the women would be easy marks. "Some of them think we are so horny that we'll go with anyone. They don't even bother to inject any romance. I can see why though. There are women like Wendy over there. She just comes here to get laid."

Wendy, a buxom woman with a wig of long shiny curls, was in the center of the floor, knees bent, skirt raised to show her red garter belt. She was swaying and lowering herself while pointing her long red index fingernail toward her crotch. Arnette pointed to a young Woody Allen look-alike watching from the corner. "He took her home from the last dance and had sex with her *twice!*" I was curious about who was keeping score.

She continued, "I'm here to meet a nice man who won't judge me for my fat, but also who won't *pick* me for my fat. I'd rather it not be an issue. I am afraid that some men come here thinking we're easy. I guess even at a regular singles dance there will be some interested in relationships and some there solely to get it on."

The Woody Allen clone turned out to be Marty, and he was very eager to tell all. I heard directly his confession that he'd been with Wendy last week and "screwed her twice." He was excited to tell me that he *loved* these dances and viewed fat women as *goddesses* loaded with fertility and sensuality. He'd known he preferred big women at age thirteen in the orthodontist's chair. His doctor was a big-breasted woman, and as she brushed against him, he was mildly stimulated. "I crave that comforting female flesh."

As he continued, he got more excited. "I like to fall in and melt. It feels very animal to me, like I am a rutting bull moose. These women love it. They get wet so easily. They always seem ready and have orgasms easily from thrusting. It goes without saying that they give great head.

"They are much more into sex than thinner women. I find them much more feminine. I think they have an abundance of female hormone, like the ancient fertility goddess thing. It goes along with a tendency to gain weight. It's part of being female. I just assume each is enthusiastic about being female and likes what is masculine. It makes me feel even more like a man."

Marty proposed that he felt it was unnatural to go for a skinny woman as her size indicates a lack of fertility. He felt that fat women were more natural about sex, seemed happier and easier to get along with than thinner women he'd known. "There's no bullshit here. I'm kind of a neurotic Jewish intellectual, and the women I meet here are nothing like my day job. I love the escape. Here it is all sensuous and a bit 'swarthy.'"

He waxed philosophical. "I guess this is part of my owning

my dark side. I know I enjoy the raunchy sex, but sometimes later I feel vulgar and embarrassed about succumbing to my baser instincts. I sometimes will sleep with women I wouldn't take out in daylight. Not because they're fat, but because we have nothing to discuss."

Unfortunately, there are scarce venues where we can see heavier women celebrated for sexuality. When I told colleagues about the premise of this book, some recoiled with the comment, "A book about fat ladies having sex sounds repulsive." Fashion magazines show anorexic images of "waifs" and "heroin chic," but there are only a few magazines that show lusty, full-figured women, full of power-strutting stuff. Are these figures relegated to big-mama catalogs or porno shops, and if so, why? I once saw a lovely magazine cover of a busty big woman at a kiosk on Broadway in New York City. I didn't buy it right away, but I returned the next day to purchase it to display at my seminars. I searched every kiosk for ten blocks and could not find the magazine. After deciding I was on the right corner, I questioned the clerk repeatedly. He finally pulled out the magazine. While I paid for my purchase, I asked why he had it hidden, and he told me that passersby the day before had asked him to put it away. They found it offensive. They weren't offended by the countless spreads of thinner women. Those thin women were posed to be more demure, more vulnerable, more open to victimization. The heavy woman was powerful and possibly intimidating.

Though I find these prejudices appalling, I am still not on a soapbox with the "fat-acceptance" movement either. I want eating behavior limited, not for social acceptance reasons, but because I want your body, your listening tuning fork to be more resonant.

I appeared on the *Sally Jessy Raphaël* show along with the president of the National Association to Aid Fat Americans (NAAFA). This group politicizes the problem. They argued that although the culture expected unrealistic body standards, they (NAAFA members) wanted to accept themselves with heavy bodies. They filled the audience in support of a young man named Michael who lived in upstate New York. Weighing more than eight hundred pounds, he was moved with a forklift. I traveled upstate to his trailer and, like Richard Simmons and Godfrey Cambridge before me, made many attempts to help both him and his mother. Their anger at the system kept them from helping themselves. Soon after the show aired, he died of complications from his obesity. What cause did he serve? What purpose does your body serve? I want your body juicy but also slightly empty so it can resonate well, so you can use it to go to higher vibrations. Whether the culture approves of your body size or not, you need that healthy, resonant body.

Body for View or Vibration

Even more important than the look of the body is the energy it radiates or collects. Marilyn Monroe was popular for her perfectly shaped body, but she was also expert at tapping into her radiant sexual energy. Susan Strasberg told a story about walking down a New York City street with Marilyn, who was dressed down, with no makeup, sunglasses on and a scarf tied around her head. No one noticed. She turned and asked Susan, "Would you like to see Marilyn?" Susan nodded and then watched as Marilyn made slight adjustments in the tilt of her head and her walk, and a crowd started following them. She *created* Marilyn.

I have been a collector of Marilyn Monroe memorabilia since I was twelve years old. Although at first she terrified me, ultimately, she saved my sex life. Junior high was mortifying, showering with those skimpy little hand towels. I scrutinized every other body, all the while madly trying to cover my own.

Before that time, the only naked females I'd seen were my mom and my aunt. Both these women had pendulous breasts with large, brown nipples. But the girls in my gym class all had small breasts, tiny pink nipples and bodies that were straight up and down. My own body curved in and out, which, at the time, caused me to feel too fat and rounded. Large nipples dominated my prepubescent chest. I saw them as a major disfigurement. I just knew that the women in my family suffered some hereditary curse. I hid my nipples at all costs so no one would see what freaks the women in my family were.

Then I saw that calendar photo of Marilyn on the red satin bedspread. My world changed. Marilyn had big nipples! She had a rib cage, and her body curved in and out. *This was sexy? I was sexy?* Scared to death, I proceeded to eat ravenously for the next seventeen years!

I was taught to attend to body shape and form instead of function and vibration. I never learned how to practice using sexual power to hook up to the cosmos. Accessing that spirit enhances a sense of childlike wonder. That's what really made Marilyn sexy—her air of childlike innocence and her sense of play. She portrayed sexuality as sensual, and powerful, and still a lot of fun.

Being playful involves developing a loving sense of humor. We respond to people who bring out the playmate in us. We have to get more comfortable with that sense of fun. It is okay to laugh in bed as long as you don't point. . . .

In recent years, all of my lovers have liked muscular thighs, buxom hips, small waists and a big smile. I have exactly what they want. I don't associate with folks who don't prefer and freely choose exactly what I have to offer. I know that I have absolutely no time in my life for anyone to criticize any single part of me. I'm too busy, have too much to do, find it meaningless conversation. My response is, "I'm not really available for that right now. Just not available. No vacancy. Gone fishin'. Be back later. Whatever negative comments you have to offer, I'm just not up for it." If you aren't up for criticism either, you are a very unusual woman. Have you ever sat with groups of women who brag to each other about what they *like* about their bodies? Usually we find it easier to talk about what we *don't* like.

Womb Envy?

When Sigmund Freud taught women and their shrinks that we looked down, didn't see a protrusion, and so immediately assumed something had been cut from us, he never dreamed that instead we might have thought, *Oh, how safe and compact we are.* He led us to believe that we suffered from a malady known as *penis envy.* Many who followed Freud tried to diagnose our problem as a secret wish to be men and assume male power. We don't want to be men! Sure, there are surveys like the Gallup poll in the summer of 1996 that found women more likely than men to say they would choose to be reborn as the opposite sex. None of the respondents said it was because they had no penis and craved one for themselves. The reason was that their *societies* favor men over women. When asked if the society at large would be better if there were more women in politics, women and men both say yes. These are political and sociological considerations, not sexual ones. I like Marilyn Monroe's attitude best: "I don't mind living in a man's world as long as I can be a woman in it."

Why don't we investigate more the phenomenon of men craving the power that women carry between their legs? Roberta reported, "As I had my seventh orgasm of an evening, my particularly attentive lover whispered softly, 'You know, every guy would love to experience those multiple orgasms.' He knew the experience was transformative and that I had left the room. He and I both knew it was awesome and possible. He knew that I had both a sensual and spiritual experience during sex. It was more than physical and more than cerebral. Our lovemaking had transformed my body into a cathedral."

When I talk to women's groups about the possibility of this truly ominous sexuality, I often face blank stares and no comments. I now realize that many do not know what I am talking about. They've been so inundated with images put forth in the popular media that they may not understand a woman-based sexuality that is quite different. So many current models of sexuality keep us hungry. If you have spent much of your life settling for hunger-inducing sex, then you may not know about satisfying, filling sex. Instead, you might have been encouraged to join in with men as they watch pornographic films of men jabbing women.

Erotica vs. Pornography

Erica Jong noted that when you watch a porno flick for five minutes, you believe you will want to make love continuously for the rest of your life. If you watch for fifteen, you may never want to make love again. Instead of watching, you might let your man know that the poke on the screen is anatomically likened to pushing forcefully on his scrotum. Sexy image?

Pornography usually features physical sex without emotion and often without mutual consent. It emphasizes genital close-ups and penetration. There is rarely a buildup to some relationship between the characters. Erotica, on the other hand, shows emotional connection that develops and builds between characters. I've also heard the amusing distinction "Erotica is with a feather, while pornography is with the whole chicken."

I was aghast when I attended a conference on pornography and spirituality. The porno film star, Nina Hartley, responded to a question from a troubled woman about what to do when her husband only gets turned on by looking at Nina's exposed crotch in a pulp magazine. Nina answered that wherever the man gets his erection, the woman should be grateful and welcoming and realize that he's brought it to *her* for its final journey. She cautioned, "After all, he could take it to the streets." Oh really, now! Could he? Would he? Is he looking for a repository? Are you available to be a repository? And you're supposed to be grateful?

You may be one of the countless women settling for this repository role, knowing but ignoring that his energy is not coming at *you*, but at a receptacle. He could be working out rage at his mother, disillusionment with work, midlife crisis or jock itch. Even if you don't care, your spirit does. *She* knows the difference. When you engage in that kind of sexuality, when you or your partners are not really there, showing up fully, the real you sneaks to the fridge when it's over. When you do, you feed the wrong hunger.

If sex is used as a utilitarian function to achieve gratification and pleasure, eros can be destroyed. Rollo May wrote, "By anesthetizing feeling in order to perform better, by employing sex as a tool to prove prowess and identity, by using sensuality to hide sensitivity, we have emasculated sex and left it vapid and empty."

As a wise woman, you will have to take more responsibility for your sex life, guiding your men in these simple ongoing pleasures. You can turn to other women to learn how to take dominance, conquest and acceptance issues out of sexuality. We can teach each other how to be more "responseable," how to have more *ability to respond*. It may be your job to initiate and become more conscious of what you receive from the experience.

Maybe men aren't all they're cracked up to be. In the late Tammy Wynette's codependency lyric, she asks women to accept their man's predilections: "After all, he's just a man." Do you make excuses in order to make love? Let's face it, only the power of sex could bind us. If it weren't for the sex thing, men and women would naturally live apart. The need for sex groups two very different people together without a net. We learned the equipment during puberty without a user's manual.

You may have to see the value of women friends for some comforts and men for others. Maybe women provide comfort, but men have another purpose. Maybe you confused comfort with other issues and expected more from men than could ever be delivered. Maybe you were trying to compensate for a childhood of disappointment and resentment. Maybe a man is a man is a man. Even Freud said, "Sometimes a good cigar is just a smoke."

Both boys and girls need to grow into powerful spiritual

men and women. Sex suffers when men stay little boys. It also suffers if the female takes on a mothering role instead of a partnering one. This is a very common pattern. Witness so many daytime talk shows where wayward, adulterous men are berated by audiences of incensed reprimanding women. When are both the men and women made responsible for the spiritual connection of sexuality?

You are probably having more fun in bed than women of previous generations. If you have taken on my instruction to learn from your liaisons, you have probably learned more reading this chapter than your mother learned in a lifetime. Your men are often better trained and more interested in an involved partner. Many modern men have done their home-work and are adept at stimulating women and bringing them to orgasm. The women have also trained themselves to know what they like and to go for it with gusto. We can all get off. That's not the point at all. If it is, masturbation works as well as anything else with less hassle most of the time. It may prove to be some of the best sex you'll ever have. But, it won't offer you transit to the spiritual realm, which you can attain with a truly connected partner.

Liaisons with sexually proficient men, focused on bringing their partners to orgasm, can be some of the emptiest sex ever. But then again, as Woody Allen said, "Sex without love is a meaningless act, but as meaningless acts go, it's not bad." For the grounded, sensual, spiritual woman though, too much of that can get old quickly. If a man is busy being competent, concerned with performance, working a finely tuned instru-ment, he may have no personal involvement in the mutual transmission of energies and the organic building that hap-pens during truly connected sex. You'll instantly know if you've been left high and dry despite competence and physical satisfaction.

As your sensitive, finely tuned instrument progresses and gives up excess fat, you will be acutely aware of when your partner is present and when he leaves you emotionally and spiritually. Instead of taking yourself to conscious bed and heights of sensual, spiritual ecstasy, you might have instead joined countless others who have taken themselves to psychiatric couches. In chapter 2, we will examine how psychobabble has served to stifle sexuality.

Two

It's No Trauma

A cat or dog approaches another,
they sniff noses. They sniff asses.
They bristle or lick. They fall
in love as often as we do,
as passionately. But they fall
in love or lust with furry flesh,
not hoop skirts or push up bras
rib removal or liposuction.
It is not for male or female dogs
that poodles are clipped
to topiary hedges.

If only we could like each other raw.

—MARGE PIERCY, "WHAT ARE BIG GIRLS MADE OF?"

o you think you could really like your body for its smells, swells and furry flesh? Or are you like countless others sent to sanitized stainless-steel gyms to constrict and abuse yourself? Where do you learn to appreciate and validate your juicy temple? By making female bodies objects for barter or sale, we have disowned a wildly pulsating feminine energy. In this chapter, we will see how preferences for sameness in body shapes have not been the only way to constrict female sexuality. Here we delve even more deeply, examining quite credible scions of society: the medical and psychiatric communities. These, too, have colluded to make us all more conformist and less open to our own individual vibrations. As women have achieved more economic and political power, the effort to control and constrict us in other ways has proceeded vigorously.

If you are either obese or anorexic, you are a symbol of society's conflicts about indulgence and abstinence. The same conflicts exist in bed. Masturbation guilt is replaced and interchangeable with carbohydrate guilt. These conflicts are even more visible in a society that espouses "free love" and supposedly open promiscuity. Food used to be natural, but now is forbidden; sex used to be forbidden, but now is commonplace. Gluttony does not mean you enjoyed your meal more, and wanton sexuality doesn't mean you enjoy sex. Both these overindulgent behaviors produce loneliness and isolation, as well as numbing and inauthentic experience.

In the 1950s, we were into romance and melting. Tammy got the bachelor. Troy Donahue found *A Summer Place* with Sandra Dee. In the 1960s, we were swept away by one-night stands. Sex therapists focused on painful intercourse, premature ejaculation and preorgasmic women. In the 1970s, we worked hard at having simultaneous, no-strings-attached, multiple orgasms. In the 1980s, all forms of sexual experimentation were encouraged, with or without drugs, and we diagnosed inhibited sexual desire alongside "love addicts." We were diagnosed at both ends of the spectrum—feast or famine, all or nothing, fat or lean. By the 1990s, we got scared of sex, as it could cause death, and anyway, we were all overworked and, quite frankly, tired. We went from examining inside plumbing to running the streets to fearing the morgue to roaming the kitchen, but bypassed intimacy. You may find it much easier to dish out ice cream late at night than approach the arduous work of mounting or melding with a partner. Busy or bored lovers feel lonely and eat instead. Things are so turned around now that you show how sexy you are by not eating and by restricting and dying. Sex used to be about celebrating and continuing the life force. The once-prized intact hymen is now replaced by a size-four dress.

In the 1950s, when water was clean and sex was dirty, we held to a restrictive sexual standard even if we sometimes indulged ourselves with a chocolate malt. We did a lot of petting, rarely "going all the way." We played "baseball" in backseats of distinctive cars. There were certain "bases" to cover in sequential order. You went through first, second and third base, and then you scored! It worked well then. "Girls" were the gatekeepers, and we held out for romantic encounters. If you were one of those "girls," you are now close to fifty years old and don't know how to balance all the sexual conflicts. Your psyche is a rock and roller of the 1950s, but the media tells you to be a " '90s woman." Rather than acknowledge and respect your sexuality as a gift and call to awakening, you are forced to view it as yet another demand in an already too busy life. "Not tonight, dear. I have a career. . . ."

Well, get busy getting sexy. Sex is the solution to many of your unresolved problems. I know this might sound like upsetting news, but it's better than learning that doctors have to amputate your leg. Let's face it, many had large sections of their abdomens cut out to lose excess weight. Compared to that, a little good sex can't be all bad.

Since treating my own obesity for four decades and working to treat others' for three, I've had ample opportunity to study the myriad reasons for why we "get fat." I became a psychologist to figure out the answer to that one question, and everything I learned drove me straight to the fridge.

One of the most current causal theories is the idea that we never received enough "unconditional love," which we all supposedly need. Can anyone tell me what that looks or feels like? Anyone out there who is not from a dysfunctional family filled with fallible human beings? Were you loved unconditionally? Ever stop to ask what that is supposed to mean? Well, the theory goes that as long as you don't get this elusive experience, you will have an "insatiable desire for food to match your insatiable desire for unobtainable love."

Then, not loved enough, you can become quite angry. Some will tell you that foraging for food is an expression of rage and hatred. Then some will take you back to Thorstein Veblen and his essay at the turn of the century, "Conspicuous Consumption." They'll tell you that your eating or starving represents the conflict we all face, and you act out gluttony or ascetic denial in the face of consumptive consumerism. Susie Orbach, in *Fat Is a Feminist Issue*, tells us that you refuse to compete in a society that disempowers women, so you withdraw from the race and let your skinny sisters go for it. Others will say that we accumulate girth to gain power, in order to feel more like a man. Some say our overeating expresses a desire to be pregnant, or if not that, then a fear of becoming pregnant. Others have said it is a way to feel powerful because we feel so pumped up on such false power. We're really egomaniacs with inferiority complexes. Then some say it is our defense against adulthood and responsibility, a way to remain a child—helpless, dependent and clinging. Or it could be a way to leave home, reject parents, make them suffer with guilt that you turned out so bad. And then, of course, it could just be too many carbohydrates, or eating a steak alongside a baked potato, or eating too late at night. Recently, many say it's a defense against sexuality because whether we know it or not, we were probably incested or otherwise sexually molested.

Well, they're all right! Any reasons can be right. However, *Time* magazine ran a cover story called "Girth of a Nation," showing that "right" creates more fat. They reported that we know more and more about calories, pulse rates, fat grams, Prozac and our dysfunctional childhoods, and despite more knowledge, we're getting fatter and fatter. We can safely say that eating is a pseudosolution to a multitude of personality problems. Despite what we know, we eat for comfort. Life is hard and food soothes it. Knowing the "right" food to take has nothing to do with that insatiable need for comfort.

Sex comforts, also. It comforts a hunger we can't readily identify, a longing, an ache. Those of us in the treatment field say, "What we see as the problem, the patient sees as the solution." What we call their symptoms, they call their salvation. The symptom is self-cohesive, meaning it provides a container, or safe harbor, for the patient to store all her feelings about herself, her life and her therapist. Unfortunately, by the time a binger or starver gets to see me, what once *solved* the problem has now *become* the problem. Therefore, as a therapist, I can't take away one "solution" without first acknowledging how hard giving it up will be, inviting the patient to feel the pain, then replacing the old "solution" with some alternative comfort.

I now invite you to reduce food excesses, substituting conscious sensuality and mindfulness. You will replace excessive filling with a long-disowned spiritual/sensual vibration. You will feel hungry, but not eat. You will feel your aches, and not eat. You will long for a higher vibration, and not eat. You will accept that you are born to ache. Breathe into that feeling now. Feel the hollows—the spaces between your cells. Lean into the whole experience. You may never learn precisely what the "cause" for the hunger or aching is, but you will find a comforting solution that isn't self-destructive. What could be bad about that?

Sex as curative is not necessarily an unnatural idea. Sex has solved many problems among the bonobos, a humanlike ape species initially discovered in Zaire in 1929. This breed walks the most erect of all nonhuman primates. Females are dominant in their society. Life is so mild and unobnoxious that there seems a relative equality between the sexes. Researchers call it a codominance.

The bonobos have sex all the time. Social harmony is achieved through all manner of sexuality. They are amicable, sensitive and, basically, quite humane. They do it all, including French kissing with anyone and everyone. They do it for appeasement after a fight, cementing relations and relieving tensions.

Dr. Frans Waal, primatologist at Emory University, is author of the most extensive study of their behavior, documented in his book *Bonobo: The Forgotten Ape*. He notes that these primates are so much less hostile than chimpanzees: "The chimpanzee resolves sexual issues with power; the bonobo resolves power issues with sex." One from Mars, the other from Venus?

Just as I mentioned earlier regarding dolphins and humans, these primates use sex far beyond just needed reproductive purposes. Also, the females are not competitive, but instead have close-knit alliances. Think for a minute if we could approximate bonobos. Sexually powerful women could resolve power struggles with sex. Not a bad idea.

At one of Dr. Waal's lectures, an indignant audience member confronted him on why the males don't rebel to gain an upper hand. He answered calmly, "They seem to be in a perfectly good situation. The females have sex with them all the time, and they don't have to fight over it so much among themselves. I'm not sure they've lost anything except for their dominance." Isn't dominance an issue in our society? Could the battles stop if there were better sex for all?

Your Engine Wants to Drive on Home

Efforts to control both food and sex are efforts to control all of life. Food and sex perpetuate the species and the life force. Giving in to sexuality helps you float easily to your intended selfhood and home. Food is the fuel; sex is the starter. Though past programming may have taught you to control, control, control, now is the time to learn to let go. As a habitual dieter, you've been well trained to fend off temptations. However, denying the ravenous appetite for food has also trained you to hold back, cut down and keep hidden other parts of your sensuous self. Your diet progressed, but your sex life suffered. When you starved in the kitchen, other appetites may have also been suppressed. At some point, your dieting may have awakened a deep sexual hunger. Maybe you saw both eating and sex as indulgent and giving in to emotionalism. If you give in to the eating or the loving—both of them life forces— you may judge yourself as weak-willed and totally animal. As you read along in this book, ponder these issues. Remember, food is the nurturer, sex is the battery charger, and your authentic life is at stake.

"Too dramatic!" you may say. Well, when you take away excess food, a true longing emerges.

Map out Your Journey

You want to be fully seen. You long for visibility, yet recoil from it like the plague. Facing your fears brings you closer to making sex a truly intimate act, opening up to vulnerability. But as you are a truly conscious being paying attention, the closeness you say you want can bring up more questions than answers. Is it more intimate to have sex with a partner or alone? Is intercourse more or less intimate than mutual masturbation? Does oral sex seem intimate? Is it somewhat easier because there's no eye or "I" contact, or is it intimate because of the vulnerability of being so open? These are questions of visibility *and* perspective. While pornography objectifies us and puts all at a distance, some acts, like oral sex, put us so up close and personal that we really can't see the fullness of what we're doing. We lose perspective. Sometimes eliminating distance really puts us *too* close. We need visibility tempered with perspective.

Leona shared the following at a "Hollis Hollow" retreat: "In my early life, I would certainly tell you that I found 'getting head' just the best. I saw it as more intimate, parting my lips, letting him smell, not being in control of what he could see. It was so, so intimate. I didn't find intercourse very intimate as it just seemed like a lot of pounding and thumping and gasping. We seemed to leave each other and leave the room. Now, in later life and with an older man, I find intercourse more intimate and usually more enjoyable. I don't like oral sex when I feel that cold draft at my chest when he's 'down there,' away from me instead of wrapped around my body. With intercourse, I like how we have to wait for each other and learn how to move in sync and get coordinated. It helps me slow down to a smooth build. It helps me stay present with him."

You may face the dilemma of how to own your sensuality without feeling sleazy. You may want to be erotic, but fear verging on pornographic. There are no models. Avoiding objectification, you may have chosen to hide out in your eating disorder. John Stoltenberg, in his book *What Makes Pornography "Sexy"?*, tells us, "The anorexic body is sexually safer to inhabit than the pornographic." How do you find the way to celebrate yourself without being misunderstood? You want some power, but not as an object. Stoltenberg organized Men Against Pornography (MAP) workshops, to show men what happens to women who feel objectified. He wanted men to understand what it was like. He asked men to look at pictures of women posed for cheesecake camera shots. The men were later randomly selected for a fantasy photo shoot, some as models and some as directors. They were asked to pose in a similar fashion. At first, John remarks on the men's expressions just looking at the pictures. Just looking made them fearful. Later, those who played the parts of models stood before a gawking audience.

Most of the men responded that in posing to replicate the pictures, they felt "vulnerable . . . awkward . . . humiliated . . . uncomfortable . . . embarrassed . . . degraded." He attributed most of the uncomfortable feelings to what he called the "alienation effect," an experience of "self splitting that female models perform in order to qualify as sexy in a camera's lens."

Your work is to keep yourself sexy, enjoy your presentation and keep from splitting. You can accomplish that by staying focused on *your* experience, not on the viewer's. In fear, you might turn off or turn away, or hide your head in the sand. You must replace such "ostrich sex" with full-frontal, engaging sex that goes deep to the core of your childhood programming, but also calls you to your higher spiritual Self. The spiritual and sexual path is not for sissies. You are now investigating an important aspect of growing up and maturing into your intended life. You'll be spiritually leaving your childhood home. Sexual preference is something you develop independent of your parents. You will have to make friends with your bonobo so you can meet your goddess.

As your pulsating temple has been inviting you to more and better sex, your social and media contacts are bombarding you with messages about restriction. Good girls don't eat dessert. Your mind is battered with intellectual, scientific information, while your body and soul seek sensation. You are seeking a form of relatedness that enhances your being.

But so many warnings abound. Yes, you may need to learn all you can about sexually transmitted diseases, prophylactics and prevention, but this information shouldn't paralyze you and shouldn't be the only focus of your sexual discussions. Today's excessive focus on the ill effects of sex has silenced our celebrations of the glories we can find in it.

Let's now take a look at the medical model and see how much we're warned about ill health from indulging the senses, whether eating or bedding. Then we'll see how much our sexuality is relegated to topics of abuse and incest instead of celebration and joy. We are investigated as survivors of trauma instead of trained as agents of pleasure. Body image workshops at many treatment centers focus on body acceptance instead of sensuality training. Those who comfort your victimhood must also train you to stay in connection and power.

What You Want, What He Wants

As you give up excess food, it stands to reason you'd want more sex. Some women, however, report the opposite. You may wonder how this could be. These women report that they shy away from sex; some are even repulsed by it. Some report childhood sexual trauma, rendering them repulsed by sex today. Most clinicians have accepted these reports and spent most of their time focused on their patients' pasts.

Jean-Paul Sartre said, "Freedom is what we do with what was done to us." Your past trauma may be a call to awakening, creating you as more aware and responsive than others. In that way, you may be more aware of connections, when they are made and when they miss. According to a 1997 survey in a popular women's magazine, it's not childhood trauma, but present-day life that causes sexual turnoff. *Mademoiselle* magazine, in its annual sex survey, found that 81 percent have sex when they don't really want to, 47 percent still fake orgasm and 27 percent are celibate. The respondents attribute their lack of sexual interest to job and life stress and having no time. These young women see relationships as stress and too much like work. If you suffer from disordered eating, you have to do this work!

You need to make contact and be seen while enjoying sensual stimulation. That's where a partner comes in. You want to make sure that you are personally involved and connected to the experience. Your body needs focused, intentioned sensation. Remember, you are animal and also spiritual. If not given focused attention, you'll revert to excess eating. Eating is just a substitute. Food doesn't pay attention. It is passive, so you feel in control of the merger, but you really don't get much out of it. Eating is the safest and easiest merger experience you know. Food comforts while it makes little demand on your time and no demand on your intellect. It is readily available at any time or table, and it doesn't ask you to present any image. When you feel there's not enough of you to go around, food is there for you, not taking, but giving. It provides instant gratification with no commitment of Self. In a sense, it's really a free lunch, but you pay double in excess pounds when you aren't connected and fully sated.

Fat Unhealthy?

We have been bludgeoned with warnings about the danger of overeating. Yet, the warnings don't change the behavior. Psychologically, weight loss is sometimes contraindicated. Some extremely obese individuals, up in the seven-hundred- to eight-hundred-pound range, coped very well at high weights, but after they lost weight suffered major depressions.

When I was fat, I rarely had any physical complaints. When I lost weight, I needed back adjustments to correct the scoliosis I developed as a result of my spine growing crooked to accommodate the excess weight. When I lost weight, the balance shifted, causing new pain. As a fat lady, I had scoffed at any woman who complained of menstrual cramps, but when newly thin, some days I went to Midol with the best of them. I'd previously eaten to soothe any cramping pain. So, you may not want to face some of the new pains that weight loss brings. According to that longest-running, twenty-five-year Framingham study, thin was not necessarily best. Thinnest men had the worst life expectancy. For women, moderate excess weight was not a mortality risk. It's the moderate excess weight that most of us struggle over and complain about. Naomi Wolf refers to it as the "one stone problem" (a stone is fourteen pounds in the British weight system). That's where most of us struggle.

Just Say No!

You certainly haven't been encouraged to enjoy sex for its own sake. At a recent conference for marriage and family counselors, a concern arose that parents not say too much about enjoying sex for fear the children would want to do it—as if not mentioning it would make the itch go away. The speaker's recommendation was that while discussing sex, parents must also discuss "values." Their values related to morality and love. There was no value placed on pleasure. Why not really teach children about pleasure and the *value* of connection?

We usually think "values" means waiting for marriage or holding out for love. Instead of "just say no," I recommend we teach "wait 'til you feel a true 'yes.'" Why not teach the value of keeping a vulva vigil, waiting to feel connection before consummation? You could teach kids to hold out for the good stuff, just like they can wait for the best dessert rather than bingeing on cellophane-wrapped junk. Why not teach about

the emptiness of meaningless involvements and how wonderful it is to hold out—not for moral reasons, but for personal preference and integrity? Children can benefit from
learning about good lovin' for its own sake. You can talk
about the frustration, but then ultimate satisfaction of waiting for the best.

It is important that you take a long, hard look at yourself
and your programming in order to understand who you've
become and why. You have probably been raised to believe
that your goal is to be a good girl and get married. That's still
basically true in the 1990s. To do that, you have to monitor
yourself, both sexually and gastronomically. Women experiencing pleasure of any kind are usually sent reeling with guilt
and remorse. All that deprivation training influences the kind
of package you bring to your partner. Instead of bringing your
lover welcome entrée to heavenly pleasures, you may instead
bring him your conflicts between indulgence and abstinence.
Your sex life and your dining habits reflect the mixed and
inhuman messages of a sick society.

So much has been made of sexual abuse and incest in the
last two decades that you find little opportunity to look at the
exact nature of the kind of sex you want. You want empowering,
soulful sex that takes you to a higher level of consciousness.

Intimacy doesn't mean sharing deep, dark secrets, but
rather, bright, light experiences. You don't want to make your
lover into father confessor. Think about how much of your problems or difficult past needs to be shared with your lover. Even
molestation or damage is not necessarily immutable. In other
words, even if you were invited or coerced into activities against
your will or judgment, that does not *automatically* mean that
you are irreparably damaged. You may have been told what you

should feel and never stopped to ask yourself what you *do* feel. Examine closely the current thinking of our culture, and then go inward to Self to find your own answer. How bad was it really? Were some parts of it good for you? Can you admit to that? Is that scary? Were you traumatized or slightly repulsed? Does the perpetrator still live rent-free in your head, or could you boldly flick him away so you can now flower?

Even if you've been abused, that doesn't mean you can't like sex. The trauma model of life tends to trivialize us as beings: when we "traumatize" our experience, we don't see how heroic and courageous humans are. We aren't just knee-jerk reactors to our unhappy childhoods. We are resilient and flexible. Love shakes our tree. We seek relationships, not for safety, but for growth.

Let your trauma go. Let it go for the sake of better sex. Let a little love in your heart. It's fine to delight in other pleasures and joys as long as you don't limit yourself. Allow your sexual life, your erotic and intimate self, to also provide fulfillment. Learn to drink from the well of your own desire.

Don't worship your neuroses. Freud did. He believed we were immutably programmed by age five and that our sexual repressions would haunt all aspects of our lives. Freud believed that no one ever improved, let alone healed. Newer thinking is not so pessimistic. Joseph Glenmullen, instructor in psychiatry at Harvard Medical School, wrote in *The Pornographer's Grief and Other Tales of Human Sexuality*, "Sexual identity is incredibly plastic and changeable." You may have watched yourself in a number of sexual growth spurts. With early maturation, desires for sex are often like desires to relieve yourself, like sneezing. Later, as you matured, you coupled the physical release with a sense of wanting intimacy. The desire to share intimacy happens for both men and women as they age and accounts for many women reporting that older men are better lovers. Men, too, want closeness. So, even if you were abused early in life, and then lived through a marriage consenting to painful inter-course, that doesn't mean there's no hope now.

Most eating-disorder specialists have studied your infantile sexuality and abuse instead of looking at your current func-tioning. They have come up with a fairly commonplace "wall of fat" idea, explaining that you erect walls to ward off feared sexual advances. They'll tell you that most women who struggle with food have been sexually abused and, therefore, fear sex. However, too many fat women who weren't sexually abused refute this. From my sessions with some of them, I'd say the wall of fat serves to ward off *unsatisfying* sex, not nec-essarily abusive sex. That's a different issue. Think about *your* issue now.

Psychobabble Stifles

I realize what a can of worms we open here. Millions of women enter therapy every year working on relationships or sexual dysfunction of some kind. They usually show up asking, "What's wrong with me?" Instead, with sex, the fault, dear Brutus, lies not in ourselves, but in our society. Maybe your discomfort signals not what's wrong but, rather, what's *right* with you. Why not ask yourself how you adjust to a social structure that teaches you to beat up on your natural self? Maybe the correct plea for eating disorders is not insanity, but self-defense. There's got to be some natural repercussion somewhere. In your case, constricting sexual juices shows up *on* the body. You live in a society that doesn't support your sensuality or growth. Your neurosis may be your last saving grace. It may be the righteous rebellion of a delicate flower snuffed out before its bloom. D. H. Lawrence, noted novelist and author of *Lady Chatterley's Lover*, was upset with a schizoid culture that overvalued rationality and thus promoted emptiness in relationships. Lawrence felt that to counteract the strong power of the female, the fear of a dominating mom, modern men had come up with a male-dominated sexuality. Male-dominated sexuality seemed to focus more on the attainment of pleasure and performance. Lawrence and others wrote less about the goal than about the journey. He found focus on the goal unnatural and limiting.

Ezra Pound said of Lawrence, "[his] use of the word 'touch' isn't epidermal but a profound penetration into the core of someone's being." That is the focus you will take with a vulva vigil, paying attention to penetration as a wise and conscious woman. Intercourse isn't all there is to sex. I trekked the Amazon with a botanist who pointed to every stamen and pistil of the lush tropical plants with, "It's all sex." I studied acting with movie stars and commercial directors instructing me to make love to the camera and the product. They too advised, "It's all sex." Your local newscast blares out the latest presidential affairs each evening, questioning whether he did or didn't have sex. When does sex begin? It's all sex. Are we having sex now or what?

You'll do well to admit that it's all sex. Nature loves to thrive. As you eat, you will accept each moment, each morsel, each crossing of your boundary as pure, unadulterated sex. Accepting this sexuality of eating can help you open up to yourself as a sexual being. It might make the word *sex* go down "a little easier." Your sexuality has something to do with early infancy training. If you were raised in this dieting, restrictive culture, you learned early and well to disown the body. Dr. Hilde Bruch asked mothers of obese children about infant eating episodes. Moms reported the experiences as "uneventful and rather bland." In normal development, eating is where the infant exercises independence and owning power. The exercise of eating, allowing in or refusing food, is one of the first opportunities for humans to exert power and influence over the universe. It's your first chance to negotiate how your boundaries are crossed. You need to control timing and styles of entry. If you were not in some power struggle with mom and the spoon, you may have become overly compliant, sensing mom's needs more than your own. Now as an adult, you battle this out in your own plate and bed.

For both men and women, sex is our true expression of individuality; yet, in many ways, it is beyond our control. What constitutes your attraction to a white T-shirt at age twenty and then a pin-striped business suit at forty? Can you sort out your own preferences from what has been programmed into you? Just know that when your sexuality is born in a culture that exalts male power, both you and your men have not been schooled in valuing the female. You may be with a man who gets scared at the power of your eroticism.

He may say he feels controlled. If you've touched his heart, he may have to retaliate. Feeling that he thinks too much of you, he may shut down his desire. At the same time, you might be afraid to let go, show yourself and truly be seen. You may not want to show how much you really crave sex. It's not the ladylike way. You might not want to look that vulnerable, or you may fear he'll suspect you're using him. On some level, you lessen your desire so as not to look too "castrating." That word has surely served well to limit female sexuality.

You may feel overburdened with a sense of responsibility to boost the male ego. If he is strong in his own desires, not holding back because of this powerful mother thing, then you could let yourself go without fear of emasculating him with your desires. Is your lover interested in licking you or his own wounded ego?

No wonder so many eating disorders came to women during the adolescent growth spurt with the onset of puberty and sexual longing. Having sex in our society is a strange and forbidden right of passage to adulthood. Having sex is a way to separate and leave home. We offer no rituals around entering puberty or the onset of menarche. Instead, sex is our right of passage. If you had realistic ambivalence about growing up and leaving home, you probably had nowhere to share it. With so many rapid changes in modern society, parents' homes can often feel safer than the future unknown. Who wants to grow up? Instead of facing that conflict, you might have taken it out to lunch. Taking it to bed doesn't solve the conflict either.

When Sigmund (I-don't-have-penis-envy-but-you-do) Freud wrote about how much females felt like "failed males," he always wondered about "what women want," but he never asked. He had to admit that mental illnesses are rare in cultures where girls are more free sexually. Even his own daughter probably suffered an eating disorder, writing him letters from camp about how "fat" she felt. Freud noted that women found food a comforting substitute for erotic pleasure. He wrote of "disturbances of eating," which we today call "eating disorders." These problems were only seen in women. In a paper entitled "Female Sexuality," he wrote about the divisions among his followers on this topic. He noted that women more than men were greatly in fear of losing control. (Remember, food is a comforter we *can* control.)

Two of his most ardent dissenters were Karen Horney and Melanie Klein. Klein didn't buy the Oedipus complex. Freud said girls feel bad as a result of the "narcissistic wound" that we have because we can't feel mastery in urination. He wrote that we are inhibited because we can't stand up when we urinate. This makes us feel weak and out of control because we can't command admiration of our stream. Excuse me?

He's got to be kidding. Is this something you've actually considered at any time or in any way? Puhleeze! Unencumbered by underwear, in our natural state, we definitely *can* stand and urinate. It requires a slight parting of the legs and no pointing. Squatting makes it even easier. Perhaps ours is the more efficient anatomy and the men feel jealous and urinarily challenged.

I have not found one woman who can describe feelings of penis envy! For the guys who suffer from it, however, women would gladly recount this old proverb: "It's not the size of the boat, but the motion of the ocean." Women seeking conscious coitus might add another: "You can never tell the depth of the well by the length of the pump handle."

It's not just in elimination, but also in procreation, that the males may actually be jealous of females. In the paper "Dread of Women," Karen Horney suggested that Freud underestimated how much males have "womb envy." The rooster may crow, but the hen delivers the eggs. Ever since Eve offered the apple to Adam, human history recounts tales of sinister, mysterious, tempting, fearsome women to be dreaded and feared. Horney believed that men masked this dread with love and admiration, and then secretly defended against it by conquering, debasing and diminishing the very objects of their desires. No wonder we developed the Madonna-whore mentality.

While Freud taught that "anatomy is destiny" and that all our basic programming was set by age five, Horney believed in the life-affirming, positive strivings of the human organism and that we could be shaped by new situations and remain open and responsive to our environment.

Childbirth is one area in which men can envy women, and orgasm is another. As a woman, your orgasms offer great variety and changeability. If you just keep at it, you will be opened to infinite variety. Stay tuned for surprises. Men's experience is pretty pat, straightforward and repetitive. No surprises. Males led the debates about vaginal and clitoral orgasms. Women were too busy enjoying all of them. Male orgasms might be likened to eating boring fast foods. There's a rush of sugar or fat, but it all seems to taste pretty much the same. Women have so many more variables. The clit comes and goes. Sometimes the earth moves, and shudders occur incessantly. Other times it's a slow, rumbling type of earthquake.

There are so many different ways females feel pleasure, and men who pay attention know about them. One male workshop attendee noted to a group composed predominantly of females, "It is okay with guys if you gals masturbate, because you may be getting into more complicated machinery. We know that it isn't always as easy as tightening a few screws or delivering an oil change. Sometimes you just may need full maintenance."

At age seventy-six, in a lecture about his findings on femininity, Freud apologized, ". . . it is certainly incomplete and fragmentary and does not always sound friendly. . . . If you want to know more about femininity, inquire of your own experiences of life, or turn to the poets, or wait until science can give you deeper and more coherent information."

Sorry, folks. The best science has been able to come up with is a further constricting of the wild woman by focusing on our dysfunctions rather than our functions. It took the intricate research of Masters and Johnson with probes and sensors to finally tell us that the two "types of orgasms," vaginal and clitoral, were "not distinguishable on a physiological level, but have different psychological factors." Their expert "scientific" studies have still not identified the mysteries of that goddess experience. Women call in the spirits to unite body and soul. Can you stand to own your power and still assert that you are a mystery? Isn't that juicy? We're still mysterious; we are not yet explained to death by science. Isn't it great that female sexuality is still so elusive?

If you've been in therapy for a long time and remain fat, then please continue reading. You may feel that you are not really into sex because of painful first intercourse experiences, incest or other traumas. You may be admitting yourself to treatments focused on your past traumas instead of treatments that are invitations to your future awakening.

It is important that you trust and listen to the experience of other women. As more women become willing to celebrate and talk about their sexuality, we will change the nature of all sexuality. In *Ordinary Women, Extraordinary Sex*, Sandra Scantling and Sue Browder documented what women reported as the results of their peak sexual experiences. They reported a feeling of total absorption, a sense of connectedness. They felt that their spiritual and sexual selves were no longer separate. They had a feeling of confidence and a zest for life, as if they were transcending self-consciousness and self-judgment. It was similar to having achieved a state of grace. Many reported feeling healed or transformed beyond the physical body. They described themselves as feeling "powerful, high, floating." Now, it's important to determine whether the man gives this feeling to you, or whether you have the innate capacity for power and he merely helps tap it. In other words, do you carry the power and simply need him to "recharge," or does he "give" you power? Is he a source or a booster? Is he the battery or the charger? Your answers to these questions will greatly determine the course of your life. As you own power, you don't need to overfill your tank with excess food. Can you live with the power *and* its mystery?

Is This My Diagnosis or My Life?

Some professional interventions might have helped you avoid, rather than claim, your sexual power. You've been diagnosed instead of motivated and stimulated. As a female therapist, I have both participated in and observed the gradual progression into deeper diagnoses of women. As women achieved more power in the workplace, medical staffs helped us deny power in the bedroom. The female success wave of the 1980s was transformed into female failure. A reactionary, low-self-esteem psychology was born. Big businesses of weight loss, beauty and feminist psychotherapy were born. Some of this was actually set in motion by the very treatment centers that were formed to help women.

In 1975, I started the nation's first Twelve-Step eating disorders unit at San Pedro Peninsula Hospital in Los Angeles. It evolved from my work with early addiction-treatment centers and my involvement with the U.S. Navy's alcoholism programs, treating Betty Ford and other prominent figures. When Betty bravely admitted her problem, it helped thousands of women accept help for themselves. Before her courageous admission, women were dying in back bedrooms, while families mourned, "Thank God, it's over." Following Betty Ford, hundreds of thousands of women have entered treatment, and many have remained sober for many years. Now they want to make love consciously!

Admitting alcoholics to hospitals, fitting them with an arm band, and having an official person with a stethoscope and white lab coat tell them they were truly sick helped them recover. They were able to stop blaming and judging themselves, got off their own backs and were willing to accept help. They came to see that they had tried their best and all their efforts brought them right through the doors of our hospital. We taught them that they were not bad people trying to get good, but sick people trying to get well. We taught them about the progression of the illness, the family dynamics, the psychological profile and the road to recovery. They moved from the *sin* to the *sickness* model.

I saw that what worked for healing alcoholism could work equally well for overeating. By interpreting the diagnosis for bulimia, adding a nutrition and exercise component, and emphasizing how overeaters had to make friends with their substance, I adapted what had worked for alcoholics, and opened my first Helping Overeaters through People and Education (HOPE) eating disorders unit. Shortly thereafter, hundreds of units spread throughout the country. Many suffering people found recovery. Chronically obese dieters gave up the food obsession and went on to live productive, aware lives. For both the alcoholic woman and the eating-disordered woman, however, little attention was paid to lustful, adult sexuality. Though we'd been eating and drinking excessively since puberty, we assumed that once in recovery we'd instantaneously know how to have great sex. We didn't. No one did. Many had been eating and drinking in order to cope with lousy sex.

During the first decade such treatment centers existed, rapid changes occurred that created many of our current problems. Insurance company executives began to see the tremendous payments made for both alcoholism and eating-disorder treatment. Many doubted the efficacy of such treatment, the necessity of lengthy hospital stays and the actual severity of the illness. They began to question aggressively and push for shorter inpatient stays with more outpatient follow-up. Based purely on economic considerations, they instructed treatment centers that $1.30 per day for an anti-depressant pill was, in their opinion, much wiser than the exorbitant staffing and operational costs of full-counseling programs for all family members.

Battle lines were drawn. Hospital treatment staffs argued and held out for longer "lengths of stay," while insurance company clerks insisted that only cases of "extreme danger to self or others" warranted inpatient admissions. The treatment staff knew that if the chart described the patient as extremely damaged, dangerous and chaotic, needing intensive therapy, the insurance company would pay for another few days. When a patient mentioned some horrific event in childhood, it was sure to be attended to and written up extensively. Trauma was important. Subtly, counselors started "charting to catastrophe." Daily life problems, the broken fingernails and shoelaces that many of us binge over, were sloughed off or

ignored as "nonreimbursable." Insurance companies deter-
mined what was important and worthy of note, and thus
extreme cases of terrible abuse were mentioned in staffings,
written up in charts and published in professional papers. The
"normally neurotic" average case was not worth mentioning.

It became a game. First, counselors hunted down abuses
and extremes. Then patients competed with each other in
groups, vying for attention, catastrophizing: "I am sicker than
thou." Finally, treatment staffs came to believe that the population was actually growing sicker. That was not the case; it
was just that we had all been subtly coerced into noticing only
the worst-case scenario. Eventually we came to believe in
what we had hunted out, cultivated and developed. We
believed the "ain't it awful" catastrophe model. We focused on
some "causal event" that must have traumatized the person.
We hunted down a cause and then ended our investigations.
We abandoned the complex, multifaceted individual, relegat-
ing her to a limited diagnostic category. Then we could chart
a treatment plan with goals and objectives and prove to insur-
ers that we had "fixed" the problem. We functioned like auto
mechanics. We taught the patient to believe she had a mechanistic personality, that she had developed some knee-jerk
reaction to a past event and become entrapped by it. This was
so simplistic, but safe. The tragedy is that we stopped looking
at more current, present-day lifestyle changes that could be
curative. Patients and their counselors began relishing the
recounting of past traumatic events. Subtly, the issue of
"choice" was removed from the conversation. If you've done
this to yourself, please ask now, "To what end?" What did you
leave out? Is there other life in there somewhere?

Any facility that wanted to stay open had to conform to the

insurance companies' dictated guidelines. Insurance clerks became the arbiters of a patient's fate. Families were rarely involved. Drugs were the logical solution to any problem. Teamwork and community self-help groups were devalued and disrespected. Often insurance companies authorized admissions for patients and then later changed their minds. Once hospitals went to the expense of providing treatment, the insurance carriers would later renege and refuse to reimburse, basically shrugging with, "Go collect. Our lawyers are tougher than your lawyers."

Insurance companies just stonewalled. Finally, in 1996, after several years of observing my competent, dedicated psychiatrists spending much of their days arguing on the phone with clerks, I closed my last remaining treatment center.

The tragedy of all this is that the insurance world dictated that health care providers had to *prove* sickness. This made it doubly hard to convince a patient who was already in denial. Whereas earlier we had labored to convince alcoholics and ovcreaters and their insurance carriers that they were sick and needed help, we now had to *prove* it! This component helped many stay out of treatment. In short, it wasn't enough to be living a life of pain. Patients had to show that they were truly damaged, in need of crisis intervention and intensive care.

Thousands who never had an inkling of such a thing suddenly remembered sexual abuse. Sexual abuse was horrific! Attention was paid, and so was the insurance bill. Counselors attended weekend seminars where instructors told them that 95 percent of eating disorder sufferers had been violated as children. They were instructed that patients amassed great flesh to avoid sexual overtures and that such avoidance tactics were unconscious. They were instructed to push clients to remember damaging incidents. If patients couldn't remember, counselors were instructed to confront the patients' denial systems.

This hysteria wasn't quite justified. Some patients weren't traumatized. They just chose the comfort of food over other comforts that require more conscious connection. I'm not trying to minimize anyone's trauma, but even if traumatized, you may have to cultivate adult choices anyway. We all can live in the face of horror. If you have been abused, you may need a lot of help, and this book may be only one of many tools. This book is for the countless, moderately disturbed dieters who didn't suffer such abuses but are still fat. The situation is bad enough without anyone making it worse. For example, I remember Anabelle, who couldn't stop eating. She decided to stop attending OA meetings because she felt *they* were not working. She was not following any disciplined food plan. She expected prayer to dissolve her fat. She had an inkling that "Even though I don't remember, I must have had an incest event that caused this. I am going to Sex Addicts Anonymous to uncover what I am hiding." I, on the other hand, felt that a few weeks of disciplined eating would teach her anything she needed to know. *Not* eating would have brought to the surface whatever trauma she needed uncovered. At last report, she was still fat.

Many who were not able to maintain a "weight loss" food plan turned to such groups to unite as victims of abuse. They saw themselves as sexually damaged, in need of extensive counseling, at extremes of either asexual or overly sexed beings. Again, if this alternative proved healing for you, maybe it can help you cut down eating. I, however, found too many who were not truly damaged sexually. They had normal, healthy, lusty-lady sexual urges and didn't know how to live with them. By the way, this was also true for those who'd been abused. Quite honestly, just because you've been abused doesn't mean you don't like sex or that you shouldn't. Nor does it mean that because you do, you will participate in your own abuse. Maybe you enjoyed some parts of it even then, and you need to make friends with that side of yourself now. This is wonderful and so potentially healing. If you want to make friends with yourself, read on.

Currently many eating disorder clinics are tied to trauma centers. Yes, we may be treating the same clientele for both issues, but no doubt there is some teaching going on where counselors convince patients that they have been damaged, are responding poststress and as a result are fat. Maybe yes, maybe no, but saying this will get insurance companies to pay the bill. Your psychological diagnosis may be an economic convenience. What if we are not damaged and traumatized, but just unable to cope in such an inhumane society? What if we have no training in growing to sexual maturity? Maybe it is harder to think of surviving the daily abuses of this life than it is to think of surviving trauma.

Finding out that you are actually a super person, blessed with greater sensitivity, intuition and clarity than most might be harder to face. What if you are actually more sexually responsive, awakened and available than "healthy" folk? At a 1997 eating-disorder conference, Dr. Bessel A. van der Kolk, psychiatry professor at Harvard, gave a slide presentation that showed the actual brain changes produced by trauma. He noted that sexually abused girls have three times as much testosterone as nonabused girls, secrete twice the amount of sexual hormones and mature sexually two years ahead of the norm. As they naturally turn to sexual activity, we label and diagnose them as "acting out." What if we shifted the lens and took another view of these young ladies, perhaps applauding their head start on learning about sexual pleasure and possible connections? I know this might be difficult, but just allow the concept to enter your thinking process. I'm just asking you to try another view of "significant" events. We have no machinery for aiding and applauding sexually maturing young women. As a result, we diagnose their behavior as problematic. Truly, their problems are culturally induced, based on someone else's idea of when to start having sex, and then how often to have it thereafter. We're concerned that they are starting young, so we look for dysfunctional causes. Their problems are cultural. They live in a society that fears female sexuality. Are we too threatened? Are clinicians threatened or jealous and thus overly diagnostic?

Food Is Good Girls' Sex

Your therapy should help you to celebrate what is right about *your own* behavior instead of focusing on what was done to you. That would make you active, not passive. If you want to improve self-perception, just look to current success. Let's look at what is right about you, instead of getting out that big burgundy bible, the *Diagnostic and Statistical Manual* (DSM) from which therapists glean diagnoses.

In looking for what is "right," we might have to accept parts of ourselves we formerly judged: our sexual longings, for instance. In our society, we just can't stand to say that women love sex. Any alcoholism lecture you hear will talk about alcohol loosening inhibitions and how male alcoholics then run amok, doing whatever they feel like. We believe that for men, but not for women. Anne Geller recently spoke at New York University's recovering day for women, explaining the gender issues in recovery. She discussed the elaborate "scripts" women try to play out. Dr. Geller related that women get drunk and then "act" promiscuous, hinting that they are not as sexual when sober. She lamented that women "get a bad rap" for being hot to trot, which is not their true state. Yet, this refutes every other statement about the effects of alcohol. If we say that alcohol lowers inhibitions in men, allowing their true nature to emerge, why can't we say the same for women? When inhibitions are lowered, can't women be sexy, too? Maybe some women have to drink in order to show this lusty side. Wouldn't it be nice if they could show it without drinking?

Most people you ask can recall a scene of a drunken woman embarrassing herself. Even if she's sexy, she's often laughed at and disparaged. Fat women are also noted, objectified and ridiculed. You might think, *Well, if they don't want to be talked about, they shouldn't put themselves in that situation.* Instead, consider that you, along with most women, live in fear of appearing like those women. At all costs, you want to avoid looking the fool. You don't want to let anyone see that you want or need sex. *Need* is embarrassing. This could inhibit your sexuality.

Shoshana races down to see me from Monsey, New York. She has just become engaged to what she calls a "nice Jewish boy." Very Orthodox and wanting to maintain a current weight loss, she sees that she has to resolve sexual issues before she can consummate this marriage. As we talk, I find that there are sexual issues alongside maturational issues. She wants to grow up and birth herself into her own adult life. She is grateful at this point that the Orthodox community in Monsey discourages physical contact for men and women before marriage. For her, it makes things easier.

However, she is concerned as a result of the Shabbat dinner she recently attended with her fiancé's family. "I was so swooning and slain in the spirit. I was sitting next to him. The rest of them were singing and joyous. Everyone was having a good time. All were reverent and celebrating God's gifts. I was orgasmic.

"I felt every note of the songs in every capillary of my blood system. I thought I was going to faint. I was so scared that they could see it all over my face. I couldn't look at Herschel because I was afraid I would grab him and kiss him right there at the table."

Shoshana had lost a lot of weight as a result of diagnosing her own eating disorder and going to Overeaters Anonymous. Now, her sexuality was brimming. She was seeing a therapist to explore her "issues as an incest survivor."

She was also, at age thirty, still living at home with her parents. Though capable, she had trouble finding work, so instead of working, she spent two days a week visiting an elderly lady just to be "of service." Within a few minutes, she felt comfortable reporting to me how sexual she felt. I suggested that her "incest issues" were not about victimization, but about fully feeling the power of her brimming female sexuality. I suggested that she feared her own lust, rather than approaches from men.

She smiled sheepishly and then told me that she was afraid she lusted more than most. Women were "nice" in the religious community, and she didn't know how to grow into that while feeling such uncontrollable physical urges.

I suggested that she was just more honest about it. I also intimated that her inability to find satisfying work could be tied to her repressing her sexuality.

That stopped her short. She stared intently at me for a few minutes. Suddenly, she grew painfully honest with herself. "Why am I spending two days a week visiting this old neighbor lady instead of getting on with my life? I think I am re-creating and reliving the bad scene I lived with my grandparents. I'm sort of waiting for Grandpa to come in and violate me again. I am anxious whenever I am over there."

"Why might you think you'd go to that experience at this time?" I asked. I hate shrinklike questions, but sometimes they are helpful.

"I think I'm supposed to be looking to the future and to my future as a sexual, mature woman. I need a job and a life. Instead, I look back to a time when Grandpa was in charge. Somehow it feels safer because it was a time when I was less responsible. Now, I am the sexual predator. I am so afraid of showing myself in all this womanhood. I don't want to appear foolish."

There it was. . . . A woman who is sexual is foolish. She will be left alone. No one will want her because she wants. She represents that insatiable, hungry, prowling female. She has to effect a dishonest stance pretending she doesn't crave what brings her ultimate satisfaction. Her only sexual recourse is anorexia. . . . Deny the hunger. . . .

Shoshana lives in a society that restricts sexually expressive females. She feels foolish for wanting, not realizing how many other women are feeling the same way. In fact, early in 1998, the *New York Times* ran a number of articles about Orthodox communities in Brooklyn, where very sexy intimate apparel was sold in basements to very religious women who hid their ankles and hair by day, but were seductive temptresses by night. Why is it all kept so hidden? An ancient

Jewish law known as *onah* requires that a husband sexually satisfy his wife. Women are allowed to encourage this in any way they see fit. The religious are not opposed to sex at all. They are just opposed to making it a sacrilege. They want it conscious and spiritual. So do you.

A strong group of feminist clinicians write and teach that the psychology of women needs to be addressed differently than that of men. They argue that Jungian ideas teaching individuation, separation, differentiation and autonomy are true for men, but not women. In my last book, *Fat & Furious,* I followed some of the Jungian perspective, suggesting that daughters' work was to individuate from their mothers. Our work is to grow up and leave home, to learn what we can from our parents, how we are similar and how we are different, and then grow into the Self we were meant to be. That often means leaving behind outmoded values that no longer work. It could mean rejecting rules your mother taught you, but does not mean that you reject *her*. It means you separate from her life in order to live your own.

Once individuated, and thus knowing who you are as a separate self, you are ready to choose partners for healthy and growth-producing reasons. You have to be a separated being before you can truly mate. The clinicians with the "new feminist perspective" tell us that men are the ones well trained in separation (mostly seen as a negative trait) and that women, instead, long for and are adept at "connection." They say that failed connections are largely the fault of men. They say that women are instead expansive, resilient and move out of themselves to encompass and include everyone as one. They don't seem to see any vulnerable men in their practice, but only women as victims. They also don't see the many women I do, who, to paraphrase Greta Garbo, "vahnt to be alone."

It's a Gal Thing?

Some writers want to convince us that women are the saintly sex seeking love and connection. Men instead are described as boorish animals, causing all our problems. Some of these women actually rant like sailors, showing one kind of power, while they ignore the gift of female sexual power.

When I first saw Jane Campion's movie *The Piano*, I wanted to run out and buy hoop skirts! If you saw the film, you surely can't forget the gentle seduction with which Harvey Keitel eventually got under those hoops. The sweetness of his respectful yet sensual approach to Holly Hunter was lustful, but poignant, sexy and erotic. She resisted until she couldn't, and then she was in love. Her mean-spirited daughter turned her in and caused shame and devastation about the adultery, but that motivated major change in the story, creating its intended ending. She left her intellectual, power-driven husband for a sensual woodsman who adored her piano playing as well as her sensuality. He admired her art as much as he craved her body. Her music was her only passion, until his love integrated it into her body. He waited until she could give her soul with her body.

I was shocked to later read feminist writers criticizing the film, citing misogynist rape fantasies for both men and the woman, and Holly's inevitable "surrender" as likened to what they saw as director Jane Campion's surrender to the money interests of Hollywood. These women saw the lusting men, one a husband who worked to be patient and tender, one a lover who only wanted her if and when *she* wanted him, as the enemies, the colonizers, men who trivialize women and their art. Give me a break. These men helped her birth herself. They helped her hear. Amazing grace moves us from "blind, but now can see." What do the critics want these men to do? Worship at the trough? Supplicate to fornicate? These guys were both gentle and sexy and worked to win her love. One could touch her art, and thus could go in for her heart.

Sometimes, seemingly supportive women may be doing you a disservice. They can keep you focused on men's abuses instead of redirecting you to your own passions. They don't acknowledge that women lust after and also need men. They buy into the old myths that men give love to get sex and women give sex to get love. If you are a woman who herself *wants* sex, that doesn't make you more like a man, but actually more like a woman. Women love sex! When men find this out, they can panic first, then act more respectful when they come to bed.

Erica Jong, whose books are repeated bestsellers, is a sexually powerful, man-seeking woman who is scoffed at by many feminists. Some feminist writers and teachers condemn her candor. They argue that she sold women a male fantasy of uninvolved sexuality. Yet, her portrayal of women who admit to really liking sex is admirable, even empowering. Sex need not be uninvolved. In fact, it's best for our purposes that it be even more intense and immediate. It just doesn't have to last all the way to the altar. Think about who is more involved and true: the coquette romancing men for marriage and security or the seductive, sensual woman tracing every moment of titillation.

Erica Jong's early bestseller became almost a manual for newly liberated women in the early 1970s. In *Fear of Flying*, she described a woman aboard a train in Italy who watches a scruffy stranger board. As the train passes through a long tunnel, these two jump each other's bones, consummate their heat and then sit back down to emerge from the earth's orifice, serene and sated. There was no awkwardness, only bliss. There were no bras to unhook or pants to unzip, certainly no nonsensical small talk to be made. It was all smooth as Vaseline, and in those days sex was even safe. This scene gave birth to the concept of a "zipless f–ck," and women began to fantasize about things they couldn't tell their mothers.

So as a woman, you can also like sex for its own sake just as passionately as some men. You have a vibrating, pulsating body that seeks connection. Wonderful opportunities for growth and learning about yourself can arise from those connections. True connection will draw out your disparate parts, forcing you to face yourself, sometimes getting yourself rearranged and better understood. What could be bad about that?

Women can also reject closeness. Sometimes the thing we most want is that which also terrifies us the most. A man called my radio show to tell us that he'd made love with a woman who told him she'd never come during intercourse. She'd been with five other men. When she came with him, she cried and told him he could never leave her. Two weeks later, she dumped *him*.

My female clients are often disconnected, separated and unto "themselves." They don't say that at first. In fact, they usually project this trait onto their lovers, judging them, wanting *them* fixed. They don't initially see that their partners mirror them. Eventually, they do see the parts of themselves that feel safer separate. They don't want to see it because they judge it to be "unfeminine." They are not longing for connection in relationships, but would really rather be alone, thanks. That is even true of those who complain of having boorish, "rock" husbands. In couples counseling, when the men do begin to talk, the wives try to shut them up. They find chocolate much more soothing than companionship. For both men and women, that position has to be respected, understood and admired. From that acceptance, a person can decide to give up food and move away at her own pace without conforming to yet another psychobabble expectation.

But we're a country as addicted to psychobabble as we are to drugs, food or any other self-destructive behaviors. Eric Sevareid said, "The biggest big business in the U.S. is the manufacture, refinement and distribution of anxiety." This anxiety has been visited excessively upon women. We are stressed out! The greatest antidote to sexuality is stress. We have the greatest menopausal problems of any Western country, and despite a thriving porno industry, we are most repressed sexually.

All these problems exist because we don't respect female sexuality. If we can allow women to have ruthless, wanton, selfish sexuality, instead of only compassionate, caring engagement, then we can "get real." When we live in the truth, our anxiety will diminish. Focusing so much on only loving, caring, sweet, enveloping women gives no allowance for selfish, aggressive, lusty passions. It is important for women to be able to speak aloud about their own selfishness. If we can't, then we have to continue the myths of our being overpowered and carried away by studs. If we don't give selfishness its due, it has to go underground. Then it's not a learning problem, but a listening problem. It's a howl not heard.

Accepting your sexuality as a growth opportunity will allow you to use sex to better know, see and hear yourself. Not a bad way to take a good look. Because sex seems to permeate our media and is given a lot of prime-time attention, we get the erroneous impression that we have an easy attitude about it. Watching television, we would think that everyone has sex within twenty-four hours of meeting, that the deed is accomplished with little talking. We think women's work is to attract, and men's work is to pursue. If these scenes are believed, then if you are thin and beautiful, you have sex a lot and like it a lot. We see sex as a disposable consumer product. In the romantic 1950s, a lot more time was spent leading up to the act, running consecutive bases and then scoring. Today we make love like we eat: *Life is uncertain. Eat dessert first.* Sex is explored as mostly physical with little connection. It is demystified and marketed and no longer sacred. Does anyone blush anymore? Do they listen or pay attention?

Women always ran the sexual show, but we can't believe how powerful we are. Shere Hite asked a very important question, "Is sex man penetrating woman or woman enveloping man?" Such questions are more psychological than physical. Often we have done a lot more psychological work than our men, and we have to help them turn to the same page. Compassion is required. This adventure forces us to become compassionate with ourselves and our mates. It is much easier to talk of concrete things like calories instead of the vagaries of vulnerability and dependencies.

Glowing

Even though women spend a lot of time exploring romance and delving into themselves as lovers and loved, many find it difficult to be loved well. Once you start listening to yourself, you will tune in to see how much has been missing. You will feel very vulnerable. You'll come to know the difference between when you found contact and when it wasn't there.

Men talk of a woman having "that morning-after glow." They notice and admire satisfied women. In the movie *Mr. Skeffington*, Claude Rains tells Bette Davis, "A woman is beautiful when she is loved and only then." I'd amend that to say, "loved well. . . ." Famous child psychiatrist Bruno Bettelheim wrote in *The Uses of Enchantment*, "It is, in the final analysis, love which transforms even ugly things into something beautiful." Is it beauty in the eyes of the beholder, or of the beheld? Do women notice this afterglow in their men?

Why aren't we speaking to all this as a joyous celebration instead of a dark, closet thing? There are so many very good reasons to celebrate sexuality. Yes, it feels great, but that's not all there is to sex. Why should you do the work of overcoming early childhood trauma to make yourself available for this experience? Dr. Sandra Scantling and Sue Browder are also concerned that we label women who like sex as "sick." They refer to such women not as pleasure addicts, but rather as "pleasure experts." They also see that when we're doing it right, it is a rare opportunity to be fully absorbed in an experience. Pleasure experts take the event beyond genital focus to one of connection. The connection of our spiritual and sexual selves renders us no longer separate, and that very connection is healing in and of itself. When we can go beyond titillation, we go beyond self-consciousness and awkwardness about performance. We gain a sense of unity with other living things and the present becomes elongated, even eternal. We experience a zest for life and a sense that all's right with the world. All this from a little good sex?

Yes, because it brings us to ecstasy, a way of knowing and the result of knowing. When your female body becomes grounded in this way, you walk with a certain sureness about yourself and life. In the *AA Big Book*, this new sense of spiritual consciousness is referred to as "being catapulted into the fourth dimension." There is a clarity of "knowing," a feeling of rightness.

Viva la Vulva, Love la Labia

Instead of body image workshops designed to help you accept the form of your individual rolls and swells, I run "Viva la Vulva" workshops designed to teach you to listen to and dance to a personal vibration. In order to dance to that personal tune, you'll have to love your labia and get them smacking!

When you've been fat all your life, you're used to having big lips. Since high school, I'd seen all those other women with flat abdomens and no protrusion "down there." Then there were women like me who had large lips and a mound of flesh. Another fat friend once noted that when she was losing weight, she'd wear tighter and tighter jeans and the seam between her legs would create a "taco shell" effect as her sex showed through. As women, we'd never discussed the "big lips" thing. I wondered if men talked much, comparing size and position of their organs. I imagined they didn't as it was such an ego-involved matter for them. Why didn't we women discuss and compare?

It's the lips, the outer vulva and labia area, that are our sex organs. So often we say, "men have a penis and we have a vagina." Well, the vagina doesn't do that much for us sexually or sensually. Sexual nerve endings only go in one inch. Vaginas are for birthing. Anatomically, our corresponding member to the penis is the clitoris. Your greatest pleasure happens outside the vagina. Those lips slurp and slide and move the clitoris. Lips are for loving. I want you to like your lips. They may, as Norman Mailer asserts, have a personality all their own. In an interview with Charlie Rose, Mailer told of how he'd had a lifelong fascination with seeing a certain face on a woman and then discovering a whole other being to her below the waist. Let's pay attention to what he's suggesting: Have you even looked "down there"? Could you tell us the personality of your labia? That's part of your vulva vigil. Know who guards the gates.

Notice what Virginia wrote during a group exercise where participants examined the "lay of their lips":

During most of my preteen, teen and early adult years, I had a fat apron covering my mound. When I first lost most of my weight, my stomach still hung down. I went to a surgeon to see about a tummy tuck. Thank God he didn't need the business. He told me to exercise and sent me packing. I'm happy to report that my belly has receded nicely, but a consequence is that my pubis protrudes. Invitation or curse?

The area stayed quite fleshy and bulbous for more than ten years after my initial weight loss. No one mentioned it, but I saw it. Then I started a small running program in conjunction with a new commitment to grow up.

As I exercised, developed my career and became more content to live a simpler life, my pubic area tightened up. By all laws of gravity, my lips should have been hanging more. Even Marilyn Monroe said, "Gravity gets the best of us all." Instead, the whole area was tightening, almost standing up and coming out. She was sticking herself out for the world to see. She was up and eager for visitation!

With varying weight losses and exercise programs, I've had the opportunity to examine my lips and my relationship to them. There is a lot to be said for keeping them hidden. Once exposing that area, you're awakening a call to eroticism. Now, my yoga teacher instructs us to walk as if our upper torso is a large vase resting comfortably on the pedestal of our hip girdle. Here I am now thrusting my pelvis more forward than ever in my life. I greet life, not with the linebacker's shoulder thrust, but instead with a graceful glide of my hips leading me into my life. It's a whole different ballgame.

I invite you now to ask yourself:

> Is my fat covering my pubic area?
>
> How does that serve me?
>
> What does it say to anyone approaching me?
>
> How will it change my life to lead with my pubis?

These questions are not here for debate. You have the flesh that you have. For whatever reason, you have a fleshy "mound of Venus." The teenagers at the beach may not. So be it. Moving into a womanly appreciation of your abdomen is a part of leaving your parents behind. You hope that you'll be with men who like the same things you've got.

I never thought I'd show up at a nudist camp and surely never thought I'd disrobe. I finally took up my uncle Sam's offer to visit him and Aunt Myra at the "clothing optional" camp where they lived. I was soon sans smock on a chaise lounge in the sun, peeking out above the large newspaper I was "reading." I learned a lot about bodies that day. It wasn't so much the form as the function. I saw many varieties of structure and flesh. I watched how forms hung on frames and I watched how the muscles moved. Size wasn't as interesting as the movement of the organism in space. I liked watching how flesh moved aligned with or opposed to the being inside. I was fascinated watching the movement of energy. That's what you have to embrace and admire in yourself.

You can see how, if you live by this credo, you can't complain about being "swept away." You become master and creator of your own energy field. You know what you are doing, and *you* are responsible. Instead of seeking validation as an art object, it will be better if you are connected to your own energy field. I've recently begun taking tango lessons, where I see many large women strut and gyrate and revel in their sensuality. Size is not at all a factor. Grace, style and energy win out over slimness.

If you are in your forties, you are entering a peak time. The famous designer Coco Chanel said, "A woman does not become interesting until she is over forty." In early agrarian societies, women were used up by then, but now women have fewer children and stay sexually active into their sixties and seventies. There's a lot of fun to be had. In *Anatomy of Love: The Natural History of Monogamy, Adultery, and Divorce*, Helen Fisher noted that, "Never before in history have so many women been free to express their sexuality." In the Alfred Kinsey reports of 1948 and 1953, only 26 percent of married women had conducted affairs, while 50 percent of married men had. In the 1990s, studies show men still at 50 percent, but women have moved up to 41 percent. I'm not inviting you to commit adultery, but rather, I want you to note that women are seeking more and better sex.

Perhaps eating or not eating has been your only way to exert power. You may have been eating to defy competitive standards you dared not confront directly. You're seeking control of a world you didn't create.

PMS

Rather than celebrating your body, you've probably heard a lot more messages to suffer with it. From menstruation to child bearing to painful, dutiful intercourse, you're taught that being female means misery and pain. Many have been taught to accept being "nice" over being successful. "Good works" will compensate for an unrewarding life. Most important, you've learned that you can't trust that demon body. You must control it. It must be sanitized, cosmeticized and limited at all costs. You can never let it grow out of hand or be free to wander. It will turn you on and turn on you!

Many have been pleased of late that the medical community gives so much attention to premenstrual syndrome. We've accepted our natural function as a medical malady and lost touch with the wisdom of our wise woman's bodies. Before the onset of menses, we go into a slight mourning period. This may be a last hurrah from the unfertilized egg lamenting its lost chance. Unfortunately, many can't stand any mournful message from the body. They'd rather find her voice discordant and abhorrent, so they turn to disempowering diagnoses that they call "healing." Be careful of this orientation. Trying to exorcise these hormonal messengers is not too far removed from distrusting the female and putting her into some "other" box. Just because you seem "edgy" does not mean there is something wrong. Maybe PMS is what's *right* with you. What if there is no such thing as PMS and this is your true self showing up? You might only discover PMS and your mourning female when your food intake is limited. When you stuffed these natural longings with excess food, you never had a cramp or cry. When eating is curbed, you'll listen to these natural messengers.

There are other cultures that welcome and glorify the female's apparently crazy monthly oozings and mutterings. They stay tuned in and listening, rather than medicating. In some Native American tribes as well as among the Balinese, menstruating women are barred from religious ceremonies. This is not because menstruating women are considered unclean. Quite the contrary. They tell us that, during this time, women channel such high spiritual energy that they act as a lightning rod from God. They are sent away from the ceremonial tent so that others may partake of this energy. In their view, menstruating women would channel all the energy, leaving none for others. In Lakota tribes, women go off alone to menstruant tents where they and their children are cared for by other women. They are instructed to listen to the rumblings and high spiritual messages their bodies send. They are left alone to listen and watch themselves freak out. Encouraged to withdraw, be more introspective and go down into their dark shadow sides, they then report back any messages from the cosmos. This is when we are most like a raw nerve; but a very clear, vibrant transmitter. Unfortunately, in modern Western society, we decide instead to medicate this altered state. Earthbound cultures instinctively give women this time of no distraction to be involved in prayer and meditation. We "moderns" instead label this wonderful experience a medical malady.

Diagnosing PMS is tragic! The medical establishment shuffled the validity of grave concerns into some sort of hormonal malfunction. Gloria Steinem said that if, when premenstrual, we have more testosterone, then the only malfunction might be that it made us act more like men.

When you treat your PMS like a sickness rather than a gift, you are buying into the culture's dictates to sanitize yourself and exorcise your animal. If you want to stop eating compulsively, you will have to reclaim and delight in being such an alive organism. Maybe PMS is a heightened-awareness state. Aren't animals in the wild hypervigilant and alert? Maybe this is when your animal comes out to pay more attention to how you are living your life. Maybe if you feel like killing your husband, he'd better cool it. Maybe you should attend to your feelings rather than medicate them. You need not feel guilty for having complaints. When premenstrual, you are just not able to keep pain under wraps. The animalistic rumblings howl loudly, and your guard comes down. Thank God the guard left.

Your concerns merit attention. They don't need to be sedated with Valium, Prozac or any new concoction. How easily we'd rather ascribe all of life's ills to something made better through chemistry. Instead, maybe it is really the divorce you're upset about. Maybe it really is the kids leaving home that makes you weepy. Maybe it's watching your mother deteriorate and not knowing how to face the whole aging thing. Maybe it's your friend's illness, your lack of sexual contacts, your failures at work. Maybe it's anger and sorrow at going along with unsatisfying sexual contact. These may be feelings you are able to sublimate as long as obsessively working, starving or bingeing, but when the body becomes needy, your other neediness crops up. It's not your period. It's your life!

Strut Your Stuff

It all comes back to owning your life as an earthbound animal as well as a wise spiritual goddess. Either these messages from the body deserve attention, or your body is just a receptacle, depository or dumping ground. How do you see it? Your body *knows*. Your body knows on a deep and intimate level about what really happens with the sex act. As you act consciously, your body can feel more participatory. You must stay attuned to how your batteries get charged.

In the early days of the women's movement, you might have actively explored your body using workbooks like *Our Bodies, Ourselves*. Much of the information and attitudes presented in these books helped women know and protect themselves. They helped us look at our bodies without embarrassment but didn't teach us much about the joy of sex. Betty Dodson was a pioneer, organizing workshops to teach masturbation. Betty was teaching women to find out and know what they want. She assembled women in circles with vibrators, helping them to learn the look and feel of their sexuality. Her seminars were often sold out.

In the 1980s, we became interested in packaging again. As a result, not too many women take the time to investigate their own bodies and vibrations. How many women get to see their own parts, let alone other women's? Boys get to see their fathers' parts right away at the urinal. How many moms show their daughters how to insert a tampon? Did you get to see mom's labia? Did you learn to notice the folds of labia, vulva, vagina differentiated? Did you know you had parts, or did you just know you had a hole? Who named your parts?

Talk show host Howard Stern asks men if they saw a below-waist photo of a group of nude men standing at a wall, could they pick out their own member. Could you pick yours?

I'd suggest you start by getting to know your toe. That's right. Know your toe to know your vulva to know your life. Take a look at your big toe. Fancy yourself a flexible, curious infant who has just become enamored with the look and feel of your big toe. Investigate thoroughly. Look at all the indentations, calluses and curves. Feel the rough and smooth textures. Notice the nail bed and how your nail rests: high, low, smooth, rough? Now look under the nail. Get specific about what you see. Say a gentle apology to your toe for being so invasive. As you leave your focus, say good-bye and acknowledge the break in intimacy. You are now directing your focus back to the printed page. Your toe knows.

I hope by now you see how important *focus* is. Paying intimate attention wherever you look is key to later noticing when you do and don't contact your lover. Perhaps you will be able someday to pick out yours in a picture of many toes. Looking is one thing and then feeling and sensing is another.

It's not enough to know the equipment or even how it works. You have to know the subtle nuances of what turns it on. Books, charts and even videos work for a while, but as the magicians say, "It's all done with mirrors." Some self-help books read like plumbing manuals speaking to positions and techniques rather than attending to vibrating, pulsating energies. In some less industrialized cultures, such things are more easily experienced between women. South Sea Island tribes direct older women to break hymens of new brides, teaching them how to own their bodies. In Turkish belly dancing, women show each other how their bodies work. Belly dancing was actually developed as an art form for women to learn how to turn themselves on. In our cinemas, we present it as an enticement for men, with women strutting for male approval. In actuality, the guys had nothing to do with it.

Get Real, Ladies!

Question: "Is sex dirty?"

Answer: "It is if you're doin' it right."

You will not be able to achieve the heights of spiritual connection I am suggesting unless you are willing to let your body go. You will use your body and its pulsating rhythms as a barometer, as a litmus test, as a vehicle. It is not an architectural structure to be admired, but your chariot for soul travel. When you focus on that big toe, you will learn the pulse of the body and let it guide you. No matter what it looks like, it still has a voice.

Its voice sometimes speaks through fluids and juices. You cannot remain fastidious and truly savor sex. That means you must grow to love your secretions as well as his. These cannot be seen as messes to quickly wipe up, but instead as showers of ecstasy. If you don't allow yourself these sensations and experiences, you'll find yourself sopping up excess gravy in your plate. If you've allowed yourself such oozing and sucking with food, now allow it in bed.

Start in the Bathroom

Let's talk about washing your hands in the ladies' room. How conscious or unconscious are you about washing? Unless you work in food service, what is all this washing? I would actually prefer you wash your hands, but I want you to *choose* to do so rather than perform automatically for others. A recent study observing ladies' room behavior found that when others were present, eighteen out of twenty women washed their hands after using the latrine. Later, when the lavatory was empty, when they thought no one was looking, only three out of twenty washed! What is the game you play and for whom? When at home alone, do you wash your hands each and every time? Do you want to? Do you want to stop? Can you? According to the American Society for Microbiology, one in four women skips the sink. So let's get off the performance bandwagon. The handwash ritual is one of many vestiges of robotized behavior. Wash when you feel like it, but, apart from hygiene, be willing to accept your fluids. I'd just like you to pay attention and be clear about when and *why* you do it.

If you can't stop yourself, then try to find out who you are washing for and what the purpose or point is. While men have been schooled to feel pride at the trajectory and flow of their body fluids, women feel mostly shame at their secretions. I could never understand how women who had periods could feign horror at the sight of blood. Some of my patients have felt great new rushes of their animal natures as they switched back to using pads instead of tampons. We do keep clean and neat, but what is all this sanitized, secretion-free, fastidious deadness? Let's own our animal. This is the oozing body you were given. Are you going to get behind it and support it? You need to accept and attend to your own secretions in a more sacred and loving way. That prepares you for better sex.

Lust or rust! Some registrants for my workshops think they are signing up to talk about abuse and poor body image. Instead we celebrate vibration, energy and listening to yourself. Some go home to partners full of lustful energy. Others decide to prepare their own field, awaiting a new partner. In the film *Field of Dreams*, Kevin Costner's character was told to cut down cornstalks and build a baseball diamond so the spirit of a star player would materialize and play on his field. He was told, "If you build it, he will come." I say, "Till your soil, and he will plant it." There's work to do. Whether you buy into that or not, by the end of this book, you will surely see that both eating and loving have to be done with the same consciousness and intensity. I am not the first to see solutions in sex. Chip Rowe, writing in the *Playboy Forum,* advised that instead of firing Jocelyn Elders, President Clinton should have hired her as campaign manager, offering *Support for Masturbation* as a slogan. He elaborated, "There would be no AIDS problem. Unwed mothers and welfare babies would decrease. Hands holding onto themselves could not grab an uzi."

Your *uzi* might be in the form of a *cookie*. Instead of grabbing that cookie, let's go for what you're really after. Let's look at choosing partners: dating and mating.

Three

Dating, Mating, Sating

"Why aren't you married?" the talk show host asked point-blank.

"I like sex too much," I blurted out.

Where did that come from? Couldn't a person be happily married and still want and enjoy nice sex? One would certainly hope so. But, that spontaneous outburst caused me to question myself and my attitudes. I'd been both married and single, and had shopped around. But, I'd learned to survive happily alone. I realized that the only way this book and its message could have any relevance was if women always *believed* on some level that they had the right and the option to be or remain single. Any discussion of relationship had to be opened with a sense of freedom. If we *had* to be married, then there wasn't much chance of breathing in air or of movement. We'd all just have to accept that what's done is done—it's all a done deal so stop talking so much.

If we could instead feel the freedom not to wed, then we would be different in our couplings and different at our meals. We have the option of stopping a binge in the middle of a bag of trail mix. I've had wondrous moments of catching myself and quitting midbag. Similarly, no matter how married you are, you've got to know you can quit. You've got to be ready to bring the relationship right down to the line each time you look. If it can't stand scrutiny, you'll turn to gluttony.

So let's think for a minute about the whole marriage agenda. Many women of the '90s are choosing not to marry, or if they marry, they wait for later in life. Some have "been there, done that" and are choosing to stay alone.

For a brief moment in 1986, researchers at Yale panicked many by reporting that by age thirty, only 20 percent of college-educated women had a chance of being wed. After age thirty-five, only 5 percent had that chance, and after age forty, only 1 percent. This sent many to the streets or to matchmakers and sent feminist writer Susan Faludi on her own investigative journey to scrutinize the data. As a result, she and the U.S. Census Bureau's Jeanne Morrman reported back that 68 percent of these women *would* find mates. Still, that left 32 percent not marrying. Panicked and enraged, no one stopped to question the numbers of women who were *choosing* not to marry. It wasn't for lack of men or lack of offers. They just liked their single lifestyle.

Some unmarried women feel more complete than their married counterparts. They live longer, have a greater range and variety of friends, are often financially independent, and have greater flexibility choosing jobs, lifestyles, locations and loves. When forming friendships, they invest more effort and thus spread around their dependency needs, not seeking all sustenance from one mate. They have not married "breadwinners" and placed all their financial planning and security in the hands of a spouse.

Often, single women take more financial care of themselves and set up secure households. They appreciate the neatness of their homes as a refuge from work life. They like the peace. In a home of her own, a woman has a retreat, a quietude that lets her hear herself. In *A Room of One's Own*, Virginia Woolf advised that no real creativity could happen for a woman until she had a private space all her own. Married women rarely do.

A new date once asked me, "Why don't you have a man in your life?" He asked this as if I were abnormal. He called upon me to explain my abnormality. Too many women have pushed themselves to permanent monogamous relationships precisely to avoid such questions. I could have told him that, like the Marines, I was looking for "a few good men."

Can't Mate in Captivity

Therapist Wilhelm Reich said, "Marriage is designed for the sexual repression of women." Many married, never considering that sex wouldn't be a permanent part of their relationships. It was something everyone took for granted. They didn't know how to cope with his "headaches." When the sex waned, they ate. They mated but were not sated. For most, mating had been the badge of their acceptance and validity as women. If no man had chosen, claimed or *committed* to them, it must be because they lacked something. (Notice we also use the word *committed* when locking up inmates and mental patients.)

I could have answered this new date's question by saying that I had many men in my life. There was also life in my men. We just weren't partnered. I remained a woman alone. Katharine Hepburn said she chose to live alone so she wouldn't "trade the admiration of many men for the criticism of one." I could have answered like my friend Jeannie, "Why I'm alone? . . . *Why make just _one_ man happy?*"

I could have really told the truth, which was I just didn't have time. Another date once told me that I was a workaholic running away from intimacy and relationships. Why did pursuing my career mean I was running away from men? Charlotte Chandler, in the introduction to her book *The Ultimate Seduction*, postulates that "The ultimate seduction is not about sex, but about passion." Interviewing famous artists and creative types, she proposes we care passionately about creative endeavors, which satisfy us more than love or sex. "Repressed sex is more constructive for the creative person. It must get out, and so it goes into the work." What if women's working so hard on relationships is really an avoidance of our true work—other creations we need to deliver?

I know that Adrienne Rich wrote, "Relationships are women's work." Was I less a woman because I chose work over relationships as my primary focus? I certainly thought a lot about relationships—and had a few. I was a career-oriented professional person, *and* I liked men. It's just that work paid better dividends. My writing and lecturing delivered more consistently than all the effort I'd invested in the *R* word. In his book *The Seven Habits of Highly Effective People*, Stephen R. Covey writes, "Whatever is at the center of our life will be the source of our security, guidance, wisdom, and power." Work has served me far better than love. That's my story. Is it a ten-cent novel or an intimate adventure to be read and savored forever? Whichever it is, I write my own script. It's a freedom ride.

So, I answered my date with, "I expect too much from relationships."

He countered, "Do you give a lot?"

I wanted to say, "Yes, I gave at the office. I gave above and beyond the call of duty. I gave 'til it hurt! I gave until I learned more about *codependency* than I'd ever want to know. I gave a lot. I learned a lot. What's the point?"

The truth was I liked the infinite variety of meeting so many men and watching how I responded differently with each. I enjoyed learning new things about *myself* while not giving myself away.

Fated to Be Mated

Did you ever know that you had a choice about marriage? Even at this late date in our century, most women are still programmed for marital "bliss." We are trained early to sleep away from home. All that programming may be parents helping *themselves* face how difficult it will be when you finally leave the nest. Early on, you are encouraged to find another home. You'll want to develop attractive attributes. Encouragement to snare a mate starts early and is usually quite complimentary. For me, it started with my eyes: "Look at those gorgeous eyes! You've got some mankiller there." What did I know? I was destined to dazzle. Did anyone ever ask if I wanted to? Did I? Think about so many of the subtle messages that trained you early about seeking and searching for a man. A few key lines are:

You'll need someone to care for you later.

It's lonely without a mate.

All women want children.

It's best to pool finances.

Don't let him know too much about you.

Know what you say, don't say what you know.

These messages program you early for the dating game. Add in a few lines of your own and sit quietly to contemplate what *could* have been another message. Where would that have taken you?

"I Don't Want to Die Alone"

Fear of dying alone is the reason most often given for why you need to develop a permanent partnering. Why *not* die alone? Ultimately, we all die alone anyway. Are you going to orchestrate your entire waking life preparing for that one last fleeting moment? It's only a speck of time. You have many more non-dying moments. Dying is no fun, whether mated or not. Why do you want someone at your side? My dear friend Herb, in his final days, barred me from visiting his hospital room with, "I don't want any deathbed scenes." We'd shared enough in life to be complete without a send-off at death. Hospice workers report that having loved ones hanging around often keeps the dying person suffering and hanging on longer. It's often when family members take a break and go home to rest that the patient finally lets go. So, evaluate how much your life has been choreographed and programmed for that final curtain. Make sure there's your own rich script to play out on the way.

Spinsterhood Is Powerful

Those women choosing to go it alone are not longing. Despite those feminists writing about women's "affiliation needs," these women are living alone and loving it. According to psychiatrist Harold Bloomfield in *Lifemates*, "For people to be single and healthy in our society they have to have the greatest self-esteem of anyone." They are living somewhat outside the norm of traditional values, and that in itself takes a certain amount of confidence. They usually get accolades at work as they perform well, don't complain about problems at home and are readily available for overtime when needed. They usually fare better in credit ratings, auto insurance and even longevity statistics. They take on their projects with enthusiasm and dedication. They take the time and have the focus to put forth a concerted effort. She travels faster and deeper who travels alone.

A 1985 Virginia Slims poll reported that 70 percent of women believed they could be "happy and complete" without a wedding ring. By 1990, the New Diversity poll found the figure had jumped to 90 percent. In 1986, Charles Westoff noted, "The more economically independent women are, the less attractive marriage becomes." The more women are paid, the less eager they are to marry. In 1988, another survey showed that far more men than women were placing personal ads; in fact, like "ladies' night" at bars, women were offered discounts and freebies to place ads. Psychologically, single women usually fare better than single men.

Single women are often educated, self-sufficient and happy with themselves; they just don't want to play the game of love. They may know how, but just don't *want* to. Maybe these women just don't need men. Maybe they see the price they pay for love is not worth the benefit.

Maybe they just need men for sex. Even that benefit might soon be in question. In April 1994, an international women's magazine published an article describing and expounding on the great variety and efficiency of vibrators available to women. One man told me he could never compete. He didn't realize he had more to offer. We need men for more than titillation. Maybe we're here to grow and learn from relationships. We're after the man and *his* vibration; not mechanical vibrators.

If you've had a history of abusive relationships, you may refuse to enter the ring one more time. Some women repeatedly choose men who make them feel worse about themselves. Cynthia Heimel, author of *If You Can't Live Without Me, Why Aren't You Dead Yet?* reports that we tend to choose men who make us feel bad about ourselves, the same way as our parents did. It's a way to stay connected to the same struggle and thus avoid growing into spiritual adulthood. She and others are asking, "Who needs this?"

Maybe you need to keep resuffering the pains of your childhood, or maybe you need to emotionally grow up and leave home. Maybe you've learned enough. At some point, therapy ends. Life is in session, and you must be present to win.

Married doesn't make it better. Sometimes unhappily single may prove better than miserably married. At least it's up to *you* to do something about it. In 1998, 65 percent of American marriages end in divorce. It's not such a safe bet. I'm not opposed to marriage. I've been married and single, and counseled couples and individuals in and out of relationships for over thirty years. I personally have liked life both ways and found freedom all ways, but each and every way requires work. The reason the other gal's grass is greener is because she waters her lawn.

Truth That Dare Not Speak Its Name

Dare we say it? *Women want to be alone.* It isn't really true, is it? Isn't it just that those women haven't found the right match? I have counseled so many young women who *know* they like their single life and don't have one word of retort or any reasonable way to answer when friends and relatives query, "Why aren't you married yet?" With no models, they eventually judge and punish themselves for a truly legitimate and often healthy life choice. Why is it so difficult to acknowledge some women's choice to live without a man? What will it do to our culture?

We're afraid we won't have as many babies. If women find themselves content with lives they create without mates, would they be motivated to have children? Would they consider raising children alone? Maybe we need to consider our "welfare crisis." Many women find they do well with government-funded financial support for their families, and they really don't miss having a man around. Even with so many of us continuing to marry, we see how many are quickly divorced and then raising kids alone. It has to be a realistic thought on the part of any prospective mateable female: *I just may end up raising children by myself.* Recent reports show that teenage out-of-wedlock pregnancies are on the decline because young girls are opting for a better quality of life. If women choose to stay alone, if we practice safe sex and responsible sex, who will have babies? Will our population wither and die?

Nymphos

Now let's consider this and follow it to its logical conclusion. If women aren't seeking mates, then why are we dating and sleeping with these guys? Could it be that we really love the sex thing, that we want to explore our sexual selves and use men to do it? How will that affect the social order? What will happen to the world's oldest profession? Will women hire men? The marriage bed answered one form of the question by explaining that men wanted sex and women wanted security. What if she's as sexually motivated as he is?

Single ≠ Celibate

Single does not equal celibate. You can be single and still have a sex life. You may take sex more seriously and con-sciously. If not healing some childhood trauma, you might ask, "What are we doing here? What's love got to do with it?" If love is blind, why do we seek the dark side? Why do we die for love? Die into love? Out of love? Why do you want relatedness? What are you doing with all this *Sturm und Drang?* What are you after? We'll chew on these questions throughout this chapter.

I feel both blessed and cursed to be qualified to write this book. I have loved often and well. My past three great loves all have died. Feeling those losses and showing up to love again has made me expert at weathering the dance between con-nection and separation. I've had to learn about recreating myself and my capacities for loving and mirroring. Fully choosing to love again, I stay available, penetrable and still surpriseable. As I've faced and lived through these deaths, I've learned how to show up again and again for life. I know that *I* house my own lovingness and that every experience comes home to me. Nothing is wasted.

In the game of love, I emulate my roses. I'd been out on a lec-ture tour and made no arrangements for anyone to water my garden. I returned home to find all my roses wilted and hung over. I thought I'd killed everything but I decided to go ahead and water anyway. Within two days, the bushes had sprung back, full of buds and blossoming color. The roses didn't spend one minute berating me for my bad parenting and lack of care. They didn't hold out or punish. They just bloomed. It's the natural thing to do, to go toward life and away from pain. I'll keep showing up and blooming. I'll also continue to grow toward the nurturing sun and avoid droughts.

I am writing both for the single woman over forty and for her younger sisters—all of them emerging into a world where women can love themselves and their lovers. *Now* is all we have. In fact, as we age, we must realize that we have little time to waste and that we do *deserve* the experience of loving. It's a God-given right! Even though you may not want a permanent coupling, you *do* want experiences with attentive lovers.

How does it feel to think of yourself as a lover? How would it feel to say that you *have* a lover? As a lover, I want to welcome you to a discussion of sex as a sensual experience, an opportunity for psychological and spiritual growth, and a possible prescription for weight loss. It's important that you know what you are after in your couplings. Make sure that your involvements teach you important lessons.

A professor once told me that we travel to strange lands in order to learn more about ourselves. The love trip is a way of traveling without physically going anywhere. To look at your lover is to hold a mirror up to yourself. You learn about your lover to learn about yourself. We choose who we are. My lovers helped me find my varied sides. Each woke me up. I've enjoyed observing the ever-changing landscape of whom I choose as I grow. I've stretched. Maybe a more appropriate answer to the why-not-married question would be, "I haven't learned all I need to know yet." I could have answered the same way Gloria Steinem retorted, "I am lacking in the low self-esteem required to make the necessary compromises."

Disappointment

You have to be able to make many compromises, but for some it is too much to ask. It is never too late to sell yourself out. Some just go for the "okey-doke" and some hold out for more. The okey-doke is when we say,

"Oh, that's okay."
"That's good enough."
"Aw shucks, it didn't really matter anyway."
"This will be fine, thanks."
"I really don't know what I was expecting anyway."
"This will do."

Are your expectations being met? Are you satisfied? We compromise what we want of men and relationships and decide, "This is all okay. Okey-doke." Think of the old circle dance done at weddings, the "hokey-pokey." Here's a modification for daters:

The Okey-Dokey

You put your whole heart in.
You take your whole heart out.
You also give your soul and you shake it all about.
You do the okey-dokey and then sputter, stamp and shout!
That's what it's all about! Yeah!

What is the disappointment? What are you really giving up? You give up the wish to be *seen*. You want to be truly seen at the core of your being. You want to reveal yourself and know that another being you respect actually *saw* you. Instead, you settle for being invisible. Sex is where no one can hide. Many men won't even know what you're asking for. There are even women who don't know. When I proposed the course outline for "Viva la Vulva" workshops to help women achieve focused, conscious sexuality, the dean responded, "I don't need sex. I'm married." We both laughed.

Women expect so much of themselves in relationships. We have been trained to be *codependent*, to worry about the needs of others, anticipating those needs before they are even voiced. We are quick to judge ourselves when things don't work out. Some have cautiously taken a look at the compromises and benefits of both married and single life, and have decided to treat relationships like luscious desserts: "Try a few bites at a restaurant, but don't keep it in the house."

Let's look to the short-range goal of being seen, rather than the long-term goal of mating. You just wish that *he* could see *you* in the moment, no matter what the future holds. Early on in the relationship, you could believe that he saw you. You projected onto him any feelings you imagined he had. Later on, as you got to know him better, you hoped that he was also knowing you. Often he wasn't. That discrepancy between your expectations and what he can deliver reveals a great well of loneliness and disappointment. He was supposed to be your "soul mate," and to a certain extent, he doesn't even know you have a soul.

Don't blame it on the guys here. This evolved over a full lifetime. This happened because of all the times you decided from age five on to become an "as if" personality rather than an authentic being putting out her wants. Think about the many situations where you traded your nitty-gritty for an okey-doke. Here's a partial list of trade-off comments:

Okey-Dokes	Nitty-Gritties
"I understand you are shy."	"Look me in the eye."
"I know how busy you are."	"I don't pick up after others."
"I'll protect your ego."	"I didn't quite come yet."
"I will follow him."	"I might have to relocate."
"Let's be less confrontational."	"Let's call it as we see it."
"I'm too sensitive."	"I've got to trust my instincts."

When women dare to be the nitty-gritties, we're all in for a more authentic life. Feminist psychiatrists like Jean Baker Miller at Harvard report that "most women spend their lives constantly doing good and feeling bad." In my work, I see evolving women who do "bad" but feel good. These sexually energized women are a powerful threat. Early on in the women's movement, women like Germaine Greer were the wild-eyed radicals, who told it like it is—full-frontal and braless. In recent years, feminists have turned to a moral righteousness; they are less sexual, more puritanical and, in a sense, less of a threat to men. There's less sexual energy. It's a new anti-sex feminism that failed the promise of the bra-burning sixties. They've taken their gonads underground. Ellen Willis, author of *No More Nice Girls*, wrote that women could say whatever they wanted as long as they weren't sexually threatening.

We are so busy working on relationships because we're always "sorry" for something. We prefer finding ourselves guilty, wrong and, especially, "too demanding," rather than seeing the disappointment we've found in relationships. If we can find *ourselves* inadequate, defective in some way, too needy, then we can pay for therapy, assuage our guilt and keep working at things. Sometimes we'd rather make apologies than progress. We'd rather accept culpability than chaos.

But, what are we really asking of our men? Contact? Full-frontal honesty? Is that what we really want? Can we handle it? Usually, your greatest disappointment will be about his lack of honesty. The first line of my first book is, "We're as fat as we are dishonest." You have colluded in deceiving yourself about yourself. You also may have been sincerely deluded about him. You thought he was really there, but somehow both of you were probably out to lunch. Sometimes this realization comes after a major betrayal. He has cheated or revealed some long-hidden truth about something he doesn't like about you. You are somewhat relieved as you sensed a vague lack of contact. You finally get to know the truth, that you'd been right all along.

Henrietta worked so hard not to nag, not to ask Harry where he was going or why he got back late. She checked for all the telltale signs of another woman and found nothing. She smelled a rat but resorted to judging herself and her keen sense of smell. "I'm just too sensitive, too suspicious." She danced the okey-dokey. Dancing the okey-dokey separates out the women from the girls, or sometimes the mated from the unwed. Henrietta even acknowledged that she'd have to give up friendships with single women if she were going to stay married. She was right, too. It was a whole different mindset. I'd been one of those discarded. It wasn't that we broke our friendship. It was just that the subject of "him" became taboo.

At first, I'd been his most avid defender. She'd call me with tales of woe about his style, his arrogant attitude toward her, how he talked down to her and criticized her a lot. I defended him with a standard I'd used to explain such abuses to myself. "You know, Hen, we're very strong women, and our guys get intimidated around us so they start acting pompous. You're the bigger woman for all this. Watch your own needs to control and have him perform *your way*." Thus, heard and sated, she re-entered the fray. Until the next round. As much as he wasn't there for her, I was. But what was I doing for her? I was helping her to see that her power was threatening, that she'd have to cool it. Was I doing her a favor or a disservice? We both colluded in finding her wrong.

She set out, as women are trained to do, to diagnose herself. She figured it was her insecurity and need to control. It *was*. She wanted to live in truth. He wanted to live a lie. Finally, she discovered he'd returned to gambling and spent those extra hours at poker parlors disposing of their income. Betrayal. Yes, he couldn't control his compulsion, but what about her judging herself for having legitimate suspicions? That was her larger self-betrayal. Her betrayal of herself was greater than his betrayal of her. And we helped each other maintain these lies. She used my friendship and therapy to keep finding herself wrong.

Henrietta and Harry had a tripod marriage. Therapists and well-meaning friends can keep such a relationship together because they provide the third leg of a teetering structure. Would the relationship stand without this third person bolstering it up? At some point, the therapist has to let the couple teeter on their own. There has to be enough there to let them stand alone. To dance the okey-dokey, you have to stick one foot in while balancing on the other.

Stop the Manuals!

I want to yell this out like a reporter charging into the newsroom with, "Stop the presses!" This is groundbreaking news. There are no books on your relationship. That's right. There are only two experts in the whole world who can accurately attend to your relationship: *you* and *he*. You are the experts; everything else is footnote and extrapolation.

Your body will let you know what gives. Sex therapist and author David Schnarch goes along with me in asking you to focus on what is between your ears instead of the cellulite on your thighs. He believes there is a strong correlation between cellulite and good sex. By the time you develop cellulite, you are usually grown up enough to pay attention. You just have to pay attention, not to thighs, but to vibes. You have to both transmit and receive. Listen and then learn.

In family counseling, we look from session to session at what the family does with the insight and information uncovered during the prior visit. Do the family members note and take in what was said? They don't have to necessarily comment and acknowledge *during* the session. What is important is whether behaviors change *between* sessions as a result. It's similar with sex. Does he attend? Do his subsequent behaviors show that he has heard you? Do you hear yourself?

James Baldwin said that money was like sex. When you have it, you don't have to talk about it. When you don't have it, you think of nothing else.

For all our attempts to control and manipulate, we still have to do the dance of love. There are those biological urges after all. There's sex everywhere. The only question is, do you plan to go along with the program? In human relationships, the soul shows up with the body and changes things. Just like your appetite for food has little to do with hunger, your appetite for sex has little to do with eroticism or physical needs for discharge. All that is genital is not necessarily sensual. Despite Freud's formulations that all our neuroses were the result of repressed sexual longings, sex is not necessarily our most important drive. We are not driven so much to spread seed or gain pleasure as we are toward security. Only when you feel safe can you focus on pleasure. When you feel safe, get naked.

Woman as Predator

Women are feeling safer, and their lusts are leaking. Juicy women are setting out for life. We've been taught the old line, "A man should chase her until she catches him." Even though women can call men today, we still can't be too forward. If you pursue, he may be flattered, but not necessarily interested.

Most dating and mating primers teach how to "fake it 'til you make it." At all costs, we have to try not to be too intimidating. Also, according to the rules, don't be too eager. There is a lot of work involved. Don't let him know too much about the real you. I've had therapy teachers recommending this same approach with new clients. They say to hold back and not interpret too quickly, because the patient needs to develop trust. Once trust is established, you sock it to 'em. Why waste the time? Will you trust me more if I am inauthentic in the beginning?

Let's see who we are right away and call a spade a shovel. I recommend that you show your true colors on the first date. Most dating game books are clear in telling you what *not* to do. They say to find a mate "don't be yourself." What's the point? Do you have to die for love? Is this desire for merger covering up some hidden death wish, a desire to remove and eliminate yourself? It's definitely geared for you to have little effect as a person. These books fill a need for us. They try to teach us that we *can* have power over another person. We can woo him, cajole him, manipulate him, make him surrender and take no prisoners. It's a fallacy. In truth, a lot of this is up to *him,* and that's the root of the problem. Mating is such a random, insecure thing. We'd love to find out it's something we haven't done right, something we can fix. We can cure disease, but not fate.

Women read men's magazines to learn about the opposite gender, but men don't usually pick up *Cosmopolitan.* It is actually a sad commentary that although 35 percent of the readers of men's magazines are women, the reverse is not also true. The men who are really engaging to women are those who pay attention. They take the time to learn about women. They read about women. They care enough to ask us what we want. The men who ask learn a lot.

According to Bob Berkowitz, TV commentator on ABC's *The View* and author of books teaching women about men, most men rank good sex in the top five reasons to choose a marriage partner. Many rated it number one. (What do you rate it?) However, the top two reasons for divorce are children and then money. Sex is far down on the list. Bob tells us that men fall in love with their eyes and women with their ears. We have "eargasms."

We fall in love with his potential. Lois Wyse asserted, "Men fall in love with women hoping they'll never change. Women fall in love hoping men will." You might have fallen in love, telling both him and yourself, "I love the person you were meant to be." For both men and women, the tremendous value of dating is that, if nothing else, it can make you fall in love with yourself. Dating new men helps you feel brand-new and you get to see yourself through new eyes.

Once you have come through the risk, shown who you are and then been seen, tremendous fears can surface. That's when the power struggles begin. We resent the power of this attraction and how it can own us if we aren't careful. If we find true visibility *and* good sex, we're afraid of becoming *angler fish*. When angler fish mate, the male buries his teeth into the female, hanging on for dear life. His mouth fuses, his eyes glaze over and the rest of his body quits working. Eventually, he becomes a blob hanging on and only capable of reproduction. That dependency is what some crave in a relationship, and what others greatly fear.

Notice in this explanation, it is the male fish who blobs over. With black widow spiders, the female kills her mate after coitus. The female praying mantis bites off the head of her lover after sex. And women are the fearful ones? Think about it. Nature would not have it go the other way. It's a natural phenomenon that males don't kill females. After fertilization, the female still has utility. Nature wants us to keep reproducing. That means the holder of the new life will survive while the fertilizer is expendable. For male readers, no offense intended.

Both sexes seek escape from isolation but fear what it takes to get it. We'd like to believe in a fusion fantasy, that once we hook up, we harmonize and meld. In reality, for the relationship to survive, it must ebb and flow. It must flexibly move in and out of connection. We have to become resilient. You have to risk feeling the connection and then watching it wane. Can you weather waiting in the hallways? If you've landed your prey by playing a phony game, then you'll continue to feel lonely. Just like compulsively eating a piece of candy never satisfies but always leads to more compulsive eating, rigid expectations of relationships lead to unsatisfied questing.

Unmet Hungers

So, I am inviting you to look soulfully at the kinds of connections you've had and encouraging you to hold out for something more meaningful. How you express sexuality is a reflection of your total personality. You might seek sex or food to quell anxiety or depression, or to express repressed anger. Problems of appetite with food or sex have nothing to do with hunger. They have to do with how you relate to others and how you deal with your own feelings.

Accepting this means being willing to risk. You can learn about yourself whenever you risk. You get to know what your price is. You might have been trying to have a relationship without risk. That stands to reason because, as an overeater, you probably would like to have your cake and eat it too—to eat what you want and not gain weight. Well, unfortunately, it all has a price. There's no free lunch. It is told as a true story that George Bernard Shaw asked a woman if she would bed with him for five hundred dollars, to which she expressed possible interest. Then he asked her if she'd do it for ten dollars. She got huffy with insult, "What do you think I am?" she blasted. "Madam, we've already established that. I'm just quibbling over price." You can learn valuable lessons about who you are by watching your choices. Alice shared with me this letter she wrote to Bill after the breakup of their cheating love affair, when both went back to their spouses:

Dear Bill,

I may or may not mail this, but I find I need to make some closure to our relationship. I'm still quite brimming and a little overwhelmed. While in this mode, I'd like to share some insights with you.

First, you were a gift I allowed myself. Thank you and thank heaven. This richness you and I shall always treasure from this time forward. I brought it to you, we touched and flowered.

You and I were both very good compromisers. Neither of us could go for the gold, but instead went for what Judi calls the "okey-doke." Our respective marriages are examples of this. Our affair is, too.

I knew I had to end it because the back alley is no place for what we had. I could not contain it in a neat little corner of my life, tucking us away and pulling it out at will. I got to see my own power and couldn't be bridled. I had no idea the depth and intensity I am capable of. I have a deep and serious side. In the past I trivialized myself so much and allowed me to hold me back, canceled myself, toyed and put myself down. I was a dilettante . . . a spectator in the game of life. Through my love with you, I began to touch myself and raise myself up.

That's why now a friendship between us is out of the question. That would be too okey-doke.

It's funny how things work out. Through working on attachment, separation and loss, I have come to grips with the real me, going for gold now. Through a lot of piercing pain, appetite left me and the language of my heart shouts out. I accept my clarity, my oneness and my power.

We're so alike that I know you'll benefit from hearing about some of what I've learned. My struggles are your struggles. It's hard for me to say, but I think I know why your wife is "withholding." I believe that you say things that you know she wants to hear. You sincerely mean them at the time . . . and then, if it's too hard to follow through, or not convenient, or makes you too vulnerable, then your fear takes over, and you forget what you

said or promised and you fail to follow through. After a few dis-
appointments, she gets hardened a bit and excuses you a lot
and it all serves to divert intimacy.

And in the meantime, you both go for the okey-doke, never
getting what you really want, never feeling deserving. I know
this is none of my business and that it smacks of my own judg-
ments, but I'd love to see you go for the gold and stand up for
your own agendas, insisting that you will both work together.

Alice saw that Bill had recreated the same style of relating
with her as he had done with his wife. She didn't want to stay
in the game for the same outcome.

Talk Dirty to Me

You might learn something about what you want by noticing
some things about your style of lovemaking. As your animal
unites with your soul, unconscious needs are expressed. You are
seeing yourself. I've asked women for years, "Which do you find
more *intimate*: intercourse or oral sex?" "Which do you find
more *enjoyable?*" These questions speak to connected sex. Are
you in it for pleasure or to really engage and interact with this
being? Do you desire this man for satiety, the same reason you
choose food, or do you desire connection with this particular
partner? The most interesting answer I got was: "Do I have to
choose right now?"

Are you looking for any likely man, so you have a trophy on
your mantel, or do you want this unique individual? Could you
stand the scrutiny of *his* answering such questions? Do you
want him to answer these questions? Where is your focus? Do
you like a hard thrust inward, a slow pull outward? These are
much more interesting topics than fat grams. By examining
these questions, you gain an appreciation for the sweetness

and greater meanings of your sexuality.

Unfortunately, we live in a culture that represses such discussions. As far as programming to disown wants of the flesh, sex has definitely gotten more bad press than food. It's difficult to speak so openly about a subject so repressed. When I started work on this book, I feared being misinterpreted, being suspected of wanton sexuality and promiscuity. But, encouraging women to seek enjoyable couplings was not about hunting down and conquering flesh, it was about learning discernment.

For years I've watched women get up at OA meetings swearing off sex, joining celibate sisters. I'd thought them out of their minds, not understanding how they could imagine giving up food and sex at the same time. Many were cutting down on compulsive eating and closing down other "animal" activities of the body as well. This led many to ask "Why bother?"

"Why bother?" was best answered by Jane's new lover, Tim, when they were having those endless contemplative discussions about why he wanted to stay over. "I don't want to sleep with you. I want to wake you up. I want to *keep* you awake." He wanted an experience that brought them both more into *life*, more focused on the *now*. He wanted it exciting and invigorating as well as enlivening. He wanted to unite their two energies to create a third force.

So, you may be inspired to "bother," but wait to make sure you're in the right arena. Making love is very serious business. Some think it's just a simple act of copulation and pounding. Instead, it's digging into the core of your being. It brings us to the edge of facing who we truly are. On a body level it awakens the same responses as we get when under siege and gripped with fear. We feel weak in the knees and a strange euphoria sets in. Just as with a fearful, flight-or-fight response, our adrenal glands secrete madly, we sweat, our hearts pound and our breath quickens. Members of the self-help group Sex Addicts Anonymous talk about becoming hooked on the excitement as it peaks and depressed when it wanes. They use sex like a drug.

There is the chance to make contact and the fear of being misunderstood. Most women I see struggle to be taken seriously. They are afraid that making too much of sex will make *them* too much for their men. They don't want to talk with their lovers about their sex lives. They'll ask me, "But can a leopard change its spots? Can you change a lamb to a tiger?" My answer is, "If you truly want to be with *him*, you will make the effort. If you don't, you are secretly writing him off. Sex is too important to let yourselves give in to mediocrity."

A few years ago, I had a radio show in Palm Springs, California: *Dr. Jude's Ladies' Locker Room.* The locker room was a place for "wise women and a few good men to discuss food, sex, and rock and roll." One caller advised, "Many men are afraid to admit they could learn something from a woman." While I agreed with her, I questioned what purpose it could serve either of us to analyze the males further. In my answer to her, I outlined what is *our* work to do: "His lack of confidence or prowess is neither your problem, nor your fault. Your job is to make this fun as well as enlivening and, for weight-loss purposes, enlightening." We have to make it a big deal and put in the work.

Reach out and touch him without embarrassment. It's nice to care about his feelings, but have confidence and don't worry about offending. Don't let it become routine. A client told me, "My friend has been married thirty years and still has sex every morning. I'm jealous! My brand-new dates have headaches!" Before she lamented further, I warned that it shouldn't get to be like brushing your teeth. Her friend's marriage ended within the year. What kind of sex were they having?

If you take responsibility, you won't have to blame him for what didn't happen. It's up to you. When you are confident and fun-loving, class can begin. However, if you think about it too much, you can think yourself out of sex.

So what is it that you want from a man? Have we participated in shaping ourselves up as objects for barter or sale so we don't have to do the more difficult work of finding out what we truly want? Do you just want to be chosen? What does that offer you? How long can that last? You need to find out what you are after and where you want to go, or you can never get "there" from "here." Hopefully, you will want to touch a man for his soul, not his face, his chest or his wallet.

Fortune in Men's Eyes

You also want to be touched. You want a man who cares and wants your "booty" more than the beauty. Maybe it takes a god for your goddess. Yeats wrote:

> *Only God, my dear,*
> *Could love you for yourself alone,*
> *And not your yellow hair.*

We often look to the men in our lives and the life in our men to tell us how sexy we are, how attractive we are, how worthwhile we are. Men are ill-equipped to be the arbiters of our sexuality. They have ruled this roost far too long. It was our area of power, and we gave it up. Much new medical research corroborates this. Whereas we once thought that sperm swam feverishly, fighting one another to get to the ovum, we now know that sperm are very poor swimmers, almost like drunken sailors, and that the egg actually fans out sensors to lure the drunks upstream to unite. In *Sexual Personae*, Camille Paglia asserts boldly that "Men enter in triumph but withdraw in decrepitude. . . . Sperm are miniature assault troops, and the ovum is a solitary citadel that must be breached. Weak or passive sperm just sit there like dead ducks. Nature rewards energy and aggression." Even on basic, cellular levels, female power rules. You may not want a drunken sailor. It's time for him to sober up.

For the most part, we fear female sexual power, and women, even more so than men, try to subvert it. We'd rather be swept away. The men actually resent us for giving up our responsibility in this arena. Women continue to complain about what the men want instead of looking to what they want for themselves. They'll complain about the men who want them virginal and pure, and those who want them acting out trash in the bedroom. Who cares what the men want?

Do you want to be turned on and juicy? Wasting time blaming men diverts you from a more authentic opportunity: deciding what *you* want. When fully integrated, you will be up for all variations. If you are locked into either Madonna or whore, you may not be making your own decisions, but instead living out someone else's agenda. You may be sleeping for and with your mother's disowned self. If she acted prim, you act wild; if she caroused, you withhold. For whom are you doing it? Be careful you don't choose men to dance to mama's polka!

Wanted: Meaningful Overnight Relationship

Despite all the literature telling you that women crave per-manent connection, *you* may be the person who wants to roam. There are few models for such a woman. I once gave a lecture about this, and the next day, two clients called for emergency sessions to work on the same complaint. They were tired of "relating" and wanted some good, clean, noninvolved sex. They wanted an intense, short-lived, enlivening experience, one that happened easily without a lot of work or investment.

Both were with men who were pushing for marriage. They'd both met these men through ads in *LA Weekly*. They were ini-tially excited about the lovely, sensuous involvements these new men brought to their lives. Sandra was all excited about her new pilot and how he adored her and was teaching her to fly. Kim was very enthused about the heights of tantric ecstasy to which her unemployed tarot card reader carried her, even though his pot smoking clashed with her newfound sobriety in AA. It was not bothersome enough for her to give up the good sex.

When the pilot was in town, it would be for long stretches of free time. He wanted Sandra available to him rather than so career-oriented. She told me later that she knew after the fourth date that he wasn't for her, but boy did she like the *sex*. When he was in town, he wanted to be with her too much, took her time and attention. She was busy! She did like the sex, though. Then he told her he'd placed his ad because he wanted to "find someone." He saw her as "the one." She saw him as "the stud."

Kim felt similarly about her new lover. She didn't really like taking her tantric pot smoker out in public. If they could spend those endless sexual hours in bed, she was content, though often sore. His holding off so long to the tantric end resulted in endless hours of sex before he finally rolled over in a stupor. She was growing tired, as well as lockjawed. At a neighbor's party, she was embarrassed when he did palm readings. "This New Age stuff doesn't go too far outside the bedroom," she told me. She didn't like how he was able to "let it all ride" as long as he smoked a joint. She wanted more talking, more intimacy, more interaction. Other than sexually, she found him boring.

Larry complained that when he smoked his joint, Kim was too uptight. He felt they really talked enough. He didn't understand what more she wanted. He wanted to marry her. Wasn't that enough? Same for Sandra with the pilot. He was happy as a clam; he just wanted more of her time and was sure she'd come around soon. He felt they should settle in with each other.

It was hard for these women to talk about how content they were to use these guys for sex and that's all. Both eventually resolved that they'd like to see their lovers only one day a week. They could have some good sex, feel loved and loving, and then resume their lives. The men balked. Each of these women had more than enough of what she wanted. They didn't know how to speak this truth.

When a woman rejects a loving man, we question what's wrong with her. Can't we assume there is something "right" with her? There are many more such women who can't speak. The women who reject these men have experience, so they have developed discernment. Most have a baseline for comparison and have developed high standards. They don't convince themselves that great sexual energy means love and commitment.

What's love got to do with it? They want their own separate lives *and* satisfying sex. Why can't they have both?

Lesser Companions

Sometimes it is very hard to know what you know and want what you want. You might choose to hang out with men who can't give it to you. Then, in some strange way, you won't have to be surprised or disappointed. You may be attracted to angry, degrading men to act out your dark side. That can work for a while, but, unfortunately, if you don't own that dark side yourself and mobilize all your troops for your own agendas, you are really living out a subtle, secret death wish. You are focused on meaningless battles to avoid living up to your potential. You knew from the beginning that this guy couldn't give you what you need. You secretly knew he couldn't take you seriously. He usually can't operate on the level you have in mind. When the end comes, it's not you, it's not about power, it's just that two unrelated lives touched. Is that touching?

To live familiarly with inferiors is degrading. Rosemary Daniell, in *Sleeping with Soldiers: In Search of the Macho Man*, recounts escapades of two women on an oil rig. She addressed the issue of using men and sexuality to own your own aggression. You don't have to be equal to men in power, but you do have to recognize that you have an equal potential for aggression. Women can be just as wanton as men. Daniell saw their bedding these riggers as a class thing and a power thing. If you are afraid of your sexual power, that is definitely one way out. "Lesser" men let you feel very comfortable and let you psychologically "stay at home" reenacting stories from your family of origin. You don't fuel up to jettison yourself into your own life. You don't put your ovaries on the line.

One client referred to these as "playpen men." Others call them "boy toys." Sometimes being in a relationship is like being out of town or in a foreign country. Do you wonder about lust in the loins for men of little conversation? It's the sex thing. Paula knew what it was: "I like sex with angry men because they seem in charge, like they know where they want to take me. They are nasty and comfortable with nastiness. I can be raunchy, fully myself, enjoying sex, not overpowering them. Their anger lets me know they can take me. They can take me away, and they can endure all I can bring up. I don't have to tread lightly. They help me return to the gutter. In a second, I'll start to talk like a street guy, and I like acting 'street.'"

Battle of the Sexes

Owning power is painful. It's a war out there! It may be that a lot of your dating and disappointment has to do with seeking power. It's a struggle about performance, winning, losing, getting screwed or screwing the other guy first. Wouldn't it be easier to be a victim and see all men as out to get you? When you resolve your ambivalence about power, take responsibility for the distribution of power in your life and get on with it, your dating will assume a different perspective.

Trying to avoid the angler fish picture keeps your sex life a negotiation for power. Addicted women may seek macho men to keep them in their place, to "tame" them. Sometimes such men appear to promise a safe, quiet harbor to return to after flipping out. The woman feels that the man can handle her sexuality. Many choose macho types who seem to rule the roost and will keep the little lady in her place.

Whether you find men to make you warlike or you create

wars within yourself, it's all about recognizing and owning your own powers. Have you only been attracted to the tortured artists or macho motorcycle types? In group, Maxine told us about her efforts to date nice guys. "Nice guy? No matter how clean and sober I was, how diligently I practiced the principles—I went from one dangerous desperado to another because *nice guys* didn't turn me on *and I wanted them to!*" When they do, Maxine will be more afraid and more at risk. You may not feel worthy of it yet, but, ultimately, it will be the "safe" man who truly allows you to flip.

Take what happened to Lucille. She'd finally found what her family would call "a nice Jewish boy." She gave up what she called the "tango dancers" and, after years of therapy, had found herself actually attracted to and turned on by a solid citizen, an intellectually stimulating, caring, nice guy. She was exuberant when first going out with him. After a few months, their sexuality started to ignite and consume. She came to me bristling with excitement, but filled with tremendous terror.

"I can't believe how scared I am of this man. His love for me, his passionate caring, his attention to me makes me feel so safe, secure and tamed, but at the same time, I find myself letting go. I am willing to melt down all the walls. I don't 'perform' during sex at all, and I don't expect him to. He's so loving and accepting that it makes me sort of freak out. I forget myself, and I forget to play roles. I'm just letting myself be. He's letting me be. It terrifies me. What if I truly love and relish this and then it changes? Maybe he'll just one day stop loving me."

Fear that he could change his feelings and withdraw his love so quickly had more to do with Lucille's mentally ill mother, whose moods turned on a dime, leaving Lucille constantly trying to catch up. When she found a man who let her feel so natural, she reverted back to childhood, feeling "at home," "comfortable," and, thus, "scared." The intimacy awakened fear. Her passion ignited sexual lust, but also repressed rage for the pains of her childhood. She would have to experience both to transcend to her spiritual domain. Her goddess had chosen this man. She chose him to heal the wounds of her childhood. She was afraid of the truth she knew. He was a full-grown adult with his own options and choices, and he could freely choose her or not. He was pretty scary. She needed him more than chocolate cake.

Many of us bought into the idea that if we felt economic power in the workplace, somehow fearful longings would wane. We have to personally and collectively rethink this. You may have swallowed a mixed message that because you are powerful in the business world, you also wield power in relationships. This is a major problem for modern women. We bought into the new paradigm of seeking male power in the workplace, and now tell ourselves that we *should* feel content, *should* feel great personal esteem and *should*, therefore, feel confident in the dating game. We somehow think professional accomplishment and personal fulfillment are judged by the same yardstick. This is a truly male attitude. You can read endless treatises about how important their careers are to men and how when they have career reverses, they suffer in the bedroom. Many a wife has been cautioned not to expect too much from her man when his career isn't going well.

But we're not men, even if we work like men. In bed, it's different. Since a woman's role in bed is not as performance oriented as a man's, we don't have to assume that work performance relates to our bed performance. Also, success on the job does not generate successes in bed. The two just don't compute and can even be mutually exclusive.

For most women, no matter how successful they are in business, when their love life languors, the whole house of cards crumbles. I have had moments of the greatest highs in work life that were dampened, sometimes flooded, by agonies in love life. I was once making an important television appearance to debate the author of the book *Responsible Bulimia*. I was picked up at the airport by a long, white stretch limo, whisked to a Four Seasons hotel with a two-floor suite, flowers and fruit baskets, full amenities and service. I handed my suit to the valet for pressing, closed the door and sobbed. I'd argued with my lover before boarding the plane, and all I could ponder was the end of our relationship. Amid all the glories of that successful business moment, I was on the phone to an AA hotline in a strange city, telling another woman about how bad I felt. Where do we do our work?

Picking Bad Apples

As women admit to themselves that they crave sex, they face men who are less impassioned. Their men may still be little boys and need to grow up. That is very threatening. Evelyn asked me, "What happens when you are too much for the nice guy?" As her weight decreased, her body contours called out for love, and she was "rarin' to get got." She described her sex life as a dead zone. She wanted to be overpowered. She wanted to tease him and get him squirming. Her lover was more into a bit of foreplay, affection and love, but then wanted to "get on with it." Evelyn's interest was more toward enticement, alluring, winning him over. Even when he initiated sex, which was rare, and even if he clearly desired her, she couldn't really feel ready unless he was going out of his mind. She always wanted to feel assured of that fever pitch from him. As the years wore on, he just didn't feel that lustful. He'd settled into a comfortable, perfunctory sexuality. She was fat and furious.

When she came to see me, she was disappointed and sad. The night before, they had started to make love, when she hesitated at his entering, wanting to wait and play more. He took this as a rejection, so stopped and went to sleep. She was livid. "Why can't he overcome a little obstacle? Why does it have to be so perfectly easy for him? I'm always operating on his timetable, waiting for him to be interested enough, and then still, I can only have sex if I'm an easy lay. What happened to the days of courtship, romance, working at it?"

In response to a discussion of this on a radio segment, a listener called to say, "I like them worshipful. I go with the seeking-the-holy-grail idea. If they're not ready to fight and die for it, I don't wanna give it." Hers is a harsher rendition of Evelyn's concerns. In some ways, you can see how a man could become upset and give up. They don't want to be controlled by big mama.

We needed to explore more deeply what Evelyn was really after. It wasn't sex or caring. Jake certainly let her know he loved her. He was affectionate and devoted. She needed to know she was worth fighting for! These might be legitimate requests, or they might be excessive. That really depends on the partner and the specific situation. We all make deals.

Evelyn was using the wrong arena for fighting the wrong battle. She was trying to make up for her feelings of worthlessness and lack of legitimate caring from childhood. Her mother had actually been *obsessed* about her, but in a very superficial way. Evelyn was a child star and her mother a pushy stage mom. She got gobs of attention and felt loads of power, but it felt empty. Since obsessive attention was all she'd ever known, she wanted it in bed as well. The agenda is not pleasure, but power. Obsessive attention rarely results in either.

Again, she explained, "I just want him to be more passionate about me. For me, passionate means *I pass on eat*. If he's not fully there to participate in our mutual awakening, then *I eat my passion*. I want him to seize me and insist and 'take' me. I don't want his sexuality to be dependent on what I'm doing or not doing."

I commented, "You complain about what many women crave. They beg for a man who attends to feelings and watches for a woman's cues."

"Well, I like a lot of that, but I don't want him to be so attentive that he forgets his own agendas. I want him to have his own cues as well. Actually, I resent that he acts like he is just there for me. I hate that!" (Evelyn didn't realize then that Jake, so apparently mindful of her needs, was really harboring deep resentment as her career flowered just when he lost his job. He sublimated his jealousy by "acting" the concerned, caring lover. Evelyn felt his revulsion in her body, sensing the withdrawal, but she couldn't explain it objectively. There was a visceral wisdom in her complaint.)

I Don't Like That Dress

You'd be surprised how many women pick men who criticize rather than compliment them. Psychologists who study hostage situations tell us of the "Stockholm syndrome." During a 1972 bank robbery in Stockholm, the victims bonded with their captors and feared that the liberating police were trying to kill them. They were isolated and abused, and they sought comfort from their abusers. These hostages, after they were freed, set up legal defense funds for their captors. Two of the hostages married captors after their release from prison! Family studies centers report that 28 percent of dating situations have violence attached to them. The women are constantly trying to understand and figure out their men, hoping to keep the violence at bay. Just like for hostages, any act of kindness is interpreted as the ending of abuse. According to a report from the University of New Hampshire's Family Research Laboratory, 60 percent of battered wives had been previously battered *by their fiancés* before the wedding. They reported picking the man because "he felt so at home."

Please don't judge yourself if you keep picking a struggle similar to the one you witnessed growing up. Any change requires a lot of energy. At least you are growing in awareness. Imagine how it could have been and what you were destined for before this point. You are struggling to birth for yourself a very difficult concept: deservingness. This struggle usually shows up around money and sex, and often takes at least three generations to turn around.

You probably keep attracting exactly who you are. If you feel unempowered, you attract someone unempowered. People who *feel* deserving often get what they want. Did you ever notice how the rich get richer? They feel they deserve it.

Let the Good Times Roll

It's hard to take the good times. Sometimes the guy is turned off just when you thought he'd be more turned on. Let's explore Nadine's situation with sexually disinterested Frank. There are many accounts of couples reminiscing about the good old *bad* days, when they had no money, struggled to survive, but were happy and sexy. As life improved, their relationship soured, and they ended up divorcing late in life.

What went wrong? We assume that prosperity bred contempt, but I'll put another spin on it. For addicts in recovery, it is the good life that is hard to take. We need to examine what happened to Nadine and Frank as they rose in economic status. They met in graduate school as struggling students and spent their honeymoon hitchhiking across the country; their simple life couldn't have been better, and their sex life—anytime, anywhere—was exuberant. Their life was a struggle, and their mating signaled overcoming obstacles and reaffirming a commitment to life.

But, sex grew dull as life improved. They moved to the suburbs, had three children and an off-road recreation vehicle, but Frank was no longer interested in sleeping with Nadine. She represented all of this good life. She'd encouraged and convinced him to have the kids, keep the job, be a "success." He hated her for it. Living this "good life" was giving in to Dad's way. When she'd joined him on the less-traveled path, been more of a vagabond into rebellious youth, he'd loved her madly, had sex as a way to die into love and "out" of life. Frank was able to maintain his anger at his father and rebel against all his father's values. Lovemaking was part of Frank's anti-hero commitment to stay somewhat on the fringe. With children, all that changed. As females are wont to do, after bearing children, Nadine became more focused toward stability. Frank wanted to feel that, too, but without therapy to work through his fears of success, his anger about success, his personally conjured "failure" in success, he was destined to transfer his hostility toward his dad onto his wife. This all came out in the bedroom as he could no longer sleep with her.

Sleeping with her meant something about accepting life. Lovemaking is a life-affirming process Frank couldn't avoid. It had previously supported Frank's secret death wish. It was no longer working, so Frank shut down.

Regaining sexual feelings toward Nadine was a gut-wrenching process for Frank, as it involved working more directly on his anger at his success-pushing dad and also, surprisingly, at his mother, who had died mysteriously when he was four years old. He had so disowned his anger that he imagined himself a major good guy and couldn't really express anger directly. All their friends thought him the sweetest, nicest guy around. Nadine bought a lot of it, but she also wanted sex. Because she came to represent mainstream life, she became his new object of hostility, replacing his father. She also represented "woman," and then later "mother," the major woman who abandoned him. He just knew she would suddenly leave. In this case, Frank initially appeared nurturing. Later, he turned out to really be a little boy wanting to turn the tables and attack a mommy. In his childhood there was never enough mommy to go around, and he recreated that lack in his adult life.

Nadine and Frank began having many arguments. She insisted that he tell her when he was unhappy, instead of "just going along" and compromising himself. She was angry that he so often bit the bullet and then withdrew emotionally and physically. By never confronting her and instead "making nice," he was able to stay in charge, secretly judging. He pouted, insisting that he resented her not "asking" him more about what he wanted, assuming he'd go along. He felt safer creating her as his "enemy," rather than trusting her to be his friend. If he were to risk asking or complaining, he feared she might then quickly abandon him. The arguments served to reestablish separation and the knowledge that they were two distinct human beings with different value systems. They approached a place in their counseling where they weren't really sure if they liked each other and didn't know why they chose each other in the first place. Nadine would not settle for any more of what she called "mercy f–cks" just so Frank could feel like a nice guy. Asking those fearful questions returned their lives to the excitement of choice. At that moment of doubt, the sex came back.

Light His Fire?

The moment when sex came back in Nadine and Frank's relationship was not the result of a shopping spree at Victoria's Secret. It was the result of Frank's hard work on himself, analyzing his own projections and animosities toward women. In this case, "woman's work" was for Nadine to highlight the complaint, hold out for connection and then, basically, step out of the way.

She had to have the confidence and patience to wait for that moment where both people are engaged and at risk, where both feel they have options, and where both feel the light of day and the breath of life. It is not something you alone can figure out and fix. I say this emphatically in the face of writers like Phyllis Schafly and others who tell women how much it is our job to "light his fire." When wrapping yourself in Saran Wrap fails, where is Phyllis?

We now have so many books teaching "enticement," and how to court and woo. Some of that is patronizing to both partners. It holds men up as little boys for moms to manipulate. Is that the sex we want?

Why do we give up? Our reason for losing interest in sex is

sometimes boredom but more often has to do with past hurts too difficult to confront. So, you become inured and give up longing. Many couples stop having sex altogether. It's like when you stop going regularly to the gym. . . . It's difficult to start again.

Why Deny?

HE: You're frigid!

SHE: What does that mean?

HE: If you don't know, I can't tell you.

SHE: I'm not frigid—you're a bad lover.

HE: What does that mean?

SHE: If you don't know, I can't tell you.

Such statements clearly draw the battle lines: When so many couples withdraw from each other sexually, why is it so difficult to discuss the issue? There's the fear that if you ask, you just may find out. David Schnarch tells us that the trouble is *not* that we don't communicate, but actually that we communicate all too well. We already know what our partner has to say. We don't ask because we don't want to know more. If nothing is said, then nothing can be blamed on you. Even if you suspect it's your weight, that's better than believing it's instead really *you*. Maybe he'll tell you something you really don't want to hear. Maybe he does find you physically repulsive. You may suspect it anyway. Maybe you feel safer sharing your past hurts with your girlfriends than with your lover. He may be the last one to whom you take your complaints. Reconnection requires a commitment to pain and hard work that most people avoid. Let's look further and deeper.

Good News and Bad

Life is no easier single than mated. Why? Because wherever you go, there you are. *You* show up, writing the script. You have choice in how you play the part.

"I just can't date!" Cynthia screamed as she plunked herself down in my office. "I'm so sick and tired of coming in here to piss and moan about some man who's done me wrong. Enough already! I keep trying to do this thing, and I end up hurting. I told Bud when he first asked me out that I just didn't have the 'kishkas' [guts] for this sort of thing. I told him not to mess with me. I told him I'd finally found a modicum of peace in my life and was content and happy. Do you seriously think he could leave me alone?

"All he said was, 'You're not that happy. You could be happier.'"

Cynthia continued, "Well, I've gone out with him. Now I'm miserable. I felt fine before I met him. And I can't even blame it on him, though you therapist types will probably find something that needs working on. I hate this whole business. For every guy I've come in here complaining about, there is probably some male therapist across town listening to *his* tale of woe about me. The dating deal is just a way for therapists to make a living."

Quite honestly, I realized there was some truth to what she was saying. As a marriage and family counselor, I spend a lot of time trying to help resolve relationship woes. If we could all survive separately as Cynthia suggested, perhaps I *would* be out of a job. Certainly, we would have less to work on, but also less opportunity for growth. I spared both Cynthia and myself those clichés: "suffering is the touchstone of growth," "no pain, no gain" and the countless motivational platitudes that keep so many hurting.

I was more interested in listening to her now, wailing from the deep. She had allowed this man deep inside her, and the pain this intimacy brought seared close to the bone. I let her sob.

She was an actress who traveled often with road shows of Broadway musicals. Her lifestyle lent itself to hooking up with vagabond types—actors, writers, artists—who were roamers more than settlers. She'd found this wonderful man who was newly a widower, had children, a house and a set of traditional values. He assured her when they first met that he was monogamous, faithful and honest. She said that faithfulness was not enough—he would have to *want* to be there, and he would have to *know* he *wanted* to be there. If not, he'd have to go. Was that "knowing" *her* work or *his?*

The men in Cynthia's life thought *being there* was enough. But for her, it wasn't. Men felt that if they showed up consistently, that should be all she could expect. Little did they know how much higher her expectations went. She wanted the soul of the man. She'd told Bud early on, "Just miss me. Leave a message on my machine, and we can play phone tag for days. In fact, it is much less complicated if we just don't talk at all. Just phone me and miss me and we can have an ideal relationship."

So why was it so difficult? The one little thing she begged for was what he withheld. She finally stopped crying. "So, I slipped a little note in his briefcase giving him the number of my hotel in Cleveland. He could always leave a message on my machine and I'd get back to him. Why didn't he call me? We've only dated a few months, so I am really careful about being a pushy broad, but I've had it. I am so tired of walking on eggshells, gauging what he can and can't handle, when he will or won't balk. I'm just sick of the whole dating mess."

Her mentor had advised that Bud had actually *picked* her because she was so honest and forthright. He knew she would push and confront to keep him honest. Instead of being her honest self, she hoped that cajoling and wishing would make it so—would make him be what she wanted him to be. She argued with her sponsor, saying, "A guy might invite honesty, but rarely can he take it. It's castrating, intimidating, makes him squirm. I remember once telling a guy when he called after our double-date with friends that I had felt jealous of his seeming flirtations with my girlfriend. He apologized profusely, saying he'd had no such intention or design. He took great pains to thank me for my honesty. He never called again."

Bud's family of origin was composed of fairly closed-mouthed people who just weren't pushy. This was quite different from her background, where people yelled in one another's faces. Instead of realizing that he'd chosen her to learn more about the other side—the enmeshed, invasive, expressive side of life— Cynthia was trying to adapt and conform to his ways. He was such a fine, decent sort, a man you could take anywhere, could count on, could be at home around. She was so fascinated and proud that he liked her. She wanted him in a big way and for a long time. That made her slightly insecure and worried.

She was also feeling professionally insecure. Her career, though once glamorous, was now a bit on the wane. She was an aging actress, a glut on the market, not quite a has-been, but also not really in demand. She wanted Bud to step in and replace that feeling she'd always craved—that smell of the greasepaint, that roar of the crowd, that affectionate and appreciative audience waiting for the curtain to rise and for her to "take stage." Bud, instead, was busy having his own life, including her in it, but at arm's length.

To an insecure, affection-craving battered child and former fat lady, his need for solitude was unbearable. She kept vacillating, from feeling righteous and indignant to judging herself as narcissistic and too needy. She knew the man adored her as she did him. Why did it have to be this way? She was looking for a big daddy to tell her that everything would be all right. She wanted to be rescued, or at least comforted. In her mind, all she needed was a few "there-there's." Unfortunately, she felt deprived and utterly pathetic. She sobbed to her Twelve-Step sponsor, sobbed at OA meetings, sobbed in therapy and made AT&T rich with long-distance calls to her sister. The result was more tears, but also a lot of learning:

> *I realize I am waiting for his call like a drug, a fix, a tranquilizer. I create the sense of devastation and loss for myself, then I move into a longing place, wailing and waiting and crying in the wind. I want him to change and conform to the wisdom of my ways. I seem to create this professionally as well, wanting all new actresses to practice "the method." It's the same deal. I call it "Cynthia's Sadism." I recreate my childhood, feeling alone and abused. What a painful dance.*

All this learning and self-examination helped Cynthia break free of her fantasies about being rescued from her own life. She wanted the fun of being in love to help cloud over more painful things she had to face. Things like what she was going to do with the rest of her life, and how to invest in a future career. It seemed easier somehow to obsess about something she could not change, something she had no power to fix.

Cynthia had to look at how she used relationships to keep

herself on a fence, to keep herself from full investment in her own life. As you struggle over men and relationships, does this excuse you from attending the classroom of life to learn other lessons?

"Cynthia's Sadism," as she called it, is an example of an adult acting out a childhood myth of Prince Charming coming to the rescue. Such stories do not create adult sexuality. Most of us date and mate as a recurrent return to fantasy. Most of us want to be "swept away." We don't want to be raped, and we don't want to be drugged, but we do want to pretend there are no bras to unhook. Real life becomes so cumbersome. But, if you are an addict, you must remember:

Reality Is for People Who Can't Handle Drugs

Let's face reality and look at what we're seeking with sex. For example, Cynthia used sex to avoid other life issues. You can also use it to seek power, validation, celebration and to easily recharge your batteries. If food is a fuel for your engine, sex can be a jump-start. With a jump-start, you need less fuel to crank up that engine.

Sex can help you celebrate life's victories. Some women have their greatest sex after major skirmishes. While fighting, powerful primordial energies are tapped, and there is an expression of self. Sex can be calming after the exhilaration of the hunt, kill or win. In my second book, *Fat & Furious*, I told of the difficulties experienced by Vanessa as she had to tell her elderly neighbor that she did not appreciate his hugs. It was difficult for this young woman to do, as she was overcoming years of watching her mother fondled inappropriately. She was changing a mold, breaking an ancient pattern. She felt so exuberant afterward that she promptly went home and fondled herself to orgasm. The power of fending him off, the intimacy of remembering her mom's pain, the satisfaction of providing a corrective encounter for them both and the pure personal joy of liking how she had handled the situation all excited her. Why not celebrate and release it all sexually? Would a bagel be better?

Shop Around

All this dating is for practice. Make a rule when adding to your wardrobe: You won't buy it unless it is equal to, or better than, the best look you have now. Let these words of wisdom also apply to your men. Have you chosen one set of men for your bedroom and another set for your living room? Perhaps you need to examine both your wardrobe and your love life in the clear light of day. A perfect lover sometimes has the ability to bring out your dark side and shine a bright light on it. He helps a hidden part of you shine. It may be a part of you that you don't even recognize. Sometimes this is why you will see unlikely pairs coupled together. You'll mutter, "What does she see in him?" Instead, you'd learn more by asking the question, "What does he illuminate in her?" She needs that kind of guy to let a part of herself come out. Maybe his boisterous way lets her act stronger in bed. Maybe his gentleness lets her explore her softness. Maybe his shyness allows for hers.

As you mature, you may find your attitudes toward and choices of men change. We all seem to move more toward baseline. We may even start taking on behaviors more like our opposites. You've seen older men take on some feminine characteristics and vice versa. Carl Jung said that what was true in the dawn of life was a lie by afternoon. You change as you age.

Develop your sex life as an avenue to weight loss, as well as a mirror to your deeper self. If you've been too focused on your children, other people's children or other people in general, then pick up a mirror instead of a magnifying glass. You need this experience. Look and learn in your bedroom.

Many overeating women were fathered by abusers, beaters, alcoholics and emotionally closed-down men. Some married into the same struggle their mothers had known. Some went for the exact opposite. Those who'd found the "nice guys" thought they'd escaped the difficulties, but many, like Elizabeth, found themselves tied to passive-aggressive perfect gentlemen who wouldn't fight or fornicate. During therapy sessions these frustrated wives began to resolve some of this. They started to provoke more direct outward fighting with their men. Unconsciously, they felt guilty about pushing their men, and they ate as a reaction to the guilt. Here's what Elizabeth wrote after a chocolate binge:

> *It didn't dawn on me until today that the rocky road chocolate bar was intended as a celebration. I couldn't figure out what was so different. This first bite felt unlike any other. It simply felt like a "letting go." "Let's just relax," I told myself. Now I see that I was celebrating. The trouble is that is an inappropriate use of food.*
>
> *It always starts in the plate. My celebrating started there. What's the celebration? I've been reverberating with it all week. The fact that I saw and felt the arrows from Jack. I saw and felt them in the moment and I said, "You're shooting arrows at me! Stop it!" And true to fashion, he said, "No I'm not," and for once I said, "Yes you are! And this is what it looks like. This is how you do it. It's disguised but dammit, it's an arrow!"*
>
> *Well, I've never done that. Usually my response is, "Really? It's not an arrow? Gosh, I must be wrong, but it hurts. Well, if*

it's not an arrow, I must be making it up."

This time I said, "It's an arrow and it hurts." This week, forty years of abuse and bullshit changed shape. And for the first time in my life, I didn't feel <u>under</u>-defended. I suspect "over"-sensitivity comes from being under-defended. The arrows go in deep and then I usually get very defensive. If I stop them early, don't <u>allow</u> the arrows to go in, I won't have to call myself "defensive" like it's a bad name. I will simply <u>be</u> defending. That's an appropriate response to incoming artillery.

I did not feel sensitive and fragile and vulnerable as I so often do, and yet, I did not feel armored either. Without the usual self-judgments, I felt strong and whole. It felt too powerful, too profound. So, I ate.

Then I punished myself for eating. I went back to the familiar. I always use my overeating behavior as a way to feel down and beaten. I know how to do <u>this</u>. My body and my spirit can handle this energy.

There's actually a lot more going on in our relationship. I'm seeing clearly how he seethes with hostility. I'm also <u>being</u> seen by other men. I'm the belle of the ball at the country dance class. Those soulful country songs can be so sexy. One of those cowboy-hat types turns me on. I'm so horny when I leave class that I could jump a house. Instead, I eat so I won't feel the sexual energy when I come home to my husband. I keep myself—my spirit, my vitality, my sexuality—down. How do I counter that energy in my body? I don't know how. It is unfamiliar. I had no model for it, and <u>rarely</u>, if ever, did I feel it. But it is coming out. I am coming out. This week has been one of total self-respect and of being <u>ahead</u> of my husband.

Our relationship carries a lot of myths. One myth is that he knows more, he is wiser. I've actually known differently for quite some time, and this week I didn't sacrifice myself to the myths. I don't know if he "respects" me for what I am doing. I know he is hearing me and acknowledging what I am saying. I also know he is very sad and frightened, which, of course, pisses me off. I think that's controlling, too. I'm stopped in my tracks *with his frightened routine. Poor husband. Don't hurt him. See how scared he is?*

I'm undeterred. I stand strong in the face of it and keep on confronting. This battleground has been a long time coming. Before this, the battles were waged in my body. It's terrifying to look at the face of it.

There's a possibility of divorce. We have such tremendous differences, and I fear the consequences. I am so enraged over the lies I've told myself. He's willing to sacrifice me for his comfort. I'm also willing to sacrifice me for his comfort. This keeps great distance between us. I don't know whether it can be bridged. I'm terrified to find that it can't. If I can't make it with nice guys like him, then I'm doomed to be alone forever, like my mother.

Unfortunately, or fortunately, my body and spirit are pressing in on me. They always do, and they speak if I don't eat their voices away. My terror now is equal to my celebration. For today, I don't want my body to be my battleground.

Elizabeth gained all the benefits of looking at herself and seeing how she colluded in her own delusion. Even nice guys can hurt a gal. She wanted a full-frontal adult relationship with this man.

SNAGs

Elizabeth's Jack was a SNAG. In the late 1980s and early 1990s, a strange breed of man appeared that most women had difficulty even talking about with their girlfriends. These men seemed so ideal, delivering all the proper words and deeds at the appointed times and rounds, and the women strangely felt just as jabbed and devastated as they had with the "ne'er-do-wells." I called these men "Sensitive New Age Guys" (SNAGs). They tried to act more like women than men. An honest male friend who plays this role well told me, "The chicks like it." The SNAGs sublimate hostility into propriety, and though they appear present, women still feel disconnected. These fellas just weren't really "there."

Harriet told me about it on a radio show I devoted solely to the topic of SNAGs. "Despite my recent good looks as a result of tremendous weight loss, a healthy lifestyle and living as I choose, I now run across men who seem really interested but rarely deliver. They think they want what they really don't. They want to play at love but don't really want to be there. They are so busy being nice and doing the right thing that you never see their true colors."

Another caller offered: "Some men just like to pine. They're doomed souls and offer me the challenge of making them happy. One of my great loves continued to pine for me twenty-five years after we broke up. He chose the other gal over me, seeing her as weak and suicidal, but me as strong and able to make it without him. Well, he spent half his life mourning that decision, realizing he hadn't really considered himself. Then there was Sylvester, who married his frigid girlfriend after he tried to cheat with me. He felt obligated to her because she helped so much with his career. He now sleeps adulterously all around the country but still calls me with, 'Baby, you're the best.' Nice guys all."

These SNAGs allow the woman to exert her strength and power, all the while encouraging her as well as benefiting from the fruits of her labors. They help women act out their managerial, controlling, cruise director selves. They can stay noncommittal and somewhat withdrawn, and they give supportive lip service to the powerful female. Eventually they become asexual. Actions speak louder than words. *Watch his feet, not his lips.*

Conscious dating involves both boys and girls playing together while growing up to be powerful spiritual men and women. Sex suffers when men stay little boys and their mates try to train them like mothers. This brings angry little boys into the bedroom. Many men report an inability to orgasm unless they are contorting or pounding their women. They want that power!

To counteract SNAGs and passive-aggressive guys, some women insist their men grow up. They don't want any appreciation for it. They want conscious coitus. They don't want grateful men. They want mateful men. Sex will be the barometer. They say, "Show me the honey!" Women who have been obese since childhood have fashioned a coping style to make themselves loved, adored and admired for *personality*. The last thing they want in the bedroom is a man who buys those goods. They want someone who sees past the act, someone who lusts after the *real* person: animal, slovenly or slim.

Men Want to Phoque with Women

A client told me, "Men want to *phoque* with women." (She used the Olde Englishe pronunciation, where *phoque* rhymes with *yoke*.) She yelled emphatically, "They want to mess with our heads, want to throw us off course." Arlene said it best to a new date: "You have the flavor of the kind of man who can 'derail' me. I have things I need to do, and I don't want to be derailed." Despite her protestations, he wooed her, they fell in love, then he broke the news that he could never be faithful to one woman. She ended up devastated and deeply hurt. Despite buying her a new condo, he had "derailed" her. When she came to me, she was spending most weekends at the new condo, sobbing.

He'd known from day one that his divorce had hurt and depleted him so much, he had nothing to give her. He knew he didn't want to commit the way she did. Despite all the good times, he was able to easily pull away. He knew he'd break her heart. He went for it anyway. She was a challenge. She was high-spirited, well-liked, the life of the party—a beautiful and sensuous woman. He was a doctor in a psych unit, she the nurse. They met when he approached her one day with, "You know, at every place of work, there is one person everyone is somehow after. You're that person here." He charmed her socks off, and, eventually, the whole uniform.

When she came to see me, she kept wailing, "Why can't guys like this just leave me alone?" She couldn't understand why he went for her when he knew he couldn't give her anything and he also knew she'd fall hard. She used that little-girl plea of so many grown women. We want to turn to the male of the species—the predator, the pursuer, the conqueror—and ask him to be our watchdog, guardian, keeper of the peace and the kingdom. We expect it, so we're disappointed when it doesn't happen. We came to accept this myth honestly. Did we ever stop to think that maybe, just maybe, "it ain't his job"?

Maybe, in fact, men see their job as somehow messing with the natural order of things, that their role is to throw women off course, discombobulate us, make us nervous. It may have something to do with how we've competed and, in many cases, surpassed many men in the workplace. Maybe some men have to knock us off that power trip, put us in our place. I personally think it has a lot to do with those guys who just haven't grown up enough, some who still have a great deal of mother work to do, but in any event, a lot of men want to phoque with women.

Some men may want to put us down, and if we want to be put down, it's a match made in heaven. A strong and successful career woman finds herself quaking in her boots when the stud snaps his fingers.

Careful of Your Therapist

Therapy can perpetuate the problem. Many eating-disorder therapists have known patients who initially adore them and then loathe them. Therapists both mirror and transfer their clients' feelings. Interesting research has been done with therapists' anger toward bulimic and anorexic clients. Male therapists were most enraged in the presence of powerful, vomiting bulimics, and less so in the presence of anorexics, women totally denying personal power. Female therapists' reactions were reversed. Women clinicians were more angry with anorexics, who represented a slap in the face of feminine power, and had more compassion for overeaters.

Before the women's movement, ladies sat high atop those vestal virgin pedestals, and the guys had to topple us. Now, the whole game seems stupid and insignificant, but they're still jousting and we're still tumbling. It's hard for today's woman to figure out why. She can't turn to the men to try to understand it, and other women don't see it clearly either. Agatha, a recovering alcoholic, told me that she didn't really get a chance to witness this phenomenon until she was well into sobriety and had appreciably cleaned up her act. In fact, she had shed many of her flamboyant outfits for a more conservative, "classy" look. She quipped to a friend who admired her new image, "Think pearls, my dear. Think pearls."

Once she started "pearling," all kinds of men came toward her, wanting nothing more than a toss in the hay. She had fewer offers when she wore the sexy bustiers and stiletto heels. With pearls, beige clothing and a neater coif, all the guys wanted to "mess with her." It wasn't genuine contact they sought—she didn't find that these men wanted to know her deeply and personally—it was just that they wanted to "mess with her." They wanted to bring her to her knees, in more ways than one. Because of her Twelve-Step recovery programs, she had fought hard to come as far as she had, and thus could not sleep with any of them. The price of intimacy had gone up.

You may be balking now, saying you shouldn't have to face such things to keep a little weight off. You may say you want to stay in hiding. However, if you are hiding in the plate, I'd suggest you take a look.

Add in the few thousand reasons you've given yourself for staying hidden and out of the love match. Now sit quietly and look over the history of what and whom you've been through. When you had what you wanted, what did you give up? Most important, when and how did you get "good sex"? What did you have to give up? Some of the things you thought you'd receive *in* a relationship, you received more of when you were *out* of a relationship.

The accounts we uncovered in this chapter were of women fearful of their own power, fearful of that high-voltage, spiritual and sexual energy, fearful it might drive men away. Well, maybe there's good counsel advising you to wait for connection. You'll want to maintain your vulva vigil *expecting* true connection. No more games! It's not a game of love. It's survival of your spirit. It is serious business. Whether looking for Mr. Right, or already with him, you may need a little back-off time. Your body and soul will lead you in holding out for connection. In chapter 4, we will look into "waiting"—making sure you can tolerate the separation before you go for the joining. You may have to wait longer than you think appropriate. Why not? Why weight?

Four

Waiting for a Go-Ahead

I said to my soul,
be still and wait without hoping
lest you hope for the wrong thing.
Wait without loving,
lest you love the wrong thing.
There is yet faith,
but the faith
and the living
and the hoping
are all in the waiting. . . .

—T. S. Eliot, "East Coker"

*A*re you ready to fall in love with your own body and your spirit and give up abusing yourself with food? Don't

163

answer too quickly. It's actually a scary proposition. You're considering upsetting a major applecart here! If it were easy, you'd have done it already. Let's face it. Struggles with food—a fuel and power source—have to do with struggles about all power. You have to face up to your own energies and, ultimately, your power as a transmitter and messenger.

Neediness

The deepest meaning we are exploring throughout this book is *neediness*. "Oh no, I hate when that happens!" Yes, we are people who decided to sublimate our need for significance in coupling into a dinner plate that was muffling. We cannot survive with halfheartedness or casualness in this area. We absolutely *need* conscious coitus. It charges all our batteries. Richard Pryor once discussed sexual differences between men and women. He commiserated with the men who, afterward, spent and depleted, rolled over to pass out. Their partners, on the other hand, were ready to vacuum the house or take on major canning projects before daybreak!

There is a physical empowerment that happens to women after good sex. Past generations of women endured a much more uptight sex life: feigning orgasms, bolstering male egos, rarely asking for their needs to be met. Now *we* need the power charge. Women who overeat are in conflict about power and sexuality. Food is a power source. Sex offers us another charge of power. It stands to reason that *more sex leads to less need for food*.

Women's bodies are the containers and receivers of the awakened energy. Sexual awareness is not to put down or build up men. We instead convert and use that energy responsibly to create our lives. Fully conscious, without excess food to dull us, we correctly understand and utilize our own valuable resources.

In the rest of this chapter we will explore:

Waiting: Staying "empty and waiting."

Expecting: Avoiding the pitfall of "settling."

Attracting: Consciously owning and attracting energy.

Risking: Being seen and touched.

Helene, who attended my seminar in Florida, wrote a letter explaining her new appreciation for sex and intimacy, and its problems.

> *I enjoyed your talk, especially the Sex Thing. I've been married twice and was very sexually active* <u>between</u> *husbands. I've never known a man who didn't have to be explicitly trained to satisfy a woman, and they all resent the heck out of any mention that the job they do might be less than spectacular. My present husband is frustrated because just when he had it down pat, I lost 125 pounds. My body is different, more sensitive, and he resents my changes. I don't blame him. I've about given up because I do have orgasms after all. How important is it?*

Again, that same question. It is devastatingly important! Helene is aware of when she is contacted and when she isn't. She's not in it for orgasm. Unless her husband can settle down to be there with the new *her* showing up daily, she may climax but remain hungry. Like most of us, she'll settle for orgasm. Then she'll eat.

Intimacy = Into Me See

It's very difficult for Helene and any of us to hear the voice of the body over the advertising blitz. In a culture that holds bodies as objects to be evaluated with a cultural standard of waiflike thinness, we've disowned our grounded bodies, full of strong female energy. That body still awaits contact, and aches for a sensual and spiritual connection. That ebbing and flowing, pulsating organism will not be sated by bread alone. Let's chew on this.

Who's Got the Time?

If you really want to practice conscious coitus you will need to consider many timing issues. Sometimes your weight loss and sexual attention will push you further than you feel comfortable going. Your soul needs time to catch up. When we interview relapse sufferers, a common story is of being approached too quickly, then jumping in prematurely, and then feeling out of sync with self and psyche. If you are a married woman, you may become terrified at the attentions of men other than your husband. This is especially dangerous when the husband stays turned off despite your new turn-ons. Unaccustomed to sexual attention, you may have a tendency to see minor flirtation as more than it is. Then, at other times, a man may come on to you while you are totally oblivious. Many who have been obese since childhood will finally learn adolescent dating games while in their forties and fifties. Perhaps you have not been well-schooled in flirting and titillation and so can be more easily hurt than most. What you took as genuine caring and interest did not end up in bed. Or else, you felt you found the love of your life, but didn't know why your bed was empty the following morning. Some women become angry—they feel teased and abused by men who were just being friendly. These are difficult issues because you are responsible *to* yourself and responsible *for* your sexuality. As a woman caring about your own spiritual connections, you can't put big daddy in charge.

Women who have lost weight quickly rush into bed, allowing themselves to be objectified, only to later find themselves hungry and depressed. Unable to negotiate proper personal timing, they regain lost weight. Men approached too soon, and the women had no training in waiting. Flattered by the attention, and hungry for the experience, they jump in prematurely, and are left unsatisfied and disappointed. These patients begin bingeing again and wind up back in the hospital.

Why? Because once you become aware and sensitized, you must listen to your body. Your body tells you clearly what you can and can't handle. Everything has a price. If you sleep where you don't belong, you'll eat. If you've spent much of your life as a yo-yo dieter, accumulating or shedding weight, this has kept you from fully owning your body and your sexuality. You may not have learned how to accept compliments or sexual attention. That inability to receive must be addressed in the kitchen and in the bedroom. You may find it extremely difficult to believe an adoring partner. Rarely can you tolerate lights on. Even though desire is high, embarrassment keeps it under wraps.

"Sometimes When We Touch"

There will be those men who really want to make contact and seek sex as a spiritual, mystical, creative union that grows majestically and develops into a third force, separate from the lovers and their organs. They can be fully present in the moment. Once encountering such a man, your life will never be the same.

Annette actually credits such a lover as the catalyst for her attaining sobriety in AA. She was on a singles vacation plan on a South Sea island and met an Australian army officer. With all the free-flowing booze and miles from home, she had no trouble negotiating a tumble with him right away. She was hotter than a Fourth of July firecracker and began to huff and puff into a frenzy.

In the past, she'd only known more impassioned men who would race her along to frenzied orgasm. She called them "peddlers" because as she looked up they seemed to be riding her like a bicycle. She'd watch them turn their heads and keep peddling. They'd rarely look at her for fear of getting lost into her. It was okay because she didn't want to be seen anyway. In these scenes, if either partner took time out to look, the spell would be broken. There would be real people fumbling with real clothing, impacting each other and taking responsibility for the spiritual gifts they enjoyed together. Instead, looking away worked out fine with alcohol in the equation.

This particular man really wanted to look. He pulled her arms in close, stopped moving and held her gently. With determination and control, he whispered while looking directly into her eyes, "Slow down and enjoy. We've got all the time in the world." Somehow this spoke to her deeper than anything she'd ever heard. She snapped back her head, and knew she was seeing and being seen. She loved it and hated it at the same time. To this day, she recalls it as the greatest sexual experience she's ever had.

Unaccustomed to ever being seen or that close to anyone before, Annette found him the next day. Like a teenager, she embarrassed herself beyond repair with, "I think I'm falling in love with you." He seemed flattered but gave her a wide berth for the rest of the vacation. She, heartbroken and terribly confused, drank herself nightly into oblivion. She didn't know how to fathom that closeness and openness changing to a casual encounter. She'd been so touched that she didn't know how to get back with herself. She was busy in her head engraving wedding invitations. She had been too vulnerable and penetrable, too expectant that one night would last forever. She couldn't weather the separation. She couldn't fathom walking away from such ecstasy. It's just like leaving a half-eaten meal. How can you? She didn't know how to turn herself off. She woke up drunk each morning on yet another Tahiti beach. Seeing herself that strung out and hopeless finally got her desperately to AA. The issue of penetration and then weathering the separation still is not resolved.

Annette had to later see that it was easier for her to let herself be seen by a man who would leave her on a beach in Tahiti after brief forays into intimacy. Staying visible with a partner who would stay long-term was a much more risky proposition.

Be Careful What You Pray For: You Just May Get It. . . .

Conscious coitus is something to think about and have in mind, but it is not the usual course of events. It comes and goes. You and your partner will move in and out of these ecstasies. It is not related as much to orgasm as it is to connection and integrating yourself through sex.

If you've been in long-term recovery from addictions, or have spent a long stint in therapy, you may find that you are about to uncover totally new answers to your age-old problems. The answers will come where you least expect them: from your sex life. There is more to learn from sex than you ever thought possible. You've waited half your life to show up as a beginner.

That certainly happened for Sally, who initially came to see me because she was approaching menopause and had trouble keeping her weight down. She was both frightened and depressed because she had found a man she thought would be the love of her life. It drove her straight to the candy counter.

She began her story with, "I was well into my fifth decade of life before I had a truly vaginal orgasm!" She described it as different from the other kind, nice and rumbly rather than shaky. She felt so at home with this man. She'd let it all go.

"All I know is, the next day I found myself sitting at the wheel of my car in the supermarket parking lot tearing open a bag of Hershey's Kisses with almonds. The sex was incredible, but I was on a run."

Sally had been seeing me for a while, had read my other books and was evaluating this experience as a *fear of success*. She'd decided that her life was too good, and she was running from love. "I knew I deserved this man. I'd paid enough dues, kissed enough frogs. What scared me?"

Need scared her. She needed him. She could master external orgasms and manual manipulation, but there was something about their ease and caring with each other that she couldn't pull off alone. Her body had surrendered to him, and she was afraid she couldn't bring her mind back to the safety of *not* needing. He took her somewhere, and she'd need him to get there again.

As we discussed this, she came back with, "I'm afraid I'll become longing and pathetic. I can see myself already thinking up little annoyances to fight with him about. That will move this whole thing back to a safer ground. I feel better when defended and combative. Here I got what I said I wanted. This man wants me, respects me, truly cares and is really there. I don't want to run for the hills, but I'm so afraid of where he takes me. When we made love, I lost consciousness part of the time. Each time I came back, I sensed my soul wanting to come back to *him*. He was the reason I would flip out to the spirit world, my agent for soul travel, as well as the landing pad that I would instinctively *home* back to like a pigeon."

Because she felt so open and vulnerable, so penetrated, in the next few weeks, Sally wanted to tell him about her battered childhood, some of her torrid affairs and her lonely aching senses of abandonment. I asked her why.

"Because we've gotten so close, I want to get closer."

"Is sharing pain closeness?" I asked.

"Well, maybe not. Listen to what happened. I did one morning tell him that I was just having a bad hormonal day and needed to cry. When I asked if he'd hold me, he said, "sure." He let me cry and rubbed my face. I felt great. I thought he'd turn that tenderness into lovemaking. Instead, he just held me quietly. When I felt better and was not in such a fragile place, I said to him, 'When I am weepy, you don't feel sexy toward me, do you?'

"He replied honestly, 'No, I feel like I'd be taking advantage of you.'"

"This was so odd to me," Sally continued. "Such a tender moment seemed perfect to move into love. For him, it felt like he'd be responsible for healing me in a deep primordial ooze place. He sensed it wasn't where he belonged.

"And I'd been programmed to believe that such a yearning and empty feeling could only be filled by a man. As I look back in hindsight, I see that it would have left me feeling more empty. He was so wise *not* to approach. It is lovely that I love this man enough to hang in to see these things, instead of running in rage and disappointment to focus on what he is *not* delivering. Experience and life lessons are what you get when you don't get what you want."

Sally's level of insight is rare. With the myriad cultural cues that instruct us to make big daddy or Prince Charming fill the bill, there is rare encouragement for a woman to face her own sense of emptiness and stay present through it. Sally's life had been empty. Her alcoholic parents dragged her from one eviction to another. Her friends were constantly changing. She'd never known security. She had a restless yearning for connection to heal childhood wounding. It wasn't just this man she wanted, but she wanted that manna from heaven to make life seem easy and safe. It wasn't his job to heal that ache.

For Sally, it was her own personal work to stay with the emptiness, lean into it, savor it, make friends with it and, in so doing, learn to be gentle with herself. I advised her to be sure to eat with dignity and consciousness. We learn to experience and survive hunger at dinner, yet we still hunger for *life*. I encouraged her to walk slowly and softly throughout the day, to just be still and *know*. . . .

A few months later, Sally had moved with him when he got a job transfer, and she wrote me the following:

> *I can only tell you that I am glad I didn't take the Prozac as my friends advised. They kind of just wanted me to stop talking about myself so much. Many said I should see about hormone replacement therapy. I know that may be an issue soon, but with your encouragement, I took this time to really stare dead on and face my own very deep, lifelong issues. I read in your last book how "mother's milk to the adult is never sweet." I don't think I really got what you meant until now. You mean we can't sweeten*

the painful past. It is a wounding that we must learn to live in and not only tolerate, but in a sense, celebrate. It's when we try to change the past, try to rewrite history and pretend it isn't so that we get into difficulties. I think I have been using men my whole life to try to create that feeling of "home" I've never known. I got into major power struggles trying to get them to deliver lines according to my script. I feel so clear, vacant and strangely at peace about this. Clarity brings me a larger feeling of safety. For today, I'd like to keep loving without hoping.

Sally had a distressing childhood, as do many addicts who come to see me. They all come by their addictions honestly, finding excesses of substance or activity as their best solution to major depression. Their addictions became their own personal treatment for legitimate depression. As part of recovery, they have to face, accept and allow their depression rather than medicate it. What many fail to ever learn is that those salving moments of eternal oneness, home and euphoria are all transitory. Enjoy them when they come, but don't wait for or expect them.

I didn't hear from Sally for many years. Then she sent the following note:

Heard you were writing a book about sex. I'd left out an important fact I need to share with you now. After that last depressive bout when I sort of oozed and watched how much I wanted Ben to fix me, but also knew there was no right way he could say anything to make me feel better, a strange thing came over me. I snapped out of my "wanting" place and moved into a "getting" place. It's like I accepted that no one will give me what I think I want. It's a job for me to take on. I have to understand my needs, have to minister to them and have to let myself be. Well, once I got that, I got strangely horny. It was different than ever before. It was like a whole different side of me showed up. I initiated sex that night, licking and pecking at his back, his shoulders, and ultimately his thighs and privates. I just wanted to devour him. I was after him. I mounted him and rode feverishly. I didn't achieve orgasm and didn't want to. It was heavenly giving to him. I know I always get mine with him, and I know he loves me. I'm so jazzed about what this has awakened in me. I'm not focused on what I'm not getting, but instead on what I can be giving.

It's Lonely on the Top

Sally, like many of us, was using sex to get home. Carl Jung said that addicts suffer a "cosmic homesickness." He said addiction was a longing in the depths of our beings, a spiritual emptiness that we try to fill with alcoholic spirits or other excesses. What if we could fill that emptiness and find our way home by conscious coitus, by a new presence in our love life? Going to God in orgasm could be like approaching Jung's "cosmic home." You are capable of such ecstasy, and overeating or starving has kept you from going there.

You've been blessed with a woman's body. You were made for this. You're conscious and flexible like the dolphins. Women are capable, resilient, fluid beings. We go farther out in sex than our male partners. No wonder you might be ambivalent about sexuality, fearful of losing yourself in orgasm. You sense you might leave the planet and perhaps never return. This fear is not totally unrealistic, as each time you couple in the ways I'm suggesting, you lose a part of yourself. But you will open up and find other parts. You will be getting more out of life, but also giving up some of your past cloak of blindness. Each ecstasy will move you ever closer to another part of yourself you've disowned or avoided. So the prospect, though exciting, is also terrifying. Why have it any other way? Some ignore this gift as too risky and choose to stay with men who make sex burdensome and a chore.

The Four Ds: Disappointment, Deprivation, Devastation, Degradation

Sex sets you up for the four Ds. Knowing how much is at stake, please remember that *you* are responsible for the conscious coitus, not him. When you put the man in charge, you are bound to be disappointed. Take sex seriously, hold it reverently, but realistically; don't let disappointment take you out of the race. Susie Orbach, in *Fat Is a Feminist Issue*, tells us that overeaters decided to remove themselves from the dating game. I say we have to stay in and create our own game. This is similar to the third step in the Twelve-Step program. You are asked to put out effort but "turn over" the results. In other words, "pray toward heaven, but row toward shore." I want you to learn to expect disappointment but continue to hope anyway. Here is an anonymous quote from an Al-Anon book: "Many believe that cynicism requires courage. Actually, cynicism is the height of cowardice. It is innocence and openheartedness that requires the true courage—however often we are hurt as a result of it."

Communicate to yourself and others your wishes and desires, but be prepared if things don't go your way. It's the same as with food: Some dishes don't taste quite the way you expected. You can have some influence over your responses. You must be mindful and conscious to make sure your disappointment does not turn to extreme feelings of deprivation, then despair, and ultimately devastation or even degradation.

When you don't get what you want, be careful not to decide that you are guilty or wrong. That will quickly move you to punishing yourself with deprivation. Then your firm resolve will weaken, and you will despair and work yourself into hopelessness. If you carry it further, you may seek out other lovers to punish you, degrade you, make you feel bad for wanting at all. All this can escalate from slight disappointment. Instead, expect to be disappointed, but hold out anyway. Dream dreams, not results.

Can You Stand the Weight?

Waiting takes *courage*. The word derives from the French *coeur*, meaning "heart." Are you ready to take heart and have the courage to both live and die?

Often, we will feel most like we're going to die at the very "let go" moment when we are getting ready to soar. Just when the caterpillar thinks she's reached the end of her rope, she wriggles free to become a butterfly. Is fear keeping you from your own sexual growth?

If you trust your body and your instincts, you can't ever be the loser. We've been taught so much about accountability to our friends and relatives that we often don't let ourselves just savor our moments with our lovers. Remember we explored how much we don't want to play the fool. We're afraid he won't call and then how do we explain it to our friends. I worked for more than a decade with media shrink Dr. William Rader. He used to say that all young men's first sexual experiences could be likened to homosexual ones. Why? Because every guy hurries back to tell his friends all about it.

Young girls do the same thing. Often our best friendships with other females involve endless discussions of "how rotten men are." We share the four *D*s with each other. *Disappointment* if he didn't feel as strongly as we do; *despair* if he doesn't follow through; *devastation* if we gave too much too soon; and then *degradation* if we crawl back to pester, not believing in the reality that it just wasn't the same for him. I believe the demarcation line, the difference between a slight despair and a transit into devastation or degradation, is predicated on *intercourse*, crossing the vulva, accessing heaven. That's another reason it is important to only play and pet until you are sure he's where you are. It's not to tell your girlfriends. It's to answer to a higher calling.

When I am suggesting holding out and waiting, it's not for manipulation, wanting to effect a certain outcome from the man. It's for *you* to wait for yourself. You need to take the time for yourself to show up and not proceed one minute before you are ready. Even if your body may be hot-to-trot, your soul may not be. You don't want to take your body anywhere your soul can't follow. You might then ask, "Well, why put myself into situations where I will be turned on, but not complete what I've begun?" Succinctly put, as some men quip, "Don't lather if you're not gonna shave."

But how would you even know if you were up for any more intimacy with this man if you didn't allow yourself to become aroused and intimate around him? Your intention is not to tease or to wantonly act out, but to find your own personal, true inner wisdom.

There are three important aspects to this waiting. You will have to become clear about morality, timing and body wisdom.

First is the issue of *morality*. Many confuse spirituality with morality. "Good girl/bad girl" discussions don't apply here. Touching spirit does not mean having morals. It is not about whether he will love you tomorrow. It's about whether *you* will. If you have been truthful and honest and listened to your inner wisdom, you will. Many are seeking religious doctrines, making sure the act is sanctioned by institutions. I am suggesting that the only deity to consult is the goddess of wisdom in your own soul.

Second is the issue of *timing*. What are we waiting for? Are we planning and anticipating a future event, or trying to be more authentic and grounded in the "now"? I am not asking you to plan for the future. I am asking you to pay *attention*, moment by moment, so that each successive moment signals what you are ready for *now*. You'll also come to recognize the signals that tell you when you are not ready.

Third is how you feel about your *body* and "its" motives. This, of course, translates to how you feel about *you*. Where is the locus of control? Can you trust yourself in this area, or are you possessed by demons? Do you believe your body's responses come from God or the devil? Do you believe that your body and soul are united and your soul will signal through your body? Will you use your body as an indicator and barometer, or will you work to control and subdue its call?

There are some things that can't be compromised because your body will "know." I know you've probably been criticized for expecting too much, but in this realm, you just can't lower your expectations. You can expect that he feel passion toward you and expect that he be a grown-up. I bet many of you are now sneering, "Oh, no, not that! I know my man's a child. What can I do?"

Well, you can begin right now waiting and holding out for the best, or at least better. Your job is to inspire you *both* to become spiritual adults.

It's not so much about what you expect from lovers, but about what you expect from yourself. You may have stayed fat to make it seem like sexual disappointment was all your own fault. That is easier than facing how difficult it is for you to achieve connection. Your sexuality carries symbolism. It is a metaphor, a sign of striving. When all else fails, lower your expectations. Or raise them.

Leslie came to me describing herself as a "sex fiend." She'd just lost forty pounds, was rounded and quite sensuous. She stroked her arms, pushed her hair back repeatedly and punctuated the endings of her sentences by allowing her jaw to fall open slightly. She appeared an open invitation with her black spandex tights. She seemed ready for action. She wasn't.

She told of countless bouts of excitement, titillation and attention from men. Losing that extra forty pounds had made such a difference in her sense of self. A dress size change from 14 to 8 was a major assist. On former shopping sprees to Lane Bryant, her mom told her that no man would want a hanging belly like hers. When she lost those forty pounds, the belly tightened up and *she* decided she was sexy. In her case, it was not her weight on the scale, but that size-tag that established who she was. She acted on that tag message without listening to the messenger within.

"I've lost a lot of weight. It's been a while, and I like the way men act toward me now. They often seem interested in watching me have a good time. When I was fatter, the few guys I got were mostly into their own pleasure. Or, I guess I should say *I* was really into providing *their* pleasure. I really never let them see my pleasure because I was embarrassed and afraid they'd make fun of the 'fat girl' later. I wanted to give good head. I wanted to be a special performer. I worked at sex. Now I like watching them work."

Leslie was fascinated describing herself as a sexual being, delighted at having a sex life. Like many others, she had not given herself permission to have sex until that overhanging belly flattened. Her protruding abdomen was like a stop sign, and when it was gone, green lights flashed in her eyes. Men saw it, went for it and used it.

After a few months, Leslie became even more honest about the sex she was having. Pleased at being chosen, making conquests, she had blocked out her own deeper personal pains.

She came to see me on a rainy April afternoon, sobbing, "I just don't like how he comes on my face. I've told him before that it gets in my eyes. Why does he keep doing that?"

"Why do you think?" I countered.

(I am sometimes revolted by such a shrinklike response, but, in this case, Leslie was the only one who knew what was going on there.)

"Well, he seems to be towering over me. He likes to sit on my chest and jerk off. It feels very erotic sometimes, but other times I feel trapped, dominated, even scared a little. He's very big and menacing."

"If you *feel* dominated, you *are* dominated. Do you like it?"

"Yes, there are parts of it that I do like. I've always been so big. I like it when the guy is bigger. I want a man to take me away. I just don't want the mess on my face. I think it is inconsiderate."

"So, you want the passion, the transportation idea, but you don't want what's left behind."

"Right. I don't like his mess."

"*Whose* mess?"

"His mess."

"*His* mess?"

She stared straight ahead like a deer caught in headlights.

I saw her reach for her purse to get a cigarette, and then she remembered I allow no oral gratification during my sessions. She stopped.

"I guess it's *our* mess."

"Relationships are messy. Sex is messy. It's not a contest. This consequence is the aftermath, the concomitant baggage of involvement. It's real life."

Leslie went on to explore how uncomfortable and "not intimate" she felt with this particular lover. She didn't like the idea of cleaning up together, of wiping up after their lovemaking. She didn't really want him in real life. She wanted him in fantasy as a prize she'd won. Instead, he was there in full-frontal, stark reality. He chose to be *right in her face.*

Leslie learned the wisdom of sexuality. She didn't really want this guy, and he knew it. He needed to touch her somehow, make an impact, leave a lasting impression. He knew she was treating him as an object, a commodity, a validation machine. He retaliated.

It would be too easy to criticize the man, make him wrong—a victimizer—and her the victim. That would not help Leslie learn about herself or her own sexual powers. When we've been fat for so long, we think sex is a goal. Instead it is a teacher that takes us further along the road. Leslie, like others, had to explore how *she* was creating her own sex life.

In subsequent sessions, Leslie decided to curb some sexual activity. She chose to self-stimulate rather than be with a man in bed before she felt ready to be with him in life. Countless other women, without investigating, have just continued headlong into sex for sex's sake. Often they regain all their lost weight before taking a look at deeper meanings.

Waiting

Exquisite Attention to Penetration

Women's bodies are messengers and vehicles for soul travel. They are resonant tuning forks. When you cut back on the quantities you eat, you will listen for the hollow echo within.

Your body is a tunnel for filling. Try to remain not quite full so you can hear your own vibration. Your man is the transmitter, and you are the tuning fork echoing in the tunnel.

The supersensitive, resonant, pulsating female body tells when you're hot or not, and it tells when sex worked or didn't. It deserves utmost respect. Your body is programmed for this concentrated work.

Don't complain about feeling hollow and empty. You're supposed to. That ache creates your need to fill it. It's the life force. It's why you're sent here. As we explored in chapter 2, many criticize this need for sex, diagnosing it, saying we're using sex to fill up that vacant lonely place. Too many doctors prescribe drugs for women instead of allowing them to recognize and respect the ache. Once you learn to stay with an empty feeling, you will be ready for a more meaningful sensual, spiritual connection. You are biologically built to be penetrated, to allow others in. Hormonally, too, you ebb and flow. We're talking juicy, needy women here!

Juicy women aren't playing games. If you are just having sex to get off, you are avoiding contact and remaining relatively alone. When you no longer want to be alone, you will want to experience penetration, paying attention to every single inch of the way. You will want to wait for soulful connection. You will open up while still holding on to the perimeters. You have to wait until you feel solid enough to let yourself melt. In other words, don't start until you are strong enough. That means you wait to mate. You don't go to your partner asking him to prop you up, make you feel better, tell you who you are. Instead, you kick out the tripod and stand on your own two feet rather than his toes. With the gift of your own confidence and sense of safety, you are telling your partner that you can take care of yourself. Then you are ready to melt. The trick is to let down boundaries and come back to center. All that flailing chatter out on the periphery was a way to protect too fragile a center. When the headquarters are protected, the outer flanks can stop bombarding so much.

You'll only know about savoring food or sex once you've learned to wait. With food diets as well as deferred sexual gratification, it's important that *you* engineer the waiting. Be sure that you're the one putting on the "wait," the one saying "no, not yet, wait a bit," holding out for the best. You'll be doing this in the dining room and the bedroom.

"Good" Is Enemy of the Best!

Have you been fighting tenaciously for second-best? Are you content with what's "okay" in both food and love? Settling for second-best leads you to ravenous second helpings.

Learn to hold out for quality. Do you even know there is another level? You might have rushed headlong into sex because your body wanted release. You settled for physical titillation. Though that's not a bad choice, if you wait for your soul and guts to catch up, the act will be even more satisfying.

Every addict knows *more is better*. We fear getting started because we may not be able to stop. Can you have a taste and then put it down? Can you touch the heavens and still return to earth? There's a lot of responsibility here. It is easier to swear off fats than to swear "on" to loving.

Why so? Because you're really afraid you might be turned on and not be able to turn off. You're afraid you're going to love your sensual, sexual self. You're afraid of teasing her. You're afraid she may take over your life. Is it a hunger that can never be filled? After all, we're talking about transcending the body to get to the spirit. Once there, why would anyone ever want to leave? You're most afraid of really seeing how much you've been missing, how you've been living your life without connection. It will make you grieve over time wasted.

If you doubt what I am saying now and argue that you are completely shut down and have no interest in sex, I would conjecture that you are still overeating or starving. As long as you are using substitutes, you can't really know what lack you are filling. Food obsessions don't really satisfy this craving. It is a spiritual longing more than physical.

If you argue that you are with an insatiable partner who craves sex much more than you, you may not be giving yourself enough waiting time. I'd propose that he is only hooking in with the animal side and leaving your spirit hungry. You *know* if you've engaged his spirit and he *yours*. Your soul knows.

When I teach sensuous eating, many cry while they chew. They realize how much of their lives they've been deprived of this kind of focused, nurturing attention. Well, the same is true with sex. You may cry a lot at first, but the alternative is to stay out of touch and *out to lunch*.

When we have a good meal, the apostat in our brain lets us know we've had enough. Studies with overeaters found that we don't care about appetite, we care about taste. If the taste is good, we tend to ignore the signals and keep on eating. Our satiety level with sex is just as illusory. We like the good stuff.

Sex brings up the same issues as all the other addictions: control, bondage, taming, getting away with "naughties," compulsive gambling with poor odds, separating partners into bedroom or living-room sweets. We have no signals to discern when enough is enough. With food and sex, we alternate controlling ourselves, controlling our partners, controlling our lives. Don't we lose our appetites when we fall in lust? Don't we eat, drink, smoke, work or shop more when we feel disconnected? What if indulging sexuality leaves you disappointed and craving more?

It is better for you to hold off. It is important that you investigate and communicate what you are after. Look at the note Estelle wrote to a potential lover:

> *Right now, without the projections and expectations, hoping that you care about me, long for me, miss me, we could get along fine. We love each other, have a lovely, wonderful friendship and certainly a lot of fun. I love to hold your arm and touch you, could certainly go for a lot more kissing, but it could be sweet and wonderful between us without the big nasty.*
>
> *I am so sensitive and vulnerable now, even without that major demarcation, meltdown, entry. I just can't imagine being able to live at all after letting you in. I'm afraid I am still too damaged to gain more intimacy right now. If I sleep with you, I will really be a goner, melt into a needy, longing little wretch who will make both our lives miserable. I'd have to be tougher, and not care so much, not feel so much. I'm just too sensitive to sleep with you today.*

When you take your lovemaking seriously, you will appreciate what a great risk is at hand, and you'll be able to communicate that to any potential lover.

Expecting

If you struggle with food, you struggle with expectations. If you think your standards are too high, you may compromise and settle for much less. You may tell yourself that you expect too much from sex. Where did you ever get that idea? You are protecting yourself from disappointment. By the time people come to see me, they are pretty much backed up against the wall, disappointed and ready. What makes them ready is the fact that their best friend—food—has turned on them, so there is not much room for bargaining. They may as well give up the food, because it is no longer working. That is the greatest disappointment of all. That old relationship with food is long gone and will never return. That truth is both a curse and a motivating factor.

You know you'll never receive as much nurturing as you crave. So, focus on the disappointment. Focus makes less more. Your body must get its due. Notice if you are feeling squeamish while reading this. Avoiding this nitty-gritty acceptance of your body as a physical entity keeps extra food in your mouth and extra pounds on your body. You are encased in a body that is organic and, despite what your head says, it wants its just "desserts."

If not satisfied, that body can turn on you or it can sometimes turn on others. Often a woman's unsatisfied sexual appetite shows itself in relationship to her children. A child-rearing manual published in 1947 advised dads that the best thing they could do for their kids was to keep mom sexually satisfied. It cautioned that the "child bears the brunt of the unsatisfied love life of the mother." Moms compensated for lack of attention in bed by giving excessive attention to child-rearing duties.

When the sex life went bad, other problems at home loomed larger. Mom became outer-directed. Children occupied her life; she needed "the kids" as her focus and often created "problem kids." It seems easier to fix someone else than to look at your own troubles.

This is not to blame moms for "problem kids," but, instead, to *invite* moms to seek better sex to save *themselves and* their children. Today, we hospitalize "acting out" teenagers without peeking into mom and dad's bedroom. A better treatment plan might be to advise parents to have more and better sex—for their sakes as well as the children's! If mom can stay focused on her mate, she can get off her kids' backs and onto her own.

Awaiting Personal Signals

Like most of us, rather than trusting your internal wisdom, you probably found it easier to fall into ritualized behavior. You know the drill. You learned how to make love by going to the picture shows. Movies mapped out the entire game plan, the robotized script. There is a fairly predictable sequence of light kissing, deeper kissing, petting outside clothes, inside, above waist, below waist. Now it's first base, second base, third . . . HOME! You scored! It is all so boring. The only thing to say for this game is that it allows total strangers to meet and have sex for a one-night stand. That ritualized, robotized, predictable cookbook is familiar, but deadening. When we love or eat that unconsciously, it doesn't awaken the spirit—it deadens the body. When you travel from city to city, you are pretty sure that every McDonald's hamburger will taste exactly like the last one. Is your sex life like a fast-food binge?

What's really amazing is how we all understand that once

certain barriers are lowered, once certain lines are crossed, it's an open field. One man referred to this as "seasoned territory"—ground he'd already conquered. It was like my mountain climber buddy's instructions, "Never give up gained ground." These men understood clearly how this applied to their mounting women. They revealed that once they'd gotten a hand up the bra, they felt entitled to get there quite easily the next time. They'd "earned" a free pass the next time out. I asked one if it was like a dog marking a tree. "Yeah, sort of," he replied.

For better lovemaking, don't give up any territory. See to it that you are conquered anew each time. When a new *you* shows up every day, you will have new responses. Hopefully, as you show up new, so will your partner. He will adapt and change daily with you. Each time there should be a brand-new entry, a brand-new crossing of your boundaries. The more you can focus on this newness, prolong it and heighten it, the more truly alive you will be in both your eating and your loving.

By adopting an expectant attitude, not knowing or predicting, you will enter a different part of life . . . uncharted territory. Are you ready to enter this dimension?

Ready to Melt?

When I teach conscious eating, I ask participants to try varying expectations of certain foods. Take something you usually have cold and warm it up. Let a usually hot dish get tepid. Just experiment with the variety. Carry this into your love life. Expect to be surprised.

You may find that all your old ideas have to be drastically revamped. That goes for your lovers' ideas as well. Some men have been shocked. Look what Jim wrote me:

I met Yolanda after she'd lost her weight. She showed me "before" pictures, and I couldn't believe it. It actually made me very sad, and I didn't want to know the suffering she'd endured. She sure is a knockout now!

Anyway, we had a great life together and great sex. As I've aged a little, sometimes I'm not as hot as I'd like. It takes a bit more time. I'd been taught that guys are supposed to walk around with perpetual hard-ons. I'll never forget that first time I went to a nudist colony, and despite all my projected fears, I had absolutely no erection. Not even a half-hard. Everyone told me that's how it is for all guys, but I had this idea that a "real man" keeps it up.

I'd anticipate when Yo and I were gonna get it on, and sometimes I'd prepare myself a little in advance. I wanted to show up with my hard-on. She really seemed to love oral sex, and I wanted to be ready for her. Well, one day recently she surprised me. She pulled back the covers, and I was limp as a noodle. She smiled, "MMMMMMMMM . . . My favorite!" and put my full sagging member in her mouth.

<u>Wow!</u> I thought my head would blow off. She just sort of sucked and cuddled with her head resting on my inner thigh. I started hardening up right away. Well, very soon we were goners.

Later I asked her, "What did that mean? My favorite?"

She smiled, "Well, I like it when you're limp. I like to get my whole mouth around you and then just stay quietly feeling life flowing into you. It's so wonderful to <u>feel</u> the surge coming in, to feel the life force and energy filling you, making you hard. When you've already gotten there, I don't get to enjoy the journey. By the time you are hard, you are also so big that it is difficult to feel <u>all</u> of you and the nuances of the energy flow. I like you first soft, and then getting hard <u>with</u> me. It's a nibbler thing. Not a sizzler thing."

Well, so much for the John Wayne movies. I thought it was my job to wow her with studliness. This little lady tells me she likes me soft so she can feel it all. What a concept! She says since she loves to eat, and loves feeling things in her mouth, she is more prone to savor and suck. She doesn't want to just go

*through the motions of up and down. She wants to feel and
taste. . . . No complaints here!*

Jim was surprised to be with a woman who so clearly knew
what she wanted. Yolanda was in touch with her sensuality,
her "mouth hunger" and her preference for a bit of control in
lovemaking. She showed Jim what was best for her to feel connected. It's important that *you* know the difference between
feeling empty space and then feeling connected. You must feel
your own inner space first. Sit quietly alone, preparing for
entry. Try to eat a little less before making love. That creates
the hollow more than anything. Your spirit needs the quiet,
sitting time. As my Buddhist teacher instructs, "Don't just *do*
something, *sit* there!" Just be quiet. You need to be alone a bit
before welcoming your partner.

This is where you learn about your own permeability and
what *your* being needs to become grounded. When you create
the empty place first, your own answers emerge naturally.
Without your own emptiness, there is no sense of penetration,
and thus no spiritual connection. This is the docking of two
full energy spheres. You want to stand firm with your own
boundaries intact and *then* be contacted. You want to engage,
not disappear.

Ask yourself if you can handle this. Are you able to prepare
and fully savor yourself as an empty vessel? In Jim's letter, we
learned that Yolanda liked feeling him *fill* her mouth. She
allowed herself to feel the emptiness first. Can you tolerate
moving back and forth between filled and unfilled? Are you
able to have intercourse and then return to your own solid
ground? For example, after intercourse, can you stand the
alone, contented feeling? Can you tolerate lying beside your

partner, starting to feel him ebbing away from you? How painful or traumatic is it? How right-on, natural and content is it? Can you move to a feeling of solitude for yourself without feeling threatened by a "withdrawal" from him?

Remember, the male angler fish hooks up to its mate and is later so spent that he almost disappears, becoming a blob attached but floating aimlessly behind her. Are you afraid this is your fate? Until you can tolerate the separation, you have no business making the connection. That is why you may choose to wait. Often when women speak of this spiritual connection followed by separation, their partners become confused. Their men nod distractedly without a clue. Men think it's about the future, about a long-term relationship, marriage or fidelity. Instead, many women are talking about the *now*, about experiencing such fullness in the moment that they don't mind it ending.

So, What Do You Expect?

I am suggesting meaningful, *momentary* sex without expectations of long-term commitment. It's about staying in the moment. It relates to *how* you eat as well. You are going for a meltdown or surrender experience. It is not a surrender to the man, but a surrender to your own inner female. You need the man desperately to help carry you closer. Your body is the tuning fork waiting to resonate with his vibration. Men don't open to entry as women do, so they don't transmit a total body radiation. We're the transmitters, but we need just the right connection, a place where the lover takes us, where the signal comes through loud and clear. You can't go it alone. You can have orgasms alone, but you can't arrive at this special place alone.

Melting can best be described as a self-forgetting. Your eyes and the top of your head will probably tingle, but you won't notice this until after the fact. You will feel boundary-less, as if your skin is smoothed away. Your body will want to envelop and slip around your partner. You won't be very interested in thoughts or ideas. You are fully functional and present, but you are somewhat on automatic pilot. This feeling is a home you've longed for. You'll feel at peace, and in that peace, you won't overeat.

Chances are you were never taught how to listen and trust the body and use it for this soul travel, to feel more grounded in yourself. Eating may have been your only safe sex. Sex is one of the most important parts of all existence, and look how little training we get. Remember when Surgeon General Jocelyn Elders even hinted that it *might* be worth considering teaching masturbation in schools? She was promptly fired. (Let's note that teaching masturbation would probably bene-fit girls much more than boys. Most boys learn about it the minute they slip on their underwear!) Anyway, Dr. Elders dared to suggest we might "teach" our children about plea-sure. Note also that she is an overweight black female. Can we accept such talk from such a being? Notice how outrageously our nation enters the millennium, denying and repressing this sexuality! The president's renunciation of Dr. Elders is tragic—particularly in light of the fact that he denounced her at possibly the very same time he was secretly indulging in sexual encounters in the Oval Office. To add insult to injury, the media then exposed the public to the details of his affair. This only served to further relegate sexuality to a secret, sin-ister place, instead of to the open, positive one that Dr. Elders recommended.

Let's try to keep this discussion open and in the clear light of day. If you are not afraid to be more open and vulnerable, you can begin to think about—but not have—intercourse. That act involves sharing and mutuality. It's much scarier than just titillation. Many report feeling safer in mutual masturbation or even oral sex than with intercourse. The mutual cooperation of intercourse is just too intimate. It involves entering a third, *unknown* place. It's a place that combines two beings. You can't get there alone, and you've never been there before. Scary? You bet!

Attracting

If it's going to be that ominous and serious, you'd better participate in the choice of partners. Let's look at consciously attracting what you want. In case you're not sure, let's suppose for now that you want someone who watches and listens to *you*, someone who pays attention. You want a man who can take his time.

Jokes abound about women taking a long time to orgasm. These help us keep thinking of sex as a chore instead of an opportunity.

QUESTION: Why do women take so long to come to orgasm?

ANSWER: Who cares?

This is not to say that we don't care *about* a woman's orgasm. We just don't care how long it takes. Why should the time involved matter at all? What's the problem? If we're really savoring the journey, why rush? Let's enhance the path so that *it* becomes the goal.

Got It, Flaunt It

You may now be saying, "I'll deal with this later. When I get thin, my sexual problems will be solved." If you feel that way, you might stay fat so you won't have to face any of it. Let's face it to make it. Whether you are still fat or have never been fat, you'll have to learn to strut your stuff. Losing weight and feeling sexy is about growing up and leaving home. It means walking into the sunset of joy. You grow up to the joy of sex.

If you're going to be waiting to have grown-up sex, you have to find something to do in the meantime. Flirting's the ticket. I'd like to see everyone flirting all the time. In my "Viva la Vulva" workshops, women express great fears about flirting. They are afraid to be sought after, afraid of encouraging rape, afraid of their own lustful tendencies, but mostly afraid of the judgment of other women. *"Slut!"* is not a label taken easily. To defy this controlling credo, ladies attending my workshops don T-shirts that read *"Sluts" for Slimness*. One participant was appalled that I thought it wise for us to be attracting sexual energy and keeping ourselves and others in a state of perpetual lust. Just as she opposed violent movies that she felt "created murderers," she railed that teaching flirting would have everyone raping and pillaging.

She'd offer the same argument that to smell a donut means you have to eat it. She'd say that once you start a meal, you must devour every last string bean on the plate. Can't we tolerate titillation without action? If we watch a *Superman* movie, do we have to jump off a roof? Sexual arousal is a pleasure in itself; it does not have to go anywhere from there. Too many shut off their flirting abilities outside the home and then lose them inside as well. I may see them for marriage or divorce counseling. I recommend that you do what it takes to keep the juices boiling.

"I Wish I Could Shimmy Like My Sister Kate"

A man sings this song. That says it all. He wishes he could shimmy. You've got to be Kate. Start practicing and acting sexy and lovable before you feel it. Take on the behavior change before the attitude catches up. Whether you make these changes while fat or thin, it's the fat head that needs reprogramming. Actors rehearse. Athletes train. Dieters weigh portions. Sexy women flirt. It goes with the territory. It's what you do. You must begin at once, whether ready or not, so you can look early—and often—at what you're defending against.

At my seminars, many women balk at the prospect of flirting because they fear looking foolish. They think they'll flirt *after* they lose weight. Some want to discuss the AIDS scare or date rape instead. I advise them and you that there are countless other books and venues dealing with those "powerlessness" topics. This endeavor is about empowerment.

Starting to listen to the voice of the body and showing off your female energy will cause many problems in relationships because these things involve negotiations for power. Maybe neither you nor your mate knows much about this power. As you practice flirting and this sexual energy is awakening and projecting, you receive responses. You may initially feel awkward, not knowing what to do. Lindsay shared this on my radio show:

> I was mortified at the first pass I got from a suitor. I didn't know what it was at first. I'd been a fat buffoon, clowning my way through school, ridiculing myself, being "one of the guys." When a "guy" came on to me like I was a "gal," I freaked!

That's why I'd like you to practice flirting even if you don't feel ready for action. This is so you develop more acquaintance with your disowned female power. In your own living room, you can practice walking and strutting to find your sexual energy. This can be an important component of your exercise regimen. While Richard Simmons has you "sweatin' to the oldies," take a few extra moments for soulful "struttin' with the ladies." Play recordings of some funky blues divas like Big Mama Thornton or Ruth Brown.

Claire attended my retreat at the Omega Institute in upstate New York and, though 350 pounds, could strut and grind with the best of 'em. She rotated her hips in ecstatic undulation. One man in our group noted that he'd never experienced so much sex with his clothes on. He marveled at how Claire's internal spark radiated out to him, how he felt so turned on, not by her form, but by her substance. Claire was more interested in watching *her own* hips gyrate, attracting herself, rather than attracting a man. However, by the end of the weekend, he was dancing with her, grinding along with the lightnin' in her thunder thighs!

This strutting involves deep self-forgetting. You have to give up any focus on your separate body parts, your rolls, your imperfections, and instead focus on accessing energy, as if there is an internal smoldering flame for you to fan. First, take long strides, walking back and forth across the floor. As you strut, focus on your breath and heave a deep sigh as you exhale. Listen and feel the vibration in your chest as you vibrate that energy. Push breath out and feel its resonance in your cavity. Your body is the container for that energy, and you control its discharge. Stick your chest out and turn your hips from side to side while letting your arms swing loosely as you walk. That is the warm-up.

You can slowly say our "viva la vulva" mantra. Elongate and accentuate the phrase: Y-U-U-U-U-U-M-E-E-E-E-E-E in T-U-U-U-U-U-M-E-E-E-E-E-E.

Now *stop!* With your arms at your side, feel little molecules passing blood out to your capillaries, to the tips of your fingers and breasts. Focus on that blood flow, the circulation of energy. Allow a few moments to feel your energy rise, and then raise your arms naturally while you pivot your hips around on axis. It's good to have a full-length mirror so you can enjoy watching the smoothness of your gyrations. Keep it smooth and melodic. Cock your head and smile at yourself.

While you flow with this undulation, rub your hands together quickly. After five seconds, hold your palms facing each other about two inches apart. Stop a minute and feel that heat and energy between your palms. You are practicing getting to know your own energy field with just a few minutes a day in self-stimulation, breathing and turn-on. You're doing this for yourself to keep the juices flowing.

Struttin' can be foreplay for flirting. Right now, you just need the daily warm-up, giving attention to sexual energy. You might later decide to project some of this energy outward toward a partner. You don't *have* to. Remember, Claire was dancing for herself. Strutting your stuff is attractive and energizing for *you*, and that's enough.

I have often taken patients out on "flirt assignments" to practice. I once took a van full of ladies to the car wash, each with an assignment to quietly and unobtrusively flirt with an attendant. Even with no one saying a word, the sexual energy at the drying rack was thick and exciting! People started smiling. They turned on to an energy that was ominous. Later, women who thought they were afraid of approaches from men found instead it was their *own* power they feared. Flirting made them feel so alive! Flirt for yourself, whether *he* gets it or not . . . you will.

This is all about *you* accessing your own joy and life force. Once you discover the truth about this power you have, anyone with any sensitivity at all to you will immediately see a difference. They'll ask, "What's different about you? Have you had a face lift?" No, you've allowed yourself to turn on to your own life force. You've had a *face life*.

When you "face life," it may bring up some old fears about being chosen, but you'll discover something else much more interesting. Rather than worrying about acceptance from men, you will become aware of yourself as more discriminating. As you tune in to your own sexual senses, you will find yourself interested only in men who can vibrate on your level.

"Fake It 'til You Make It"

Often, men report that *confidence* is a woman's sexiest commodity. Have you known a "plain Jane" woman who is a magnet to men? Why? She's a woman who is confident about her sexuality. She likes sex and is not fearful of newness and experimentation. She may not wear the black spandex tube dress, cake on eyeliner or sport a Wonderbra, but it's an inner knowing that she subtly projects outward. You've sensed it. You have it. Use it.

What would be so terrible if we all walked the streets titillated and turned on, up for sex and fun, and just didn't act on it? Would it hinder or hurt? Think carefully on your answers. Your life is at stake.

A lovely vaudeville story tells of Flo Ziegfeld ordering the Follies' stage manager to buy silk panties for each chorus girl.

He replied, "But Flo, that's a terrible expense for something no one will see. No one will even know they have them on!"

Mr. Ziegfeld smiled wryly, "The girls will. . . ."

Decide to Be Sexy

You've seen women who have this sexual confidence. They really know they've got it. They're listening to an energy vibration, feeling the *heat!* They're hot and proud of it! They are not at all concerned with fat or form. Obese European women strut the Costa del Sol. Heavy Russian women at the Black Sea wear skimpy bikinis with over-hanging rolls of flesh. Some are even topless and drooping, but they march up that beach like they own the world. They are much more accepting of overweight sexuality.

Presentation is everything. Your sexuality is about energy, not about form. Think of it as something that bubbles up from inside and radiates out your eye sockets. You'll soon be amazed to see the glimmer. That glimmer will show up if you just look dead on at someone and say to yourself, "I'm alive and so are you. We share a life force. Isn't it ominous?" As you think that way, others catch the beam. You've seen it from some screen stars. Some of the faces are attractive and some aren't, but they all *decide* to project their energy outward.

Flirt for a Day

Experiment now with your own sexual energy. Pick one day, any day, and decide to flirt your way through it. That means, whomever you encounter, just give them a dead-on direct look that spells *flirt!*

A smile will probably gurgle up, but don't force anything.

Men have told me that they find the smile of a woman to be her most sexy possession. Maybe they are picking up this vibration. Writing of her experiences as a stripper, Lynn Snowden noted, "I got more tips from smiling than I did from removing anything."

It's a look that will radiate from within. A look that says, "I'm hot and I'm in touch with it." It doesn't say you want to *do* anything about it. Just that you've read the meter. Try it for just one day, then ask yourself:

Why did I wait so long to be so alive?

Is there any danger in this? From them? From me?

Is it okay to *have* the feeling, but not act it out?

Am I inspired to anything new?

What has love got to do with it?

Don't waste time. You'll find your soul as soon as you take action. Girlish modesty and protestation are deadly now. So is ego. You have no time to worry about how you look. Do it anyway.

In action, you'll confront old beliefs. Real life isn't safe and sanitized. This is an invitation to a fuller and richer life to help you eat less and savor more. After one day of thinking sex, deciding to be sexy, you will start attracting sexual attention— whether you like it or not. You will exude a sense of confidence. Your spirit won't dare allow anyone to judge you on body parts alone.

Risking

Prove It or Lose It

You may have settled in with a particular partner simply because he was one who "wanted" you. Please don't become frightened by the prospect of asking now, "Did I really want him?" Did you ever really like sex, or was it just important to be *chosen?* Has your body been a barometer of your acceptability—a prize to be won? As you practice flirting while still large, you learn it is more about vibration than looks. You'll respect yourself more.

Driving through Georgetown brought back memories of her college days to Denise. She recounted some to me as she pointed out the Crazy Horse Saloon and then Rive Gauche and then another storefront where a beer bar had once stood. She reminisced, "I had just lost fifty pounds that summer, and I loved the attention from guys. I remember one night my girlfriend and I returned to some hotel with five married Canadian Mounties. It was the 1960s, and I usually went home with whomever asked me. I was so amazed at how easily and readily these guys were up for sex. I wondered why it took me longer to know."

I asked, "Did you know *then* when you were up for sex? Did you like the sex you had?"

"No, not really. I just liked the attention."

Maybe you learned that your body was a commodity for barter or exchange. Maybe you needed a man so you'd feel good about yourself, but never liked the *person* he was. So many women just needed to be *chosen*. Be careful of using sex as the proof that you are desirable. Obese women and emaciated anorexics both devise these tests of love, and both fail equally. "If he loves me fat, it must be true love. At least I know he's not using me as an object. If he can overcome this fat, I'm sure he really loves and wants *me*. Anyone can love a normal body." Don't use your lover as an evaluator and judge of your body. Your men like what they see. They've chosen you and want to love you.

Don't point out your imperfections. It's like criticizing their good taste. Body image doubts have to do with ego, not love. You are not a commodity for sale. Don't play into it. Don't use your boudoir as the test lab for acceptance, security or validation. Ultimately, your partner will see what you are doing and feel used.

Men constantly complain to me, "She's always testing me." Look what Stan wrote:

> *I'm so sick of being her emotional barometer, evaluating her torso to set her mood. She always asks, "Do I look fat in this dress? Am I as fat as that lady? Do you think I've gained weight?"*
>
> *What's a guy to do? It's all a test. Either way I'm screwed. I definitely can't answer yes, or I've bought it. Even if I say no, she just won't believe me. It makes me feel really inadequate because it really doesn't matter if I'm there or not. It's a hollow game, and one that I'd rather not play. There's no happy ending. On a good day, I can get away with, "I don't wanna play." If she can easily come off it, she'll laugh and be done.*
>
> *If she's gonna be depressed, she'll then whimper that I don't care, that I minimize her concerns, that I don't understand the pressure she's under. Well, I don't. I have my own pressures. I don't keep asking her to compare or evaluate my parts. When she gets into that, it just really depersonalizes what we have together. She takes it out of our bedroom and into the streets.*

If you're fishing for a compliment, *wait*. If you manipulate it out of him, it's not the real thing anyway. You'll feel hungry.

Your adult lover is not here to heal your wounds. Elaborate tests and obstacles that he must pass just won't work. You can't get what you needed long ago. It's too late now. Life is in session. Be present. Step up to the plate. Your game with him must be one of celebrating and bringing him the gift and excitement of who *you* are. You want him as a playmate, not a judge. Bringing these doubts and insecurities to the men in your life will take the life out of your men.

Objectification

No wonder men often objectify women. We do it to ourselves. In flirting classes, I've found men complaining that even though they strike up a conversation to get to know a woman, many women are too wary. The men report, "Some women are so defensive, they don't know how to play with the opposite sex in a nonsexual way." Listen to these men. Sometimes they just want to make friends but are rudely rejected by fearful women. When I've asked women about this, they reply they're fearful of leading men on. They are stifled by fear of their own power.

So often at retreats and seminars, one woman inevitably wants to discuss rape. Instead of focusing more on women developing their own power, this person wants to discuss powerlessness. Such diversions are quite telling. Rape and incest discussions may need a forum, but why when we're strutting our stuff? Whom do we really fear?

Sometimes women do like to be watched. Strippers in nudie bars report that they love the powerful feeling of watching men watch them. They are in charge. They don't feel objectified. They run the show. There is a subtle and important demarcation here between being seen and being objectified. The crucial factor is whether the woman *participates* and feels like she is part of the dance, or whether she *has* to dance for him.

You'll want to keep your body a little less than full so you can trust your vibrations, and trust yourself and your body to know where the power lies. Even if you've spent much of your life unconsciously filled with food, once you curtail your food intake, you can begin to trust your body's signals immediately.

If you pay careful attention, *you* will correctly read the signals. You will know when you are along for the ride, or when it feels like you're being ridden. Objectification slips in very subtly, even in the best of love affairs. Your body is so sensitive that it can tell when it's not personal. You must avoid impersonal contact. Don't allow it to happen. If it's already going on, don't let it continue. When you feel like an object, stop and regroup. You want him to view specifically your one and only body. That body knows.

If it seems like, for him, any good body will do, you'll later "eat over" the experience. It takes work and attention to achieve conscious sex. If you settle too many times for unconscious sex, you'll find yourself eating to compensate. Your soul aches. Careful here not to judge yourself as "too sensitive." This is a sensitive endeavor. How could you not be sensitive? You are anticipating opening yourself up to be entered. There is a longing for penetration, but also a fear of violation. You have a lot to face here. You open your legs, spread yourself for entry. The only way to numb out sensitivity is through eating, drinking or drugging. Without these, the true sensitive being emerges.

It's not just what *he* does that counts, but how much *you* stay there or leave. Are you paying full attention? This is not a game for flakes or wanderers. When you leave the scene and move to automatic pilot, thinking about work, the kids, the shopping, then stop immediately and regroup until you are really *there*. Anything else leaves you ravenous.

Patsy, a former prostitute, reported that in the midst of having sex with her new husband, she found herself lapsing into mechanical automatic pilot, interested in "getting it over with." She immediately stopped, pulled away a minute, asked him to hold on. She had to make sure she was there with *him*. She explained it very lovingly, hugged him, caressed his face and said, "I don't want to do *anything* with you when I am not fully and completely there. It's worth waiting a minute to make sure I'm with you." He loved it. It heightened his excitement even more. In our group therapy sessions, Patsy went on to tell of all the pushing toward the man's orgasm she'd done as a prostitute. After all, that's what the johns paid for. Now in a loving relationship, she was learning that men, too, can actually enjoy sex more when there is true personal contact. Remember, her agenda was not to keep *him* in contact, but to keep *herself* there. *She* was the wanderer! Despite all that's been said about men fearing commitment for the long haul, women have also been known to make their exits in the short run.

Seeking Visibility

When we seek conscious coitus, we are after more than physical titillation and more than emotional acceptance. We truly want to be *seen*. That's what we need the man for. We want to be seen as woman, goddess, seductress. We want his attention to an energy we radiate from within. If he is looking away, we feel it. Physical release is pleasant, but not satisfying. The gaze, the attention, the connection must be made.

Notice his look. If he gazes upon you as if you are just any woman, your sensitive body monitors that. Is he here with *you?* What is his purpose in this involvement? It really doesn't matter if he has good technique and rubs the right spot well. If you don't *feel* his concerted effort *toward* you, it doesn't connect. You will only be able to melt with him if what he does touches *you* and is personal to *you*. Elaine wrote this from Tulsa:

> *I was playing kissy face with a wonderful lover as he gave slight little pecks at my arms and hands. He held them in great reverence and awe. It was sweet. I loved to watch his head focus on my parts. He moved to the inside of my wrist.*
>
> *Somehow, that new kiss sent shock waves through my system. I gasped quietly. He felt it. "Oh, is that an erogenous zone?" he asked lovingly. He was an artful lover interested in knowing what turned me on. He truly wanted to know. He should only know that when the intention is right, it's all erogenous.*

Elaine went on to explain how intentions and style count most. Sure, there are some areas of thinner skin that respond more characteristically sexually, but that isn't what makes anything sexy. It's not the where, but the *how*. It's the reverent, loving, patient *way* that *he* kissed *her* wrist that made it erotic and made the zone open up. It's not the form, but the focus. It's so similar with food. It's not *what* you eat, but *how* you eat it.

Be careful and conscious of any lapse into robotized behavior. You'll want to experience each time as brand-new. To do that, you must pay attention to intention.

Russian men pound each other with big kisses on the lips. They're not turned on. They don't go at it to turn on. Their intentions are to greet. Eskimos rub noses and go into heat.

I don't think there are sexual nerve endings on noses. If you've never been taught that your nose is intimate, it won't turn you on. It's a cultural thing, and it speaks to intention rather than form.

Though you may be shy about your physical form, your inner being wants to come out. It has been said that "Love is the call from the other to come out." Your total body and being is up for sex. Babies' bodies respond everywhere to everything. So can yours. It just needs the right stroking, the right intentions. Be careful of men who go immediately for your genitals, thinking that's where you want to be touched. In the *Divine Dine* video, I teach that chewing on only one side of your mouth will leave the other side with "mouth hunger." When he's fondling your body, make sure nothing goes hungry, that the experience is connected, that all of you has shown up.

The greatest gift we give one another is focused, rapt attention. Conscious coitus involves being seen. Will I allow you to gaze upon me? Can I stand it? Can we endure it? Can you stand your lover's gaze? Can you stand to look during intercourse? Can you keep looking at the moment of orgasm? This life can't pass by unnoticed. Attention must be paid.

You have to find this knowing place on your own. Manuals can teach you how to keep your legs together. Dating primers can tell you how to be coy and bag your catch. But, who can tell you how it personally feels to you when you settle in to *be?* That is your goddess place, and no one can tell you how to get there or what it feels like. You'll know. Each woman will need to find her alone, separate space for the man to approach. It is your citadel. You invite him in. There is no true connection if all of the boundaries are down. You might have tried to avoid this work of waiting and listening for your Self to show up.

This is sometimes an avoidance of the difficult and intimate negotiation of opening the mystery of you. Many have avoided solving this mystery by claiming love for all. Perhaps if you love all mankind, you really love no man.

Women *appear* willing to be more open, to be more visible than their men, but my experience leads me to believe this is more or less an affectation. You may be biologically built to be penetrated and allow others in, and hormonally you ebb and flow more than men, but at the core of your essential being, you may have become quite rigid. You've tightened up to survive. On a very subtle level you're really scared to death. Let's now move to loosening up and using your mating as a way to be seen and see. It involves ultimate separation from childhood, secrecy and unconsciousness.

Think aloud to yourself now about the benefits as well as liabilities of being "seen." Sometimes you like it and sometimes you don't. We all long for visibility but also run to hide. Learn to recognize when you're seen versus when you feel invisible. In conscious lovemaking, the soul keeps on monitoring.

INVISIBLE SEX	VISIBLE SEX
Looking away	Eye contact
Rushing headlong	Waiting time
Acting as if	Telling what works
Cockiness	Awkwardness
Anyone will do	He knows it's you
Anyone will do	You know it's him
Controlled	Emotions rampant
Serious business	Sense of humor

Two precious indicators can let you know you are on the beam. One is eye contact and the other is movement. You will try for connected eye contact most of the time, and you will notice if movements are in or out of sync. Rarely can you sustain eye contact for long. Just try little by little. If the rhythm pattern changes and you feel awkward, ask about stopping to reconnect. Let him know you lost a feeling of *contact* with *him*.

Many men *do* want to know if you feel left out of the experience. You must let him know when the connection is present or broken. When we falter in monitoring this connection, deciding it's too difficult, we become very hungry later. We leave bed and head for the fridge. Sex with another human being is such a risky proposition, you must develop discernment. Food may often seem a much less ominous partner— one you can totally *control* on your own.

Permeability

I ask women at my workshops two important questions:

Do you like oral sex more than intercourse?
Do you like the thrust in or the pull out best?

These questions attend to deeper meanings in your sexuality. Sexual entry carries much more meaning than entry from food. You have taken the time to become aware of your boundaries. Now you risk letting them fall. The trick is to become a semipermeable membrane, opening up while still holding on to the perimeters. You must hold on and let go at the same time. We learned in high school biology class about permeable and semipermeable membranes. Some tissues allow any molecules to flow through freely. Others have a screening device, allowing some molecules in and holding others at bay. These are named "semipermeable." They discriminate. They aren't available for all entry, but they allow in the "correct" substances. That's how you have to think of yourself and your orifices.

You have to remain slightly separated, in your own private place, feeling just enough of a coating so there is something *to* penetrate. That is the space you consciously create for him to enter. How do you know when you've created the coating but not a wall? Let's compare the difference between contact and avoidance, between feeling impermeable and semipermeable:

IMPERMEABLE	SEMIPERMEABLE
closed down	excitement
stillness	vibrations
slowing energy	quickening energy
predictable	expectant and waiting
safe and foregone	exciting and tense
sureness	edginess

If you are learning to "let go," it stands to reason there is no formula. You can't have answers in advance. You and he will have to find out together. When the "wall" goes, so do you. You created it. You noticed it. You'll now watch it fall. And each time will be different. Each day a new *you* shows up. What felt right yesterday may seem wrong today. If your partner complains that you've "changed," explain that we are *all* changing and different every day. We're responding to thousands of new stimuli, whether we've lost weight, had a shave or just heard bad news at work. The key to artful and conscious lovemaking is paying attention and being aware of exactly who shows up each time. There is no clue to who you'll be today or what you'll need. Predictability is what makes so much lovemaking so unsatisfying. It has sent too many voluptuous women to the pantry.

Own Your Animal

We *are* animals, and we *are* our bodies. We are spiritual beings sent here to have an animal experience. We can't avoid knowing this, or our species is doomed. Instead of prowling the pantry, take that amorous animal to bed. Animal hunger forces us to risk knowing a part of ourselves we might prefer to hide. Conscious couplings are our destiny, a call to both wildness and spirit, and we must answer the call. Wise women get conscious and wild women have sex. Neither get the blues.

Lust you must! Go where angels fear to tread! You want to achieve godlike connection, and the body is the way to get there. Most of us know the body is the conduit. Some became anorexic, trying to feel more angelic, hoping to attain the spirit by disowning the body.

Remember in the movie *E.T.*, the creature called plaintively to "phone home." He knew he didn't belong on this planet. There was somewhere else he belonged and where he longed to be. He needed to return to a home he'd always known. You may also know that there is more to you than the daily life you live here. You don't want to escape this life, but you want to flesh it out, give it more meaning, increase its hue and volume. You are calling yourself out and can use your lover as a travel agent. As resilient and fluid beings, we go very far out with sex. Some ignore this gift as too risky and choose to stay with men who make sex burdensome and a chore.

"What's Love Got to Do with It?"

The effort I am suggesting here needn't be called making love. To require emotional investment can be too limiting. That suggests a "deal" between you and your partner. Connection in sex is really bigger than the love deal. It is a connection that grounds you in nature *and* takes you to the heavens. Mortal, earthly love on the personality level may be too limiting.

Equally limiting is solely physical titillation. That's an awful lot like eating and can be accomplished by yourself. If you are just having sex to get off, you are avoiding contact and remaining alone. There's nothing wrong with that, but when you no longer want to be alone, you will want to experience total penetration while paying attention every inch of the way.

Of course, you may not want such involving sex each and every time. Well then, say so. Tell yourself out loud you just want to get laid. Be straight with yourself. Unfortunately, you can't survive on an exclusive diet of uninvolved coupling. If done too often, you'll eat over it. Sometimes, though, it can serve as a diversion or relief. Take the opportunities you want for titillation, but always know in the back of your mind about the quality experience you long for. The key here is to be honest with yourself and acknowledge when it's not enough. When you can do that, you'll be less hungry. You will stay open for what *is* enough.

It's okay not to want intimacy. You may want the connection to the cosmos, to yourself, to the earth, but not to that particular partner. Sometimes you only want to use him to take you where you want to go. Remember the two women who wanted a "meaningful overnight relationship"? Too

much has been made of the cliché of women wanting closeness while men run away.

You may be the one who wants sex for sex's sake, for your
own sake. What has love got to do with it? Were you taught
that good sex meant love? That idea brought some women into
very unsatisfying marriages, even though the sex was great.
They ended up combative with men they enjoyed in bed, but
not in life. In marriage counseling, they complain of choosing
emotionally unavailable partners. Why pick such a man?

Because the sex is great! At times sex is good precisely
because your partner is emotionally unavailable. His avoidance helps you stay with your own experience and less with
his. When you stay with such a man, you do not risk being
seen. Sometimes, the more uninvolved, the better. Though on
one level you long for the connected intimacy, at times you
might feel safer with a man who isn't really there. You might
even choose womanizing men who are excellent technicians,
treating you and your responses like a well-orchestrated
dance, but making little personal contact. Be honest with
yourself and acknowledge when you're just there for the "ser-
vicing." Just notice and acknowledge.

It's Rare Beef

As you develop your own ability to "notice," you'll be well
tuned and know the quality of your experience each time. Not
every encounter will be "to die for." It's not going to be wonder-
fully ecstatic, "maaaahvelous dahling" every time. The kind of
coupling I'm suggesting will not usually be possible every time
or even every other time. Not every meal is delicious. It is a
special state and experience that your soul hungers for, that
you need to know about, and a place you and your lover will

journey toward and seek together. Getting there *is* the fun.

A meltdown experience only thrives when all systems are go. Of course, in long-term relationships, some sexual activity will be solely for the purpose of physical release. Some will be to stave off the superfrustrated, out-of-control feelings you are both having in other areas of your lives. At least in bed, you will be able to feel grounded, connected and meaningful. Those are perfectly wonderful ways to spend an evening. Don't dismiss or devalue any of the sex you are having. Just keep this bit of specialness in a small corner of your mind— and go for it.

Teach Me Tonight

It's your job to teach your man. Don't expect yourself to know what you're looking for. Often you will only be able to note what *doesn't* work. When you or your partner has spiritually left the room, be sure not to keep on pumping. Your soul will go out to lunch.

Help your man develop "a slow hand." You want to teach him about taking time. Most men do want to learn what a woman likes. You have to teach him *your* rhythm. Notice this sounds like a woman taking charge, and it can threaten some men. Be careful not to move into that mommy role. You want to *receive*, to be penetrated, and the mommy role often means "fill 'er up." You're here instead to melt down. He has to be guided gently as if you *both* are seeking a certain hidden unknown. It's not like you have "the right answer" and he has to measure up. It can help to coo or put your finger to your lips in a "sssshhhhh" gesture. This can signal to him that you want to go softly, slowly and more deliberately.

Remember, it is your job to monitor and report back about

connections, when the circuit is charged and when the energy flow is broken. This has nothing to do with ego; it's just a report. Your man may want progress reports and grade cards about performance. This is not about him and his performance. It is about the two of you and connection. Believing and accepting that it is your job to be the monitor of connection is a very big step. When you take charge, he'll know and wait.

This can't be done like a drill sergeant, guidance counselor or high school teacher. You can't lay it all on your lover. There is a way to playfully and gently "welcome" him. Give him this book to read, or make "suggestions" that work with him. Don't be too clinical. Practice first writing a letter about your longings. Write it for yourself, and then later for him. Let him know what works most times. Here's a letter Angie wrote. She doesn't say much about where to rub "parts," but a lot about intention. She told me later, "It's not latitude, but attitude."

Dear Dear:

I hope I can communicate to you the fullness of my longing to make and do love with you. My body and soul resonate with a longing to hold you in closeness, suck you into my energy and vibrate with yours.

I need to write this for myself as well as for you, so I can know better who I am as a sexual being and what it takes for me and you to enter that realm. It is a mutual, two-person realm. We both must be fully there. I am not talking about orgasm or what it takes to achieve orgasm. That is a relatively easy endeavor. That is something I can even accomplish by myself.

With you, I rather seek a sublime bliss that comes from real <u>contact</u> that can transport us both to another plane, a third realm. It is a spiritual place we reach through joining our energies. We must stay in contact before we can get there. If, at any moment, either of us withdraws our energies, gets distracted, *thinks ahead or elsewhere, the connection and energy changes. We lose it. We have to work to come back.*

I want to see us stay in that third place together for as long as either of us can stand it. If you notice me wandering, please bring me back. To stay connected, I need eye contact a lot of the time. I need to know it is you *there and that you know it is* me. *In that particular space and time, we are* it *and all there is. No one else need apply. We are full of each other.*

I need to know that such activity is important to you, that you take it and me seriously, giving care, thought, planning and respect. If you want my heart and soul to show up, if you want a piece of my "Self" to play, then this becomes a much more serious game. I am a sensitive, sweet little creature paying careful, close attention to penetration of my boundaries, to contact from outside. I watch closely and love fiercely and well. Such passion and careful attention cannot be wasted on the tenderhearted or scared, or on someone out for a romp in the park. If you're here to play, let me know. I can just play, too, but I'll need to close off a certain part of my sensitivities. Sensitive beings require connection. If you want connection, as well as play, then we have to work at it together. That connection is to a holy and sensitive place we both create. It takes concerted effort and concentration to get there. It's worth the trip.

I like my face stroked. It makes me feel so visible. I long for and run from that visibility. I sometimes cry, but not for sadness, just at the ominousness of the event, the joining, the energy, the contact. As much as I may run from being seen, I also crave it. I want to see you, too. I want to look and look and look until I know who we are together. What are we doing here? We *must ask that question.*

I respond to an indirect approach. My whole body is an erogenous zone, and it's all hungry. Genital stimulation is great, but it won't satisfy a deeper ache I have for a personal, individual introduction to you. If we take our time, I can surrender to the softness, open to the penetration, engulf and mold to you. We must take our time. When we do take the right time, we will both flow to an openness that waits to suck us up. The openness comes from attention.

If you wanna be inta me, you gotta be inta me.

Sweetly sweetie,
Angie

Write your own letter. Place it in a drawer and read it daily. When you create the space, *he* will come.

Lighten Up to Melt Down

How do you manage all this great new knowledge and attitude? It is now worth taking the time to meditate, become centered, receptive and prepared to create a welcoming place. Eating is the supreme merger experience, with sex running a close second. Just as eating is more important to a starving person, entry will be more important to an empty person. You need to maintain that empty, expecting attitude. Renegotiating sexuality can only happen if you have a lighthearted and loving attitude toward your partner.

If you are already terribly frustrated and at the end of your rope, you'd do better to get some marriage counseling before you try this. I know we live in the age of psychobabble and confrontation, but most men are so delicate about sex, having greatly exaggerated expectations of their own performance, that any comment can be terribly wounding. Some things are better left unsaid.

Caution! Some men have complained to me that I've made their wives into what they call a "conversation piece": a woman who talks in bed. Some women have found it is best *not* to discuss sex with their partners. One reported that when she tries to talk, her lover loses interest in sex. Another commented, "Telling them is easy, finding one who hears you is hard." It is a difficult dance to engineer. Be careful not to get so clinical that you talk yourself out of sex. Most important is that you own what you are saying as *yours* and not ascribe what you want to some "expert." When you are serious and taking yourself seriously, he will know it is time to listen.

Many men tried to listen and couldn't. Instead of waiting, women gave up on them and went for the okey-doke. A common joke explains it:

QUESTION: Why do women fake orgasms?

ANSWER: Because men fake foreplay.

It's time to stop faking and rise to your spiritual calling. As you take on this woman's work, you are actually teaching attentiveness or what some Buddhists call "mindfulness." You may have great difficulty at this juncture finding a partner who can pay attention. You may have a man who is shy, hurried, goal-oriented and fearful about his performance. He may have been your only partner for quite some time. You have both lapsed into a style that may be physically satisfying but has kept you spiritually hungry. Now you need to approach sex with an orientation toward soul partnership—a very different journey.

Men hunger for this soulful experience as well. You must stop worrying about safety and security and be more concerned about authenticity and reality. You and your partners must be ready to play with this fire. It takes courage to find yourself. No need to weight.

Not His Mother!

Remember the Hawaiian woman's story? We have to work so hard, sometimes against what at first seems like our "better judgment." We can't cast ourselves in a mother role with lovers.

How often did you get to see your mother as a sexual being? Even if you were one of those rare people raised by two cohabitating parents, you probably had great opportunities to observe your mother by day, but little opportunity to see her with a man at night. Therefore, you might have grown up knowing how to give "good mom," which is anathema to "good sex."

You'll have to decide if you want to be a mother or a lover and fight really hard to know the difference. These are two different kinds of power. Moms exert control. Lovers let go. Many married for control and can be happy that way. They just have to give up sex. My best friend in high school was Jane—prom queen, homecoming queen and captain of the cheerleaders. She had her pick of the guys. I met with her years later as she was celebrating her fifth wedding anniversary with her second husband. As two very volatile personalities, they'd had a wild and passionate courtship. Six weeks before the wedding, a terrible car accident left him paraplegic. Many encouraged her to call the marriage off. He even told her to move on. She considered the options a long time and decided to go ahead with the marriage. She's never regretted it. She took on the role of sole provider as well as part-time nurse and caretaker. When explaining some of her considerations, she became brutally honest with herself and announced, "You know, Jude, I like the control."

Your situation is probably less dramatic, but you may have made a similar trade-off. You may have to look at your own situation and see if you complain about his low libido but do actually relish the amount of control you have. It may be impossible to have both control and excitement, and you might have to consider giving up something. That doesn't necessarily mean giving up your current relationship, but it will necessitate renegotiating power. You can work on your relationship by working on yourself. You can work toward changing and monitoring your side of the street.

It was actually New York City's "alternate side of the street" parking rules that caused Gwen to take a look at her control and mothering tendencies. Jake had stayed over and they were sleeping in. They'd had early morning beautiful sex and were lying around thinking and dreaming. He'd parked across the street where the sign read *No Parking 11-2* so that street cleaners could brush by. He knew that. She knew that. As he quietly stroked and caressed her with lovely "afterplay," she began *reminding* him about moving the car. She didn't let either one of them enjoy the moment as she went into worry mode about *his* ticket.

Get the picture? Instead of selfishly and physically salvaging every last bit of pleasure *for herself*, she went into "caring" mode, acting *responsible* for him and his ticket. What he really wanted and could have used from her were a few "ooh, aah, that feels great, I love how you love me"-type comments.

She could have complimented their mutual lovemaking. She could have lain in his arms, savoring the moment. She could have sighed and fallen asleep. Those would have been lover behaviors, not mother behaviors. He didn't need mommy minders. Luckily, this guy was sensitive enough to see what was going on and balked.

"Will you please give me a break here? I know about the car. I feel like lying here stroking you a few minutes. Would that be okay?" He was able to say it with a touch of humor and a smile. She got the message loud and clear. Be careful. It is so easy and automatic to go into mommy mode. It takes a lot of effort to stave off such subtle programming.

Try to think about your tendencies to mother:

"Is this my job?"

"Does he need me to tell him?"

"Is it something he knows already?"

"Will it sound like his mother?"

You need to give up mother to be more of a lover. If you will practice for one week *not* giving any advice unless *asked directly*, you will be amazed. You may discover just how little you are actually needed. He's probably thought about things on his own. He may come toward you more sensually, as you have more of an air of mystery and are less intrusive. It doesn't matter that your intentions were good. Unbidden advice is intrusive.

Gliding or Stumbling?

As you attend to your own sexual nature, you will understand some of the awkwardness in your bedroom. Look what Maria writes from Santa Fe:

Three weeks ago, my husband and I began to take a course in ballroom dancing. When talking after the second lesson, I was commenting on how I had difficulty letting go and allowing him to lead me because he appeared so tentative and confused. It just didn't seem safe, and I had to remain very alert and occasionally take charge. I said to him how the same analogy is very much like our sex life. It usually is awkward and not at all a smooth dance. I think it has to do with him not feeling like a man grounded in his own right, so I don't feel free to let myself fully be a woman and go into my experience. I sometimes feel like I'm a woman with a young boy. He is also very intellectual, which leads to lack of spirituality in the bedroom. This all is a great struggle, especially now that I am so aware of what's going on and believe I know what sort of relationship really is possible. I'm afraid this is a violation of my spirit.

Are you poised to move on to even more visibility and sensitivity, to consciously experience the essence of who you are? All you've learned about assertiveness, independence and separation has prepared you for the joys of merger. You will consciously merge with your food first, then your love partner, then your goddess. Once you've truly acknowledged the quest for apartness, you will be ready for the terrifying but joyous prospect of uniting.

Now, we will look at how the journey back home to Self begins in your plate. When you learn mindfulness in eating, you can experience true contact. Next, in chapter 5, we'll explore how to keep each bite like the first time.

Eternal Virgins

What was it about marriage,
anyway? Even if you loved your
husband, there came that inevitable
year when f–cking turned as bland
as Velveeta cheese: filling, fattening,
but no thrill to the taste buds,
no bittersweet edge, no danger.
And you longed for an overripe
Camembert, a rare goat cheese:
luscious, creamy, cloven-hoofed.

—ERICA JONG, *FEAR OF FLYING*

---

hat makes that cheese lose its sharp edge? What makes your binges taste like pablum? Why has sex become dull? It's not marriage, it's unconsciousness. You left the room, left the table, left the bed. Do you want to get back in the room? Think about where you've been and how much you'd like to come back. Think about unconscious scripts you've recited:

WOMAN: Will you love me tomorrow?

MAN: Am I the first?

WOMAN: No, but you can be next.

She's in the future. . . . He's in the past. . . . How do we get them into the same room? Our goal has to be to get you and your partner into the same time and space. This chapter will acquaint you with skills to focus and concentrate, to keep *you* in the room with any love object, be it man or feast.

On my refrigerator blares the magnet inscribed with: "This is NOT the way to a better sex life." But then again, maybe it is. As we retrain ourselves to eat consciously, to focus on the sensual journey and ignore the drive to attain satisfaction and completion, we will learn many new secrets of love. I have been maintaining a large weight loss for more than two decades. Of all the methods I tried and all the tools I've used, the two most important are why this book is written. One is the spiritual consciousness, the opening of myself to another dimension. The other is a treatment tool I've used for two decades and incorporated into the home video *Divine Dine*. You will learn the techniques now. It is a form of behavior modification that helps you hook up to the cosmos through the very animal activity of eating. If you keep the faith and actually practice this, not just read it, you will find yourself changing in many profound ways. Some of these techniques you've known before. But, did you really do them? The key is in the doing. Doing this practice sends vital messages to your organism and your environment. Doing it will help you honor your commitment to yourself. It will also help you feel disciplined while at the same time encourage you to let go. That is what divine dining and conscious coitus are all about—focused discipline followed by sensual release. If you are ready to assume the risk of true joy and ecstasy, you've already taken the first step. Even if you don't feel ready yet, please read on.

"Ess, Ess, Mein Kind"

Every nice Jewish girl at one time or another heard this invitation to sit down and eat. "Sit down" is the important part of that sentence. In Yiddish and German, *essen* and *fressen* are both verbs meaning *to eat*. *Fressen* is used when speaking of animals eating, and *essen* refers to human consumption. If you want to tease or make fun of someone eating ravenously, you might call her a *fresser*, or comment to a friend, "Boy, can that gal *fress!*" Here is a partial list to distinguish the difference. Add in some of your own.

FRESSEN	ESSEN
Jump into meal	Take a moment's pause
Eat standing or driving	Sit down to a place setting
Talk with mouth full	Eating is your sole activity
Inhale	Savor, suck, chew, taste
Drown food	No liquids
Mass quantities	Conscious portions
Mindless about preparation	Gratitude about creation
Shallow, rapid breath	Soulful, deep breath
Rave about last meal	Focused on this meal
Shotgun approach	Laser focus

As you learn to distinguish the difference, you can change your eating from *fressen* to *essen*. Once you change *fressen* to *essen*, you can then change intercourse to soul travel. You will begin at the table, bringing dignity and a touch of divinity to this animalistic behavior. Changing how you eat can change your sex life and vice versa. Approaching *either* of these animal behaviors with *focus* automatically influences the other. Let's begin with food and see how it all relates.

Each Time Is the First Time

A Spanish proverb advises: "Of soup and love, the first is best." Does this mean that soup is better than love? Or does it mean that in both cases, whether eating or loving, the first *time* is the best? I think it's just like with comedy. Timing is everything. No matter what the experience, the first time is something new and different. It's a surprise. Savor it. Every time is a brand-new penetration of your boundaries. Now, what if you could have a "first time" every time? You'll have to pay attention to each first bite and each first kiss.

The British say, "Let us begin as we intend to continue." How you begin is how you'll end up. You begin at birth establishing the ground rules for what's allowed in your life and loves. Remember this as we now move to preparing for entry. The Indian teacher Osho tells us, "Sex is just the beginning . . . not the end. But if you miss the beginning, you will miss the end also." That's why you must attend to the first time.

In the 1960s, I worked with New York City's Addiction Services Agency. Addicts told me, "Man, there is nothing like that first hit of heroin. You're always trying to recapture the first time. The surprise is tremendous. You've never felt anything like it!" Remember this as you now want to consider creating first times every time, whether with food or with sex.

Consider what the first time means. What is your purpose? Why have you chosen to take in this food right now? What are you doing here? Just ask. You might want to consider that those addicted to illegal drugs might be different from those addicted to the legal kinds: food and alcohol. There is a difference in intention. Intentions count. Heroin addicts take their drug *in order* to get high. They *know* and *decide* to take in an addictive substance. *Intending* to get high, they begin as they *intend* to continue. Heading down a road of addiction, they orchestrate the experience to "get off." In that way, they differ from alcoholics and overeaters, who use their substances just to feel "normal." Your reasons and objectives with sex are equally important. Do you use sex solely to relieve tension, like sneezing, or do you seek something else? If you're just in it for the "sneeze," then a "God bless you" is in order. If you are in it for what I'm after, then you will be using sex to go to God, and your goddess will bless you herself.

Now you will pay careful attention to your *intentions* when you eat as well as when you love. You must stop eating to stifle sensitivities, and instead start eating and making love to increase them. You want to fuel up *and* wake up. You may often feel more satisfied when you eat well-seasoned foods. Of course, the spice mix received careful attention. With a little more spice in your sex life, you'll be more satisfied with smaller portions of food. Now, as you allow all your sensitivities to bubble up, you'll become more aware of your body as a pulsating, vibrating energy field, a battery charging as well as discharging. That's where sex enters the equation. Be careful! Once this need is recognized, you may want more "good sex." You may be too hot to handle. We'll see. In any event, it is worth taking this journey with me, discovering more about all your appetites. We'll look at *how* you eat and *how* you make love. We will pay great attention to style and dignity. The most important part of all of this is that we pay attention. We must *attend* or *pretend*. When we pretend, the mind disengages from the body and we eat. When we attend, we soar.

You will find, after doing this work, that your partners will either love you more or else become very uncomfortable. I offer this as a warning before you continue. Be careful and mindful before you proceed. You may be shaking up a lot more than your salad dressing. New and fearful opportunities may present themselves.

That First Time

Some women in my eating and sexuality groups report with awe and wonder their first sexual experiences. They focus sweetly on initial penetration. It was such a surprise. They wish they could bring their lover to stop and wait there a minute before proceeding. Why not? Pat Love, in her "Hot Monogamy" seminars, tells us that most women report the most exciting part of sex is that moment of initial penetration. To re-create that element of surprise, we must stay open. We have to work to stay open and unassuming, not expecting or judging. That means resisting comparing this experience, whether a meal or a love, with any other we've had in the past.

If we need to control, we can't be surprised. If you can't approach these experiences with openness and enlightenment, you will become robotized and expect only the same old performance from yourself or your lovers. As a habitual dieter, you might have already worked at hardening and sealing yourself.

You need to open up to let the juices flow. After years of dieting, you're probably well-trained to fend off temptations. You
might have incorporated the wrong messages about both food
and sex. You might have come to believe that if it feels good,
it's not good for you. You'll have to rethink some of that.
Denying your ravenous appetite for food has trained you to
hold back, cut down and hide other parts of your animal
nature. Your diet progressed, but sex and soul suffered.

Your dieting may have awakened a deep sexual hunger. It's
a hunger you've been trained to fear. Think about it. If you
give in to either food or sex, you may judge yourself as weak-
willed and totally animalistic. Perhaps eating or not eating
has been your only way to exert power. Maybe you ate to defy
competitive standards you dare not confront directly.
Controlling food and sex may be the only control you know.
When you control them, you feel empowered. Then how can
you let go and experience sensuality?

When you have compassion for your personal quest for
power, you can hold the reins more gently, but still firmly. You
now need to train yourself to give in to desire, to pay attention, and then to let go. Even if you have been well-schooled in
avoiding pleasure, you *must* now train yourself to savor it.
This chapter outlines a recommended "practice" session, not
necessarily meant to be re-created at every meal or every
sexual encounter. This training is designed to encourage you
to learn how to watch for what you want; how to pay attention. Meditators call it *mindfulness*. This is practice. You
rehearse and focus so that when the real thing comes along,
you will recognize it and be ready to melt. Letting go is a practiced art, like acting or singing. After first becoming deeply
focused, you can let go and relinquish. Like a professional

singer, after years of controlled study and discipline, we stand up to the mike and "let 'er rip"!

As you practice letting go and giving up, you will discover a less manipulative, softer, perhaps less "winning" part of yourself. You may lose a few battles to ultimately win the war for your own life. Now you are ready to claim your own sensitive, spiritual woman. That is your reason for being here, and she has been patiently waiting. You will have to nurture her consciously.

We have to eat and couple with the open-minded naiveté and vulnerability of a trusting infant. Come to your plate and partner expecting the best, fully present and participating. It is really natural to expect the best, but if you've been disappointed a lot, you may have closed down some. We've all had experiences that knock our natural expectations out of us. Regaining that "natural" child is what a lot of psychotherapy is intended to accomplish. A famous analyst, Harry Stack Sullivan, instructed that "Mental health is close to childlikeness." Sexuality comes out in a playful, childlike way. Some of us have lost our childlike qualities. We only know how to play with our food. Now as adults, we have to retrain ourselves to give up the fears and reclaim our sensual, animal, playful selves.

Be aware that the attempt will at first feel gut-wrenching. Whenever we experience a new situation, our body, psyche and brain go through a brief period of disorientation. For example, here's how the orienting response works:

You are sitting in a room listening to Mozart. You are relaxed. A train whistle sounds in the distance. You feel a slight startle as you have to recognize and then label the train. On brain scans, this shows up as a glitch on the screen. Your brain waves jump slightly in what's labeled an "orienting response." This is the glitch. Once you file and understand it, it falls into background noise, and Mozart zooms in to further relax you.

Researchers found that when Tibetan monks meditated, as they opened further and further to true consciousness, they experienced fewer and fewer glitches on brain scans. They were continually open and accepting of whatever stimuli came in. They didn't need to orient because there was no attachment to one sound over another. They let each new thing wash right in. Their eyes were wide and questing, like a newborn babe's. They didn't flinch; they didn't close up. That perpetual openness is what you'll practice in this chapter. You'll later carry it back from the dining room to the bedroom.

Since you are no longer in a cradle and are not on a mountain-top in Tibet, you've probably grown a bit fearful, closed off, rigid and scared—all the while eating to stay that way. It's important that you look at each new meal and each new sexual foray as the beginning and end—first time for all time. And it's true. Let's face it, though you've had similar, you've never had this before.

Even if this is the same TV dinner you always serve, or the same husband you've slept with for twenty years, "tonight's the night." At the Jewish Passover seder, the youngest son asks his father, "How is this night different from all other nights?" You must ask yourself this same question before every meal and every time you make love. Make each time the first time, a new time and extra-special.

You will now learn about eating and making love with dignity, integrity, grace, compassion and bliss. Tall order? Why not? You have the power to make it happen, *and* you deserve it. It begins both at the plate and in bed. You are connecting your physical/animal self and your more ethereal "spiritual" self.

To Dine Is Divine

You've known these behavior modification techniques for a long time, but actually *doing* them makes all the difference in the world. Maintaining your dignity in the presence of food will become your most difficult and most effective treatment tool. Eating this way connects you to your divinity. It also changes your sex life.

No matter what your "food plan" is, if you practice eating in this more conscious, centered, dignified manner, you will open up a new relationship to your inner Self. As you take in food more consciously, you'll be more open to other kinds of penetration.

I don't expect you at this point to be at all interested in learning this technique. If you've been raised as a normal American dieter, you just want to learn the food plan. Sorry, you already know more than you'll ever need to about *what* to eat. This is more about *how* to eat.

The question is, how do you survive on a tripod, balancing yourself as a physical, emotional and spiritual animal? Sabrina tried to take off her first hundred pounds just doing the diet thing. Since she'd left out retraining her life skills and avoided addressing her sexual and spiritual needs, her weight soon came back.

She was now taking the risk to try it again as she called me on her car phone while speeding down the highway back from a weekend in the woods. It was now "back to work" time. She was rushing to join her business partner/husband at their offices. She was frantic because she wanted to pull off at every exit to call her former lover for an afternoon "matinee." She and I had been dealing with her voracious sex drive ever since she started losing weight again. The last time she'd quickly regained over one hundred pounds just when her new attractiveness made her feel sensuous and available. Though she'd lost the equivalent of one total person, her husband, Ted, didn't notice at all. He just wasn't interested in her sexually. He was just as much a workaholic and complainer as ever, and he saw nothing to celebrate. She resolved to stop wanting. Rather than cheat, she'd eat.

Now this time, after regaining and relosing, she was committed to keeping the weight off. Just getting back to the basics of limiting her food intake had been a difficult process, as she was convinced it was a matter of her own personal willpower, having nothing to do with her relationship. She argued with me about how workable and easy her marriage was, how she'd made her accommodations and wanted to let sleeping dogs lie. I told her that in order to truly birth herself into her new life and body, all systems had to be awake.

All her systems were alive and well as she barreled down the expressway, screaming to me about how much she *deserved* an "afternoon delight." I didn't argue her out of this predicament. I just kept highlighting that it would be best if she could go *toward* an experience for her own pleasure instead of as an angry response to Ted and the business worries.

She called in once more when she arrived at home. "*He* wasn't in when I called. If he'd been there, I'm sure I would have gone for it."

That night she and Ted had a terrible argument. She screamed at him very uncharacteristically about the business crises he'd created, how she was tired of hearing how hard he worked while she saw him goofing off, how she was tired of his imposing deadlines on her part of their projects, while his were casually open-ended. She was mostly tired of having nothing in their lives but the business, and especially tired of being treated like a worker instead of a lover. She was ready to walk out and closed her arguments with, "If you want me to stay, I want more play."

Ted loved her, loved being with her, loved working with her, but didn't at all want to make love with her. Even though they slept in the same bed, they also shared it with toys and childhood memorabilia. She had her stuffed bears, and he had his. They took these toys on vacation, and even held them as hand puppets and talked through them. In fact, he used one the day after the fight to squeak to her, attempting to make up. He spent the next week walking on eggshells, sheepishly looking askance and waiting to see if her rage had blown over. This infuriated her even more. She didn't want a guilty little boy. She wanted a full-grown man who could acknowledge her weak and strong points, and give her some of that special attention she craved. She wanted to be courted anew. He didn't think he had to. Besides, he also didn't know how. He didn't suffer yearnings like hers. She was electric, eyeing the telephone repair man and the UPS guy in his short pants.

At her next session, she decided, "I'm giving up. I just can't talk with him or anyone else about any of this anymore. I'm done. I love how my lover loves me, and that is enough. I don't need sex in my marriage anymore! I just want to work through my guilt about this situation."

We talked about what she loved about the lover. It was his attention to detail, his focus on her and his longing for her. She hated her husband for his indifference.

I reconnected that to eating. "Isn't your husband's indifference to you mirrored in your off-handed eating?" I was concerned about the ravenous, binge-like feelings she evidenced in the obsessional need to make the phone call. The eating and lovemaking were kicking into that obsessional, driven energy. It was a perfect metaphor that she was calling me while driving a car.

During one of the phone calls, I suggested that she pull over to masturbate and get some relief.

Upset, she responded emphatically, "Don't you understand, I want someone *in* me. It's not just physical release that I crave! I want a man who wants me, thinks of me, lusts for me, *needs* me, *wants* me. I want to feel *him* really there with me, and I want to pay attention to penetration. It is transforming for me when he enters me and crosses that threshold. Even if my husband 'wanted' to make love, he doesn't want to pay attention."

This crucial aspect of eating and loving, this attentiveness, is ideally achieved with a partner. It can also be satisfying to have a personal, solitary, attentive experience with food.

The exercises that follow are intended for you to try by yourself. If you'd like to learn how to transpose some of them to your bed life, Betty Dodson has produced an excellent video showing women masturbating together. For years, she has been a champion of women's need to practice these skills as they are not learned in the culture and certainly not taught by our mothers. She encourages us to then teach them to our men.

Betty teaches about "sex for one" on video, emphasizing that "husbands and lovers come and go" while you will continue an ongoing love affair with yourself. I must caution you, though: it takes maturity to watch the video. When I'd previously recommended the tape to Sabrina, she reported back: "As I watched, I masturbated along with the group and felt a level of crotch acceptance I'd never known. I got hungry before we were done. I stopped the tape and tossed a salad. After a few bites, I went back to the tape and finished the deed. Then I couldn't eat at all. By that time, Betty was showing the group how to insert fingers to taste themselves. She believed herself to be a little like soy, as she'd had Chinese food the night before. Wow, the tape was a bit much for me!"

During Sabrina's raceway call, I reminded her of the *Divine Dine* video and Dodson's tape, wanting her to slow down and pay conscious attention to her own neediness. As she began to assimilate some of my advice, she was open once again to practicing the Divine Dine once a week. It did not lessen her resentment toward her husband. It did, however, bring her back to Self, finding fullness from the inside out. As the craving stopped, she became more available to work therapeutically on her marriage.

She went on to another of my recommendations: She read the book *Secrets of Seduction* by Brenda Venus. Brenda instructs you to watch closely how a man eats:

> *It's no coincidence we use "appetite" and "hunger" for both sex and food. A man who gobbles down his food, drowning it with condiments, doesn't even know what he ate. He probably does the same thing in bed. This is definitely not the way to please a woman. A gourmet will view a woman as a meal to be savored course by course. In dining, as in love, he takes it slow, praises what he's getting, sharing the sensual experience with his woman.*

As much as I want you to develop a more satisfying and fulfilling sex life, if push comes to shove, focusing on how you eat is even more important. It is your most essential and necessary tool. Becoming mindful in your plate will heal some troubles with your mate. Therefore, let's begin *here* and *now* and with your current meal.

The following exercise will help you become more "mindful," or rigorously conscious and attentive, to what you do with food. That will be a metaphor for every activity in your life. Then you'll transpose this focus on conscious entry to your sex life. Let's take ourselves out to dine and back to bed.

Divine Dine*

Your focused attention in the kitchen and dining room will lead to more satisfying experiences in the bedroom. Focus carefully and intimately on exactly *how* you take the outside environment into the temple of your body.

Most dieting programs spend a lot of time teaching you *what* to eat. Our goal instead is learning *how* to eat. You will learn to bring a spiritual aspect to your eating and, then, to your lovemaking. This will change all other relationships in your life, and you will be able to focus further and more deeply; you will be available for different kinds of couplings. That's all part of the project of opening up, of becoming more vulnerable, of accepting more intimate penetration from another.

Before you begin, let me whet your appetite with Marjorie's report back after she left treatment. Her story echoes that of many who initially rejected this tool:

---

* The *Divine Dine* videotape is available by calling toll-free 800-8-E-N-O-U-G-H.

Of all my experiences at your treatment center, I hated the Divine Dine the most. I think others felt the same way. When counselors left the room, we played like little kids. We'd start horsing around, sometimes blowing straw wrappers across the room or making exaggerated fun of the chewing and slurping exercises. It was probably mostly out of embarrassment, but we liked to act like kids and pretend that we didn't take ourselves, or at least our eating, seriously. We dreaded spending that time so focused on self. It seemed almost too self-indulgent. It was definitely too sensuous. It was okay to munch a burger in the car, but to actually sit quietly alone with that food made it all too graphic and real.

When I got home from treatment, I found that I missed that quiet time alone with the food. I quickly got into my hurried routine, mostly caretaking for my family, anticipating their needs, forgetting my own. Each evening as I spent most of the meal getting up for others, wiping spills, yelling or questioning my husband about his day, his concerns, his life, I felt my own life slipping away. I didn't just miss the Divine Dine time, I missed myself. I'd run away from home.

I resolved to eat separately from my family. I put on the Divine Dine video and carved out my own space of time before anyone else was served. Family mealtime came after my needs were already attended to consciously and quietly. I did this each night for a week, even though you'd recommended that "out in the world" we could do well eating this way only one meal a week.

Well, drastic things started happening. I found that while the family ate, I was much more quiet and tolerant of their minor personality squabbles. I found myself looking at my husband in a long-forgotten sexual way. He was more than his job or his role in the family. I also noticed my impression of myself changing. I saw myself as somehow with, but a bit outside, the family. I was there to serve but didn't really feel needy to have my own needs met. It was a strange feeling, involved but unattached.

By the weekend, Jack and I had more contact and more time

alone. He started with that irritable "What am I doing all this for?" kind of complaining he did so well. He was often into "poor me's," and I'd feel blamed because he was "trapped." This time, it didn't affect me. I was interested, but I didn't feel at all responsible. It seemed like it was his question to answer for himself, having nothing to do with me. Is this that "detachment" you spoke of so much? In the past, I took on trying to convince him of something. I'd convince him of how "happy" he really was. Was I convincing me?

All I knew was that I wanted his bod! As I kept eating in that sensual way, I was more undulating in the body, turning off the cerebral machinations. It was like there wasn't enough energy in my brain to hold two thoughts at the same time. I couldn't obsess about his problems and my sexual needs at the same time. I was reminded of that joke about God favoring men more than women because he'd given them two heads. The only problem was, there wasn't enough blood to supply both at the same time. . . . Well, ha ha, I couldn't get too preoccupied with worry about my family when my sensuous animal woke up.

This was a gift of recovery you had mentioned, but I never understood. I didn't realize that eating like this could bring back my sensuous, powerful female self. Savoring brought out my animal. I thought of this practice as some strange, behavior modification ceremony that you could bill to insurance companies. Instead, I learned and kept learning that I was a sensuous animal as well as a functioning adult providing service, doing functions. I saw that if I didn't service my own animal needs, I'd be thrown off-center and flailing. When I fed myself sensuously, I needed less from others. Jack and I have been having a lot more good sex lately. Call it medicinal, but it sure helps curb my other appetites!

I was also less available to take guff from others. I noticed it at the market with the checker, Alexis. She barks at everyone. Even though I could intellectually remark that she must be such an unhappy person to rage at everyone at her checkout, *always verbally critical or scowling silently, I still took every one of her moods personally. I would quake in line, wondering how she would embarrass or humiliate me. In my head, I raged, wondering why they kept her on at the store. How could any of us stand her guff? I still feared her. Something changed after I started eating with dignity. I just wasn't as open to her abuse. It was like none of that kind of energy penetrated me. I had a personal Teflon shield against her. Fear left me. I had no sense of danger, felt there was no way she could hurt me. She couldn't. It was like I was sated, full. My food had hit bottom. There was a fullness in my being. I wasn't a vacant building blowing in the wind. I walked on solid ground. My footing was just as solid as hers. There's just such a different sense about myself. It's a feeling of deservingness. I deserve to be here.*

As a result of following these guidelines, you are going to feel more deserving of good loving as well as good eating. You'll feel deserving of respectful, courteous treatment in all areas of your life. Let's eat!

Attention to Intention

Intention is everything. You will ultimately only eat or make love with intention. That will be a natural result of paying *attention*. By giving yourself this attention now, you will move from a self-destructive, battering relationship with food to a loving, sensual, satisfying affair. This will come from *awareness*, focused *intention* and *accepting* responsibility for what you are doing. You will be able to discern when you are eating consciously and when you are guzzling destructively. Oddly enough, you will probably get more pleasure from the conscious meal. What a major change that will be! It will be a much more satisfying love affair.

This will be a chance for you to take twenty minutes out of your day to be alone with food. Later you will move to taking quiet moments with other love objects as well.

Throughout this exercise, ask yourself three important questions:

What am I doing here?	AWARENESS
Is this really what I want to be doing?	INTENTION
Is this *how* I want to be doing it?	ACCEPTING

Give Up the Medicinal Focus

This is not a treatment plan. It is a *living* plan. Please approach it as a surrender to sensual pleasure. Many try to take on modifying themselves from a sickness perspective. They judge their eating as abnormal and decide to *learn* normal. I don't want you to become "normal." I'm after kinky, funky, nitty-gritty. You will descend into "creature" in order to soar up to "angel." I want you to become so "into" the food that you pass right through it and out to the universe. I want you to receive all you can from eating, so you can move on to receive all you can from lovemaking.

Approach this activity as a quest for *pleasure*. You are enhancing and refining a gift you already know. That gift is your ability to *respond* sensually. That gift is also your "response" ability. This is a thirteen-step program to develop a focus on your sensual responsiveness. You are adding to skills you already have. You are practicing sensual focus. You'll do it at the plate so you can take it to bed later.

When I developed the earliest treatment programs, our patients were asked to eat every dinner meal following these guidelines. They were instructed and coached by a counselor and later ate along with the video. Before leaving treatment, each patient took these guidelines, developed a personal script of what was most helpful to her and then led the group in the eating exercise. They each made an audiotape of themselves instructing the group and then took this home for personal instruction.

Now as you read on, truly *do* the following instructions. Find out which parts work for you and which don't. Then write your own script. You'll achieve best results if you follow the guidelines I'm presenting and then make your own audiotape instructing yourself. Following your own instructions from your own voice is a form of self-hypnosis. It is far better that you hear your own instructions than follow mine. Use mine only as a guide. Your own words will be much more intimate and effective. This will just be a spec script for you to modify at will.

CAUTION! Just reading without *doing* can be quite hazardous to your health. A few years ago, I sent the video to a publishing house to see if they'd like to produce and market it. None of the reviewers followed my instructions. Despite my warnings to *eat* and not just passively watch, they sat around a corporate conference table viewing the tape. They then raced out to the "roach coach" truck to grab some burgers and fries. They reported back that they weren't interested in producing the video as it "made us hungry." Of course! Thinking without doing, whether about food or sex, will always make us hungry. The soul longs to produce, and your creature wants the action.

Why Bother?

Many balk at taking on this sensate focus around eating. It has been aptly taught by sex therapists as a way to delay gratification. In sex therapy, we ask patients to focus on pleasuring bodies without seeking intercourse or orgasm. It's called *sensate focus*.

You may not see the point. What's the deal here? You may be like many of my hospitalized patients, who came from around the world to go through treatment. They asked to be locked up to protect themselves from choice because they so "loved to eat." So I said, "Let's *really* eat!" From day one of treatment, I asked them to do this Divine Dine exercise, spending a minimum of twenty minutes a day alone with food. They balked! I might as well have asked them to burn in a furnace. "Do I have to sit there and eat sensually?" they whined. "Why do we have to spend so much time with the food?" They bargained for reprieves. I answered, "Isn't food your obsessive love object? Why, then, is it so difficult to sit quietly with the food for twenty minutes a day?"

Ask yourself that now. If you are so in love with food, why do you guzzle it, drown it, inhale it or smother it? You might want to quickly answer, "I don't know. I just *love* to eat." Well, maybe. Try the exercise first, and we'll see. This little eating experience may help you find that you don't love food at all. Many report that they actually *hate* food and hate the *experience* of eating even more. On discharge evaluations, most patients felt, like Marjorie did, that of all experiences in treatment, they liked the Divine Dine least.

Consider now that maybe you really *hate* to eat. You hate what the act of eating shows about you. Eating forces you to pay attention to being an alive, breathing organism. It's scary. This sensual focus involves reowning your animal. It involves making friends with the fact that *we are our bodies*. No matter how wise you may get to be, when the body goes, it's over. You have sensual needs. If they are not met, you become ravenous. Can you stand to be reminded of your longings? It is really so much easier to starve and be away from the love object completely. Isn't fasting with protein drink easier than three moderate meals a day? Isn't celibacy easier than making love and then waiting for him to call? It's so difficult to face longing. Wouldn't it be a lot easier if you never had to see your ex-husband or critical mother or sassing teenager? Instead, these relationships can teach how to tolerate separateness without killing or being killed. The same is true for food—you can't run and hide. How can you be nurtured without destruction? How do you survive making love? How do we allow ourselves to be fed and in bed, but not end up dead?

If you do the Divine Dine, just one meal a week, you'll find that all the relationships in your life will change, especially your intimate relationships. When you stop slapping yourself with excess food, unconsciously guzzling and avoiding your sensuality, you will stop being available for others to mistreat you. When you slapped first, it was easier to let others slap, too. With these exercises, you develop a way to melt into your experience but, also, toughen up your personal boundaries. You won't slap yourself with a Twinkie, and no one else will have the nerve to abuse you.

Get Ready to Fall in Love

Whenever possible, take the time and thought to order your setting and logistics. Try to set an elegant table for your meal. Later, when you "can't," you'll have the memory of how it *can* be and you can use your imagination to mindfully re-create elegance for yourself. This time is just practice.

You are now operating at a threefold purpose. You want to:

Nurture your body
Gain sensual gratification
Integrate your animal and spiritual self

You are taking food from outside into the temple of your body. You will use your brilliant machinery to break it down and create *new cells of you!* Could anything possibly be more intimate? Pay attention to how naturally and sensually all this takes place. All you have to do is show up and pay attention.

Be Ready for the Hunt!

This experience is outlined to resemble a hunting trip. It's a thirteen-step journey to hunt, trap and devour your most interesting quarry—your Self. You've been engaging in a life-long hunt: a quest for your life, your true calling, your soul. She awaits. Your soul aches and hungers to be caught, make contact, merge. Food and sex have been a last chance to go home. We're talking about hunting down game, and also hunting up the cosmos. That's why you're here. Consider the steps:

1. Create your space
2. Adjust attitudes
3. Give it time
4. Crave space
5. Approach with care
6. Begin the dance
7. Prepare for entry
8. Survey the landscape
9. Take the first bite
10. Eat it!
11. Hold it!
12. Savor it!
13. Leave it!

1. Create Your Space

This is a conscious act. It's the most important activity in your life! Why so dramatic? Because you must truly take *action*, you must *do* this thing to establish your personal integrity. Doing it affirms your commitment. You can read, even contemplate and perhaps ruminate, and ultimately philosophize about how you know it *should* be done, but the only way to honestly change your relationships with food and your body is to *do* it.

Stop now and ask yourself: Do I really *want* to change my relationship with food and my body? Can I really give up self-destruction? Can I endure the embarrassment of owning my animal self? Do I truly want to feel less in control, more passive, waiting and receiving? Just reading and not doing will make you very, very hungry!

If you've decided you will *do* the following exercise, you have just made your initial investment. You're changing your food life and your love life. You are giving your animal and your inner Self personal, undivided attention. Nothing works better than investing your own sweat. Make this experience *yours*. Assemble what you need to create a personal table that is yours and a meal that is yours. Use the directions as your guide, but *do it your way*. Select your own table settings, tablecloth, placemats, napkins, large dinner plate, smaller salad plate, "fancy" goblet, flowers, candles and whatever else it takes to create *your* space. My only requirement is that you use *plastic* utensils. As a training exercise, plastic won't allow aggressive energy to foul your meal. If you eat too aggressively with plastic, it will break. Plastic utensils work best during this training.

Get your space in order, your food ready to serve, and now read along and do what is asked.

2. Adjust Attitudes

Secure your perimeter! Announce to people in your life that this exercise is important for your health and that they will ultimately benefit. Ask them to allow you this uninterrupted quiet time. You can ask anyone you like to do it with you, but they must be quiet and have a respectful, rather than mocking, attitude. Your food is your prescription from the pharmacy. Take it in fully and consciously. Treat this eating exercise like surgery. Just as surgeries aren't interrupted, don't allow your Divine Dine to be interrupted. When *you* make it important, others will follow your lead.

I have had great troubles teaching this within the medical community. Medical care is geared toward the staff's comfort rather than the patients'. If that weren't the case, we'd certainly never see hematology techs awaken sleeping patients at 5:00 A.M. to draw blood. Whose convenience is being served? I've been roundly criticized for trying to make our treatment techniques too precious and important. I've been told I make mountains out of molehills, especially when I inconvenience doctors.

When I personally went to battle against these interruptions, administrators called me a fanatic. I didn't want doctors pulling patients out of their Divine Dine exercise to have histories and physicals done. I felt it gave patients a message that the experience was not important. No matter how many times we tried to prevail upon doctors to conform to treatment schedules, they usually insisted that their random appearances required our patients' inconvenience. When we asked them to alert us of their impending visit so we could keep the patient out of the dining hall, eating alone and waiting, they wouldn't cooperate with any schedule. Rarely did anyone find the patient's eating regimen as important as a physician's schedule. No hospital worker could fathom a doctor waiting while a patient ate! In groups later with patients, I used this as "grist for the mill," pointing out how rude doctors were only preparing them for times back home with friends and family when *they* would be the only ones to take their eating seriously.

I was often expected to do business while eating, attend training luncheons and, in some cases, even expected to lecture while I ate. No one in medicine saw a problem with this. In medicine, such abuses go unnoticed. The neglected, dignified private part of ourselves eats over it. I eventually had to refuse to do any business during lunch. It's not that I was training myself in Divine Dine over the lunch hour, but if I guzzled lunch while working, by three in the afternoon, I'd forget that I had eaten. I'd convince myself that I hadn't had lunch. I needed to take that quiet break time and get back in touch with my inner Self.

If you are still fat, it's even more difficult to claim the time you need to eat. You would think others in your life would gladly welcome your taking time out to be quiet with food. Instead, they resent your eating and judge you each time you do. If you've suffered obesity for a long time, as I did, you probably live with tremendous shame about every bite you take. You imagine every eye in the restaurant watching you and every mouth whispering, "Why is that fat lady eating?" You judge yourself even more. I know when I was obese, it didn't matter *what* I was eating, I just wasn't supposed to be eating at all. When I finally started on this dignified path, I knew I had every right, every *responsibility* to be eating slowly and savoring consciously. Try not to hide in a corner when you eat. Everyone knows you eat anyway. If you make it a big deal and show that you take it seriously and do it consciously, you are telling everyone around you—and, more important, you are telling *yourself*—that you *are* doing something about it.

3. Give It Time

Whether it's a new wonder-diet plan, a new way to eat, a new exercise video or a new love potion, we are people prone to excess. Be careful not to take this activity on as yet another project to overdo and discard. For patients in treatment, we recommended the Divine Dine for each evening meal. For those of you who are the walking wounded out in the world making a living, I'd only recommend this for one meal a week. More won't hurt, but you'll get fantastic results just eating this way one meal a week.

Hopefully, you'll have many Divine Dines and many sensuous slurps in both your dining room and your bedroom. But please, don't expect ecstasy every time. Some meals will be just for nurturance. You'll focus, be involved, enjoy, but that's it. No bells and whistles. The same thing happens in bed. Sometimes you'll have a major catharsis. Your body will explode, your eyes will widen, you will feel a tingling ecstasy and quickening of energy. You'll be floating around heaven all day. But sometimes the earth doesn't move. Even if you achieve orgasm, something will be missing; you'll have a sense of unfulfillment, a haunting ache. You'll have to accept food and love both ways. It's fuel and energy to stoke your engines. Sometimes a meal is just a meal.

You don't have to hold out for the best meal or the best sex each and every time. However, if you practice this kind of focus, intention and involvement, you will be more assured of having a better experience more often. You'll glimpse heaven more times than hell, and your body won't go to pot. When you are truly satisfied, the hunger subsides. When you spend more time "being there," your appetites will subside and your body will lighten.

4. Crave Space

The more quiet you can have, the better. This is all about being alone with food. That means no TV, radio, distracting kids or business. When you first begin this experience, it is crucial that you set aside the time to be alone and go inward. Later on, when you have the techniques down, you can practice little parts of it anywhere. You'll be able to do it quietly while out to dinner at a noisy restaurant or even while at a business luncheon. Your first encounters with this exercise may feel like you're being ordered from outside. Actually, you are retraining yourself from within. *You* are choosing. Soon you will move to actually preferring a quiet, more dignified meal.

I recommend playing background music. I usually play Pachelbel's Canon (for background music) because musicologists say that the tonal resonance of its chords vibrates to varieties of people in many lands and of various ages. Could it be that on a cellular level we are all basically more harmonious than discordant? Perhaps through our common efforts to find our personal sensualities, we'll heal the planet. We will certainly be healing more than food obsessions.

Because I have been doing so many mother/daughter workshops based on my last book, *Fat & Furious*, sometimes I replace the music with a recording of sounds from inside a pregnant womb. It is not necessarily a comforting sound, louder than most expect, but it is definitely organic and "natural." With sounds from "mom's" womb and the instruction to focus on gaining nurturance, many start to cry. They are recognizing how long they have been without this kind of animal comforting, and they are grieving for the time lost. When they'd previously only found comfort in food, embarrassed, they guzzled too quickly.

5. Approach with Care

With food and sex, the approach is important. Here's where *intention* comes in, and this is often where partners differ. It is both playful and serious business. Any entry is profound, whether eating or bedding. We are negotiating passages across our boundaries. Remember to think of yourself as a noble creature, an animal, a child of God sent here to *live*. Whether eating or making love, it is *not* a sinful experience. It is reveling in the gifts and joys of the universe. It is what you were sent here to do. It is noble work.

This important statement is often an immediate stumbling block. Everyone will have to become honest about what they are doing. Often men like to pretend that they are just in it for kicks. Often women like to pretend they are just in it for love. When you bring it to the noble-animal level, you unify the sensual earth child with the evolving spiritual adult. Both parts must be integrated for you to return home. Sit quietly and contemplate going to the cosmos as your primary purpose. Think of it as you approach your plate.

6. Begin the Dance

You will teach yourself about surrender, but this is by no means a passive endeavor. This is a conscious and active step on your journey. Some people think that letting go and turning things over means it's time to lie down and take a nap. They think it's up to the cosmos to fix them. I think not. I think the cosmos is waiting to see what you *do* as a statement of your intentions. If your intentions aren't made clear through *action*, then you'll probably quickly fall back. You are what you *do*, not what you *say!* There needs to be some objective, active evidence to show that you are committed and involved in going for change, cleaning up your problems. God is not your butler. She's more like that mysterious pledge-break person when they announce matching donors on public television. The broadcaster tells you that they have a contributor who will match or even double your pledged donation. You have to invest something first. It's the same thing here. You show the universe what you intend to deliver. As the universe feels reverberations of your "movement," then you get attention. If you seem sincere, the cosmos may match or even double your investment.

First sit to quiet your body. Try to make a pact with your body that you will *only* eat when seated. Breathe consciously, but naturally. Notice how your perfect organism inhales and exhales. This happens quite naturally twelve times a minute, whether you worry about it or not, focus on it or not. It's really none of your business. It's just your business to show up and watch the dance. There's nothing for you to do but sit. Do that for three minutes. *Just sit. . . .*

Notice how easily your body settles in and how quickly it relaxes. These few moments alone are so important, so necessary, yet so neglected. Your body needs the settling time, both before a meal and before making love. Settle in. Try to discard all conscious thought. If your mind wanders to dilemmas in your life, like remembering an errand unattended, breathe out the thought and trust it will show up later. Let distractions enter the top of your head and then blow them out through your mouth. Trust they'll come back when you need them. Right now, you need the quiet, the peace, the settling. The goal here is to slow down those racing molecules. You want your breathing to become modulated and steady. Just relax. You deserve to be here. Your body needs the time with you. Quietly whisper now, telling yourself, *Relax. . . .*

Sometimes you can focus your relaxation by taking a fantasy journey through your body. If at the table, settling in for a meal, do this with yourself, quietly instructing each body part. If you are doing this settling in bed with a partner, take turns instructing each other in each segment of this dance.

Use the following as a script you read to yourself to instruct your body in relaxation. Don't just read over this part. Read it and *do it!* If not, you'll lumber headlong into the abyss, missing the experience completely. You *are* your body, and your body wants to dance. Join it. Feed it. Love it . . . *do it.*

7. Prepare for Entry

Focus on your toes. Whisper to them, "R-E-E-E-E-E-E-E-L-A-A-A-A-X-X-X-X." Feel the capillaries at the bottoms of your toes. Feel the molecules of blood circulating. Tell them to slow down and relax. Move your consciousness up to the balls of your feet. Appreciate them for carrying the weight of your body, your day, your life. Ask them gently to relax. Focus now on your heels and ankles, thanking them for balancing you and keeping you erect. Offer them this time to take a break and rest.

Now move up to your calves. Flex them tight and then release. Throughout the relaxation exercise, whenever you feel tightness, tighten up that area harder and then let it fall away. Now focus on your thighs and buttocks, noticing how your body settles into the chair. Take notice of the weight of your being and how it sits. Move your consciousness to the small of your back. Notice support or lack thereof. Now move forward to your internal organs, telling them all to settle down and relax.

Move up to your chest and diaphragm, and consciously watch your breathing. Throughout this exercise, whenever any distraction moves you off course, immediately move back to focusing on your breathing. Watch the undulation while relaxing. Watch how your breath moves in and out. Tell yourself again softly, "R-E-E-E-E-E-E-L-A-A-A-A-X-X-X."

Now move up to your shoulders and tell them to relax. Roll them forward and then backward, hunching them tight and then releasing. Bring your focus up the back of your neck, squeezing and then relaxing. Now move up over the top of your head. Feel the tingling as breath fills your head. Blow out strongly, giving away any cares of the day. Blow it all out and relax. Focus now down the front of your face, your neck, arms, down to your fingertips. Capillaries again. Feel the tingling, notice the blood flow, tell your fingertips to "R-E-E-E-E-L-A-A-A-A-X."

Now refocus back to the chest, watch your breathing, let the breasts rise and fall. Bliss out and relax. Now you're ready to eat . . . or make love. . . .

8. Survey the Landscape

Take stock now by asking yourself some important questions about your day, your life, your time and your partner. Notice how your day has been. Notice who you've been today. Even if today seems like all the rest, each day's a bit different. Did you notice? Take notice now. There has to have been something new today. It may be something new in *your response* to the day. Did you find yourself going through old experiences with a new attitude? Have you found someone's attitude changed toward you, or has your attitude changed toward someone else? Did you learn something you'd never known before? The more you are able to notice newness in your life, the more you will be able to bring new attention to your mate and your plate.

So, back away a minute and take a look at what you are about to consume. If at the table, look at your meal. If with a partner, scan the terrain. Take a long, sweet, savoring look, imagining what it's going to be like. Remember other times you've had this experience. Bring them into consciousness so you can make them concrete and then forget them. This time is not those times. This time is the first time. You've never had salad like this before, and you've never known a bald man like this before. Both are brand-new.

The reason both are brand-new is that *you* are brand-new. Remember, in taking stock of your day, you looked for the newness, the learning. That's why you've settled in to this meal and this lover. You're here for a new day. *You* approach anew. No expectations. No preconceptions. Nothing to prove or evaluate. It's a new day.

While you are *looking* at your meal is the time to drink all the liquid you'd like. It is important not to drink *during* the meal as you will tend to drown your food. You will use liquid to push it down faster rather than letting your own juices orchestrate the digestion process. This time, don't drown it. Let yourself work with your love object. You want your tongue, your mouth and your juices to do the work and feel the textures.

Now is the time to bring more physical reality into your

psychic ruminations. Note any expectations you have of how this food will taste. Let these expectations go. This is the first time. No expectations. You take a long, slow, visual read of the landscape, looking over the entire meal set before you. While you look, keep remembering your breathing focus. Notice if there is a quickening as you anticipate the meal or the man. Slow down. That's one of the most difficult aspects of both eating and loving sensually. It's hard to slow down, but it's worth it. Most people don't like to practice such control. They'd rather race at breakneck pace than modulate the slow, steady, deliberate, boring but grounded rhythms. Notice now if you feel frustration or anticipation while these words are dragging out your sensual experience. This is purposely intended for you to experience this *delay* between anticipation, wanting, longing, enduring and, eventually, fulfilling. You are learning how to weather deprivation. As Nietzsche said, "That which does not kill us makes us stronger." You will approach both food and love from a stronger place. You will know what you want, but also know you can live without it.

One more important step before chowing down. Serve yourself all you want from a large dinner plate onto a smaller salad plate. Know that you will be able to continue serving yourself throughout the meal. You can eat all there is on the server plate. Eating from the smaller plate retrains your eye so that you become satisfied with less. We are plate cleaners after all. Make sure as you serve out your first portions that you give yourself a variety of choices in texture, color, taste and smell. Think of your man the same way. His body offers an infinite variety of sensual experiences.

9. Take the First Bite

In praying before a meal, Buddhist monks say, "The first bite is to heal all beings." Now, that may sound a bit grandiose at first, but consider that each of us, when we own our animal selves while eating or loving, is really interacting with the whole universe. If we each pay exquisite attention to *how* we enter or consume another, how we savor and digest the experience, that first bite could heal the planet. If we each slow down and pay attention, fear subsides. We find in the moment that we can be fully present, alive, pulsating, vibrating, energized and in love with life. All that can happen at first bite and first blush.

Look how long you've been at this now with fork poised. You haven't had your first bite yet. You are finding infinite ways to enjoy this experience. There's more than just chomping in the mouth. About 90 percent of taste is *smell*. Whether it's our meals or bodies, we somehow avoid truly inhaling. Animals don't have this problem. They spend a lot of time sniffing. What's happened to us? I remember when I worked with addicts. They'd comment when someone was developing a new crush, "Man, your nose is open. That gal sure got up your nose." Were they talking about sniffing drugs or inhaling love?

As you now move ever closer to eating, pick up your plate and smell your meal. Again, notice the excited rush of anticipation. Slow down. . . . You must work hard to keep this experience brand-new, not compared with others and not consumed too quickly. See how much there is to smelling. Sometimes smelling is enough. Sometimes smelling prepares us to eat. In love, smell usually rushes us closer to copulation, but often, with foods, if you really concentrate, one sniff is enough. I've found this very true in shopping malls with those cookie booths in the food court. I think they purposely position those fans to blow out into the walkway. Then we're overwhelmed with the aroma and wander entranced to the counter.

Try this experiment sometime. Go by there again and smell with intention! Smell that cookie smell. Sit right down in front of the stall and let the aroma waft over you. There will be a first rush of madness where you think you need a dozen or so. Wait. . . . Sit a minute. . . . Inhale. . . . Notice how much just smelling satisfies you. It's often better than the taste. The *smell* of chocolate is much deeper and richer than the actual taste. If you sit there a few more minutes, you'll start to inhale the back smell. You'll smell not butter, but a heavier, lardier smell. Soon it will take on an industrial kind of flavor. It will move out of the realm of sensuous savorings and almost smell like a car repair shop. Trust me—do this test and see. It is an excellent training in waiting to see what is *really* in store for you. Developing this sensitivity will also help when you're caught in a binge. Focusing on smell can help you stop in the middle of a bag of potato chips!

Now as you smell your meal, you may decide that smelling is enough. Pay attention here because once you start chewing, you may move to automatic-pilot and start guzzling. You'll keep chewing even if you don't want to. You'll forget this moment and forget the choices you have every second. Keep smelling throughout the meal so you'll know if you really *must* eat, or if smelling is enough. In making love and eating, stay conscious each moment of every possible choice.

Now evaluate. Is this meal enough for you? Is it what you really *want?* Don't be squeamish here. It is better to send it back, start anew or regroup than to go along politely eating what you don't favor, growing resentful and ready to binge. Now this may be a "diet" meal, *not* your favorite, but you are resolved to a *choice* that's best for you. You *choose* to eat this way. But if you are eating with resentment, renegotiate! You must find a meal that feels good enough so that you can say, "Enough is enough."

Now that you've looked at it, smelled it, and evaluated it, go ahead and—

10. Eat It!

If you couldn't resist and felt compelled to leaf through the previous pages until you saw this heading, STOP! You are ready to evaluate some important lessons. What did you learn by reading instead of doing? Do you still *think* you will *think* your way into new action? Thinking it through has never worked before. I know how much you'd like to believe that. Sorry, in this case you only learn by doing. You can't think your way into right action, but you *can* act your way into right thinking. I'm telling you what I know works. When all else fails, DO IT!

> STOP!
>
> TURN AROUND!
>
> GO BACK. . . .
>
> DO IT!

Contemplate another Buddhist prayer: "We must think deeply on the ways and means by which this food has come." Consider all that has gone into bringing this plate to you today. The more involvement you had, the better, and the more time you spent *consciously* involved, better yet. It's best to use whole, natural foods, not packaged. Try to avoid cellophane wrappers. Prepare your own meals when possible. If you are actively and consciously focused and involved in shredding that cabbage, you will have a much more satisfying experience with your meal. When you finally eat a salad you chopped yourself, it is a full culmination of what all the ingredients and players were supposed to be doing here. It feels organically correct and quite satisfying. It's almost like the same feeling you get with good sex. It was meant to be; it was the next intended step. In Yiddish, the term is *beschert*, meaning "intended, meant to be." When eating or loving, you want to evaluate always if this is actually what *you* were intended to be doing. Do the best you can.

When considering how your food came to you and whether it's truly *intended for* you, there's a lot to be learned from other cultures that promote eating more consciously. When Native Americans hunted the plains, hunters paid homage to their prey before slaughter. It was known that both hunter and prey were part of an intricate and divinely orchestrated dance and each had a noble part to play. Before consuming the buffalo, hunters bowed down in reverent prayer, welcoming this beast and its spirit into their beings. The animal was not seen as a big mountain of meat out there, but instead, the spirit of the bison was taken in. The hunters felt a part of the earth and at one with its laws. There is, in that consuming moment, utmost respect for the bison and the dance of life. The hunters take the spirit of the bison within themselves. They have accepted and incorporated their prey. The hunters loved and respected the bison, and thanked him when welcoming him into their own bodies and souls. Neither hunter nor beast was the greater or lesser being. Both were part of the life-death dance.

Consider another Buddhist prayer, "We eat lest we become lean and die."

Even though we are having a sensual experience, let's remember that food and sex are fuel to stoke our engines and recharge our batteries. Any sensual gratification is a secondary gain.

Good taste is a secondary gift. Speaking of the gift of good taste, please remember that the only place you have tastebuds is in your mouth. Once that food drizzles down your gullet, the whole sensual thing is done and gone. Therefore, try to keep the food in your mouth as long as possible. Allow conscious entry, then savor.

Now take a deep breath, pile as much as you can on your plastic fork, and take in that first bite. Immediately put down your fork.

This is a receiving experience but far from passive. You are putting food in to create energy. You are joining a mate to vibrate energy. Your entered body will transform either food or man. Let the food or man in slightly, just past the orifice, into the mouth or into opening lips of your vulva. Allow entry and then gently stop and pay attention. Your temple has just been entered. Pay attention. Observe. Don't move.

Notice any difficulty stopping to pay attention. Do you rush headlong to gratification? When the waitress brings the meal, do you finish your sentence? Is all that waiting, anticipating, focusing just too nerve-racking for you? This is the heart of the matter and exactly what needs to change. It's that slowing-down-to-smell-the-roses stuff. In your eating and your loving, you must take the time. What else is there? Don't try to figure things out first. Just follow. I know it's difficult, but, ultimately, it will be much more satisfying. Remember, this is just training.

Now that you watched the entry, put down that fork and chew. Change focus from entry to savoring. Feel the foreign object in your orifice and circle it slowly. Think of each bite as being chewed to liquid. When it's liquid, that's your signal to S-W-A-A-A-A-L-L-L-L-L-O-O-O-O-O-W-W-W-W-W-W slowly. Then that will be the signal to pick up the fork, take in another full bite and again C-H-E-E-E-E-E-W-W-W-W.

Think of savoring your man's entry the same way. Circle slowly, paying attention every inch of the way. . . .

11. Hold It!

If you haven't noticed already, there *is* even more relationship between food and sex. Hold off pushing the penetration. Make sure every inch of your lips makes contact. Think of swishing your food around or swiveling your bottom. You have to hold the food in your mouth as long as possible and make sure all areas are fed. Breathe. . . .

Cecelia, a businesswoman in New York, told me how much she enjoyed oral sex with one particular partner. She most enjoyed how he slowly moved in and out of her mouth, how he explained to her that the way he was moving was the way he would move inside her other lips if they finally "did it." He was explaining and training about how he liked to move. Cecelia found she loved the titillation in his explanation. She laughed, "It was like a preview of coming attractions." She was a woman who waited many months before "going all the way" with a man. She decided that this could be a lovely sort of "test" she'd devise to observe how men moved. "If I like his moves in my mouth, I'm sure to like his moves later on," she asserted emphatically. He was showing her his timing strokes.

Your whole mouth and your whole being are hungry. As soon as you *smell* the food, your entire mouth secretes digestive juices and gets ready to eat. As soon as you think a sexy thought relating to a particular fellow, juices start to flow. Many of us, for dental or habitual reasons, only eat on one side of the mouth. The other side experiences "mouth hunger" and feels it never ate.

Make sure now that every taste bud touches that bite in your mouth. The only place you *taste* food is in your mouth. Savor the taste. Make sure every cell in your tunnel makes contact with every morsel of his member. Don't let any pleasure elude you. Go for it. Swish the food around to all corners, up around the gums, under the tongue, up on the roof and at the back of the palate.

Some find it helpful to count to twenty before swallowing. I think chewing to liquid is easier. It's just like sex. When you can't hold out any longer, when the explosion has to go, there is a burst and a trickle. Don't rush it. When you chew your food fully, it will just melt down your throat because it can't hold out in your mouth any longer. When you feel that gulp, when your mouth is clear, that's the signal to pick up your fork and go for the next bite. Begin again and chew. . . . and breathe.

Continue eating at your own pace for ten minutes. With each bite, evaluate how much you like it, how it compares with what you'd imagined and how satisfying or disappointing it is. Stay conscious. Don't go into automatic pilot. Pay attention. This experience at the plate will be transferred to the bed.

With each bite or each stroke, you have the right to change your mind. Notice what keeps your attention. If you drift . . . stop and regroup. With your bite or your partner, keep determining if you feel satisfied or resentful.

Is this fully occupying your consciousness, or are you drift-ing? If you drift, STOP! Regroup and determine if this is the meal or partner you want to be doing. If not, leave. Be present or vacate, but don't be halfhearted and don't lie to yourself. Your life is at stake!

12. Savor It!

Keep noticing. Notice wherein lies the spice of life and what is truly bland. You may now crave liquids or more seasonings. By drinking, you try to get the food out of your mouth faster because you really can't stand the sensuality of it. You are having difficulty owning your animal self. Perhaps you seek more seasonings because you can't believe how truly boring food and eating really are. You thought you loved this so much. It's really just food. Sex is better.

Whether eating or bedding, you can always take a breather and reorient yourself. Purposely stop yourself after ten min-utes just to evaluate your experience. This "time-out" is quite helpful. You may have lapsed into automatic pilot. Stopping will help you slow down to refocus.

If you are out at a restaurant, now would be a good time to excuse yourself to go to the restroom or make a phone call. Don't worry about your food getting cold. You did so much psychic preparation before eating that you learn to eat things in a different manner than expected. Issues of hot and cold won't matter.

As you walk past other tables, notice what everyone else has ordered. Notice your sense of longing for the choices you didn't make. We just can't have it all. It's important to empha-size this sense of loss. Just say it to yourself and notice the longing. You also might register a sense of competition about who at your table had a larger portion than you, who is eating more slowly and thus has more left, etc. If you don't pay attention to these secret thoughts, they disintegrate into the black hole and show up later as resentments. You'll eat over them.

13. Leave It!

Bring your consciousness back to your own meal and continue eating. Ultimately, you will reach an important, decisive moment . . . when and how to leave. . . . With sex, your decisions are often negotiated through orgasm. With food, you can be more independent and decisive. You will *decide* to stop eating. This doesn't have to be when the plate is clean, though it may be. Try leaving just one string bean.

If you like the taste, you may be a plate cleaner. Maybe serving yourself to the smaller plate can help, but there is a spiritual, sexual hunger that gets awakened while eating and must be acknowledged. Hiding it from yourself is often why you keep eating way past full. Overeating keeps on long after the appetite is satisfied. The mouth yearns, the gums ache. It is a craving for sensation, for feeling.

Continue eating at a slow, methodical, sensual pace until you have decided you've had enough. That decision is crucial. Make it carefully and, once made, try to follow through quickly. Notice the immediate longing. You are probably feeling it at this very moment. Just considering saying "good-bye" means you are ending your meal. You may be mourning, "Is that all there is, my friend?"

As you contemplate ending, think of leaving when you still feel a bit empty. I recommend eating to "half-full" so that you can be a lean machine, vibrating and signaling. A full glass doesn't ring a crystal tone. If you decide to leave something on your plate, give it a long look and actually say "good-bye." This can be an audible or purely reflective closing. Think to yourself, *I could have had it all, but I decided to leave this much.* As you say good-bye, heighten the loss by saying to yourself, *I had this coming to me, but now it's over. I will never have this particular meal again. When it's over, it's over.* You may think this is wacko, but it's actually very important. These are all mournful cries we've uttered unconsciously. Later, we go back and eat over them. I am asking you here to make conscious closure with the meal so you won't have to return.

It is so easy to begin the unconscious nibble. We've all known those mindless moments. Recently, I had eaten all I wanted of a large, luscious salad in a favorite restaurant. I'd asked for a container to take leftovers home for the next day's lunch. The very busy waitress was taking quite some time getting back to our table, and my companion noted that I kept picking at the salad. I was done, but still picking. It happens unconsciously and automatically. That is some of the worst kind of eating. It convinces you that you are *not* eating. You are! Every bite counts. If you don't catch yourself, you can put on great weight from nibbling.

Make a gesture of your good-bye. You can push your plate away, cover it with a napkin or bow your head in prayer. Have a signal to yourself that says, "This meal has ended." Notice how it feels now to have stopped the eating experience. You might feel vibrations from your "happy puppy" body. She's been fed. She's sated. She's put to rest.

You may now drink your water. That's your signal. The meal is over. . . . There will be more food in your future, but no more right now. Notice how you change gears from receiving to now leaving the table, going out into the world to *produce*. Eating is your receiving mode. Notice the difference changing from fueling energy to discharging energy. All this unconscious process has to become conscious.

If you are leaving a love partner, first savor the wonder of closeness, the wonder of meeting in that third place between the two of you. Feel your vibrations and the discharge of energy.

With both food and sex, think of the last videos of Elvis Presley's live concerts at the Las Vegas Hilton. Some of you may remember how wild and euphoric the atmosphere was as Elvis strutted his stuff, kicked karate chops high into the air, gyrated and swiveled and swirled that cape. He wiped his brow, then threw out wet towels. He gave his all. It was ecstatic. He shook his white-satined hips, swooped the stage with that billowing cape, and shimmied and shook as that thunderous band banged on. The crowd was electric! Then he left. . . . He left the arena. . . . He left our table. . . . He left the playing field. . . . It was over. . . . We saw him get into the limo to be driven away. After a long wait, a deep-throated voice announced mournfully and repeatedly, "ELVIS HAS LEFT . . . THE BUILDING."

Ultimately, the music stopped. The quiet was deafening. . . . That's how you'll feel after a great meal or great sex. There will be exuberance, thunderous heat, focused concentration, intense involvement, stimulation, ENERGY!

And then all is quiet. . . .

Done. . . .

Still. . . .

ELVIS HAS LEFT . . . THE BUILDING.

Six

Listening to
the Hollow

Love is not all: it is not meat or drink
Nor slumber nor a roof against the rain.

—EDNA ST. VINCENT MILLAY, "LOVE IS NOT ALL"

Although sex is not all there is, it becomes more important when it is disowned and avoided. When you make friends with your sexual self, you regain contact with your spiritual Self. In this chapter, you will explore the necessity and responsibility of treating your body as an instrument serving your spirituality. It is a temple, a shrine at which to bow, as well as a tuning fork for picking up and transmitting your personal messages. Instead of overstuffing your body, you'll want to keep it slightly empty so that you can hear the resonance. You must first discover that hollow place.

269

It will appear quickly as you limit food intake. You want your body to be a slightly hollow cavity so that the sound vibration, your internal messenger, will be heard as clearly as a bell. The by-product will be weight loss.

In Hemingway's novel *For Whom the Bell Tolls*, Maria comments to the gypsy, Pilar, about her first sexual experience: "the earth moved." Pilar was quite impressed and discloses that for most people, that never happens, and certainly no more than "thrice in a lifetime." About those rare moments, people report feeling like they've transcended self. It is a feeling that can both enliven and destroy us. Some report that they feel high, physical ecstasy, tingles, floating, delirious, falling up, turning inside out, a sweeping release of body. Compare this to your feeling "full" after a large meal. You are after the same thing. Good sex is tension-releasing, serves as a sensory treat that adds zero calories but may burn a few. It can be a nightcap, or a wake-up call, and also does what food can't. It enhances intimacy as an expression of tenderness. It is not proof of your femininity or worth. It will not make up for lack of fulfillment in other areas, and it will certainly not resolve marital conflict or boredom. It will, however, bring you home.

Conscious lovemaking involves nothing less than survival of our species and saving the planet. Sex—not food—is the power base. Food is a physical nurturer, and sex is the battery charger. As mentioned earlier, today we see inhibited sexual desire (ISD) in epidemic numbers. Even though anorexia has the highest death rate of any psychiatric illness, ISD is dangerous to all society. Anorexia does not mean loss of appetite. If you are anorexic, you know how hungry you are. You are not devoid of appetite, just restrictive. However, with ISD, you actually *lose* all sexual appetite. Even if we get healthy bodies, we may have no energy or longing to carry on the species. Many "modern" discussions of sexuality have been relegated to plumbing charts and acrobatics. Classifying human sexuality into biological categories is deadly. Your sexuality is not just a life function, like excretion, growth, nutrition or even reproduction. When you make love with another, you are sharing a knowledge of a *way of being*. You are not sharing techniques. You are sharing patience, attentiveness, waiting. You need commitment and intentionality. As that disappears, desire wanes, and that threatens the survival of our species. You need conscious divine dining and conscious divine loving. If deprived of either, you may develop daily living problems as well as addictive acting out.

Gateway to Heaven

Some Hindu traditions refer to the vulva as the "gateway to heaven." According to their teachings, when connection is made, a couple starts the journey to the cosmos together. As your children are birthed, they leave heaven to learn the lessons this life has in store. We've all traversed this gateway far too easily and casually. We need to learn to respect and savor each passage. Only by paying exquisite attention can true heaven be reached.

The Sanskrit language elevates the experience. A woman's privates are *yoni,* meaning "sacred space, jade gate, palace of heaven, pleasure place." A man's member is his *lingam,* meaning "wand of light, jade root, arrow of love." These names refer to space and light. They speak directly to what we cherish about sex. Sex is for illumination and penetration. It is for joining in a third, more enlightened place.

Unfortunately, we have been schooled in avoiding these

passages and calling the act itself dirty and sinful. Both eating and loving, our two most sensual diversions, are considered sinful. Our belief that our sexual and spiritual natures are in opposition wounds us. It alienates us from our true, innate essence.

We must instead see the body as a temple and bodily functions as spiritual. Both Hindu and Hebrew texts tell the story that when man and woman were created, they rejected their divinity. The council of angels decided then to hide that gift. They pondered whether to hide it in the earth, the sea or even the stars, but decided humans would find it in any of those places. Then one angel said, "Let's hide divinity deep within man and woman themselves. They'll never think to look there." I am now asking you to look, smell and taste for the soul within. Instead of roaming the earth, we need to look to our partners to bring us home to Self. The path to God is through the body. We are not walking toward God, but *with* God.

Initially, humans fabricated a competition between spiritual ecstasy and sexual ecstasy. It was believed that males had limited energy and if doing the correct spiritual work, there wouldn't be enough energy for physical connections with mates. It was the limited capacity of the *males* that made the whole split necessary. If you wanted to have serious spiritual power, you had to control your sexual power. There would always be that competition between the spirit and the flesh. A distinct line was drawn, dividing the sacred from the profane. Even though sex was a gift from God, behaviors were either sanctioned within the church or outside the church. Sex stayed outside.

Later, Indian mystics prayed to the god Shiva, who carried Shakti, or combined sexual/spiritual energy. They believed that sexual ecstasy was the doorway *to* the spiritual. The vulva was gateway to heaven. Sexuality was a means to transcend the personal and participate in primordial time. The line was starting to blur.

The Jewish tradition had for a long time believed in the sacredness of sex, holding that sexual ecstasy was a God-given joy and responsibility. The Christian tradition, however, kept sex sinful. The medieval church clearly limited female sexuality: Powerful women had to be virgins. Joan of Arc was a valiant warrior who had to remain a "maid," and Queen Elizabeth could rule the world as long as she was the "Virgin Queen."

Jewish rabbis at the time were teaching that paradise and life everlasting would resemble whatever heaven we created here on earth. In paradise, one will taste ecstasies no more and no less than one has been ecstatic in this life. Enjoying life was a requirement of spirituality.

Jewish and Hindu writings explored passion. In the Jewish tradition, women were not permitted to renounce their sexuality as they were highly valued as sexual beings. Many Jewish laws were written to help men renounce the strong pull toward females, but *female sexuality* was never to be limited. In fact, the Middle Ages produced the first Jewish sex manual, detailing how men could give women pleasure. Though in Orthodox circles all sexual expression waits for marriage, once mated, the partners are almost ordered to enjoy sex. The man must focus on his wife's pleasure as a blessing. A client who had recently converted to Judaism told me, "Any religion that tells you to celebrate the Sabbath by praying and then napping with your husband is the dogma for me!" If left unsatisfied, women overeat. Perhaps the tendency to obesity in many Jewish women has more to do with sex than chicken fat.

In the Christian tradition, there are also occasions when sexuality can flower as a God-given right of passage. Before and after the Lenten season, revelers rejoice at festivals like Mardis Gras in New Orleans and Fasching in Germany. These are festivals when humans are encouraged to lose themselves to sacred erotic spirituality. As addicts facing the millennium, we have to find a way to transform our sexual energy from rutting rams looking for tension release to seekers after uplifting spiritual energy.

Spiritual Beings Having a Human Experience

We are part animal and part divine. Life would be easier if we were grounded in one form or the other rather than vacillating in this insecure, ever-changing place. Angels have it a lot easier. They are born angels and will remain so. Cows have that same luxury. They are born, live and die a totally animal existence. They chew their cud, have a little sex and then leave the planet. Humans are placed here between angels and cows, possessing a little of both, juxtaposing and balancing the two states. Most people pass through this life not at all aware of this dilemma. Those who are super aware may become caught up in self-destructive behavior like bingeing, drinking or drugging. Addictive types are more con- scious of this quest and more aware of the loss of connection between their animal and spiritual natures. Powerful women have to stay fine tuned and aware of the struggle. Struggles with food keep us constantly moving across the boundaries of our animal and spiritual beings. If we don't stay conscious, we escape into the saintly asceticism of anorexia, or we run to base animal grossness by bingeing and purging. We were meant to go to a calmer, blissful, midline, more human place.

Keeping Our Senses

While alcoholics can "plug the jug and go to meetings," if food is your problem, you have to go *toward* your substance. You have to sink right into the realm of the senses. Fritz Perls told us we had to "lose our minds to come to our senses." You must pay attention to your senses. The first sense to ignite, *touch,* is often the last to burn out. To live consciously, you *must* reach out and touch. Long after our eyes fail, we're still "in touch." Even at the last moment of final departure, there is talk of losing touch. Are you willing to touch and be touched?

When you become willing to be touched and seen, you'll stop filling up with donuts and instead seek out more spiritual fillings. There is an important connection between sex, food and our spiritual paths. To truly honor each of these endeavors, we have to remove *sneakiness*. We can't afford sneaky food, nor can we have sneaky sex. Both experiences have to be full bore and on the table. We partake systematically and consciously by being fully alive. We savor and relish the experience. We love it! We take sneaky food out of life and put real sex in. In other words, reach for a mate instead of a plate!

We've been blessed with this conflict between our animal and spiritual natures so that we can constantly be reminded to stay grounded. While in my first book, *Fat Is a Family Affair*, I explained extensively about the "disease concept," emphasizing that we needed help to recover, I now see that rather than "sick," we are actually truly blessed beings, perhaps what this society would call "overly sensitive." We are blessed with this sensitivity to remain ever aware of when we lose our connections. AA literature explains to the addict about "loss of conscious contact with God as you understand God." The spiritual leader Ram Dass once said, "Just because you are communing with the gods and goddesses is no reason not to know your postal ZIP code." Whether using the mails or males, *stay grounded!* You were given this particular body in order to stay grounded as well as to travel higher. We need to soar to heaven with feet planted firmly on the ground.

As we discuss sex as a spiritual union, a way to go to God and fulfill our purpose here, let's not forget that we got into this whole exploration because of looking at our fat. We want to pay exquisite attention to what and *how* we eat, and keep our vessel slightly empty, a little less than half-full, so that we are available for entry and vibration. We must always pay attention to that mind/body connection.

What happens for you when someone looks and really sees you? Do you start to vibrate with tension? Do you turn away? Do you sweat? We are talking about vulnerability to penetration, along with visibility. It is really the issue of seeing and being seen. This may be just as scary for your partner as it is for you. Some men get terrified when a woman becomes yielding and soft. This might be what he said he wanted, but not knowing how to be in relationship to such a woman, he might become a worshiping wimp or a self-righteous bully.

It would certainly be easier if it were all up to you alone, if you didn't have to depend on another. In the love affair with food, you gained sustenance and a bit of ecstasy from food which you believed you could *control*. With another human being, you can't even maintain that fantasy of control. They have their own ideas. In 1920, the humorists James Thurber and E. B. White published an essay titled *Is Sex Necessary?* There they explained, "While the urge to eat is a personal matter concerning only the hungry person, the sex urge involves another individual. It is this 'other person' that causes all the trouble." This is why masturbation seems a viable alternative and is certainly a pleasant activity while waiting for mating. But, you'll need true mating to take you home.

You must be fully grown to mate. Your body needs more conscious coitus and less eating. The body I'm referring to is an adult's body. Children can do just as well to masturbate. If you plan to meld your juices and spirit with another being, it is important you make that decision as a grown-up. You must have grown psychologically even more than physically. That means you have to have accomplished certain developmental tasks. You must be selfish. You must know your own needs and differentiate your needs and wants from the wants and needs of others. That is what you need a true lover for. He will love you with your wants. He will love your real self. Show it to him early.

Keeping a vulva vigil assures you that your spirit—your inner sensor—approves of this coupling. All you have to do is listen to the wisdom of your organism. Your body won't lie. Your vulva will signal correctly. This is a personal way to fill the hole in your soul. Ponder now what might be in store if you use sex instead of food to create that unified feeling, filling that hollow place. The next time you contemplate making love with a man, take these ideas to bed with you and see where you go. Use the same focus you developed from the Divine Dine. Take the same thirteen-step journey into your cosmic vulva.

Always keep in mind that the most important part of this process is *focus*. You must pay attention and stay awake.

Attention and love are deeply related. Focused, concerted attention is one of the greatest gifts you can give another. That coupled with knowledge and wisdom is what most therapists give to clients. Don't take any attention lightly. Giving focus is an act of love.

Be mindful of the love you get, but also of the love you give. As a full-grown spiritual entity, you will grow in discernment. That may mean you don't love as freely as some others. Some spiritual movements prize free lovers who espouse love for all humanity. This form was popular with the "flower child" movement of the 1960s. That's not the kind of love I'm suggesting.

I am suggesting mindfulness and love that is not a vague sentiment for all of humanity. It is instead a demarcation on an individual journey. You seek a *specific* individual who creates within you a *specific* vibratory level that calls you somewhere else. Like E.T., you want to phone home. At the same time, you know that it is a unique experience when the two of you are together and you are loving an unrepeatable person during an unrepeatable experience. There may be others, but they will be different. Even other times with the same lover will be different.

It is important to be with a man who wants the same thing. If *any* body will do, your soul knows. You won't really open up. You've got to know he's after *you* as the specific woman *you* are. Some men want to worship a pure goddess or debase a "naughty" woman. You are neither. You are a pulsating, vibrating being. Can he let his masculine energy penetrate the specific animal-woman who is you?

You might have forgotten by now who your real self is. It is easy to turn against your own true nature. Sometimes you realize that if fully yourself, you may be quite erotic. When that truthful, you may not be liked. Some may be jealous. Some may take advantage. You may become embarrassed by your own eroticism. It seems safer to turn to a focus on looks and body image instead.

Though you need mindful connection, excess food has suppressed that need. You've grown to believe you need all that food, but the need is false. False needs can never be filled. See how appetite suppressants will fail here? They address the wrong hunger. They can suppress a minor irritation or ache, but they won't help point you in the direction of your own personal growth. They could help if you are only craving "tension-release" sex. They won't quiet the longing to fill the hole in your soul.

If you don't know who you are or what you want, you'll overeat to have false needs met. These symbolic needs are generated by the head or the marketplace. You rarely consult the *body* for direction. That is where sex can help. It will help you refocus and turn to your body for its signals. Trust the wisdom of your organism. If you don't, you'll keep stuffing but never be filled. We all came by this honestly, but how do we escape? It's going to be difficult to turn this around. As the famous British psychiatrist R. D. Laing said, "Where everyone is false, the real is not going to be convenient."

So, how do you find that real Self? You can only find her by first experiencing the hollow. If you are here to follow yourself into yourself, there are no guarantees as to who will show up. Hopefully, you will be able to maintain a dialogue with your lover about this. You have to let him know when and how you open up and when and how you shut down. You can move in and out of these states continuously. You may have been taught that you are supposed to protect your man's ego, that if you aren't careful, you could be castrating. Remember my Hawaiian friend and what happened with her two loves? Viewing men as weak egoed and in need of tending is very patronizing. If you play that game, you may find yourself growing tired of the ego you've protected.

Why can't we talk straight about this and call a spade a shovel? Isn't sex a natural act? Sneezing is also a natural act. Do you fabricate elaborate stories about your sneezing? Should he take your sneezing personally? Your honest communications can both strengthen and end a relationship. There's a risk. There's a similar risk if you decide not to communicate.

You have to be willing to surrender to that open, empty feeling, facing the void. From that void, you enter the cosmos, learn your divinity and enter paradise. It happens in bed. Why do we speak of sin in church and sex in bars? Shouldn't it be the other way around?

Why is this society so much into sacrificing and repression? Why do we question pleasure? Why is it gracious to give to others, but selfish to give to self? Sins of passion are repented in the same way as overeating. For gluttony or promiscuity, the purifications are similar: fasting or celibacy. Both these solutions don't address human beings, but foster denial and repression.

Some will teach you ideas contrary to what I taught you with the Divine Dine. They'll want you to renounce taste, to make food your enemy, to care about just the mechanics of fueling your engines. I ask instead that you totally taste and devour— taste fully. If you try to make food and taste less important, you will become deadened. . . . you will just be in your head. Conscious coitus cannot happen in a dead body. It's not philosophical—it's a body/animal thing. Jungian analyst Marion

Woodman said, "Body without spirit is a corpse, and spirit without a body is a ghost."

Conscious coitus can help you awaken your dead body and enliven your spirit. If you are thirsty, you may have a dream you are drinking water, but quenching your thirst can only continue if you stay in the dream state. As soon as you wake up, you'll be thirsty. The same applies to eating in the dream state and loving in the dream state. To be truly satisfied, you must be fully awake. Keep your sensual experiences reality based. Remember the prospective lover's invitation: "I don't want to *sleep* with you. I want to *wake* you up."

The Taste of Awakened Spirit

So, what makes this sex thing a spiritual experience? This very question has made this whole book, and especially this chapter, extremely difficult to write. This is something we don't want to codify or characterize into a box, diagnosis or expected behavior. The danger is that with too many suggestions, you might want to copy others. Instead, I want you to find your own ecstasy. *Ecstasy* is derived from the Greek *ek-stasis* and it means "standing outside self."

Carl Jung referred to "numinous" experience, something holy, sacred and standing *outside* the ordinary. Many report orgasm as another state of consciousness, where the inner world is magnified, we need less sleep, nothing frightens or threatens. Again, it's standing *outside* the ordinary.

Some find this state in celibacy, and some go for it in sensuality. Since you have the food problem, you have to go the sensuous route. You have that body that needs sating. You won't be satisfied with head trips. Your body wants to rise to a new frequency. According to Chris Griscom, director of the Light

Institute in Galisteo, New Mexico, "Sexuality is not what separates us from enlightenment; sexuality is an inherent quality of our earth experience which merges us *into* enlightenment."

You are charged with electrical energy. It needs to discharge. Haven't you felt that flip when aroused? It's a little jump inside just below your pubic bone. That quickening happens, and you want to go higher. This is the closest to ecstasy that humans allow themselves. When you allow this experience, you will feel outside of time, less personally important and a part of the natural wonder of life.

That sense can come from meditation as well. It comes from focus. You can create it on the subway, in a monastery or in the holy cathedral of your bedroom. It is your attitude that will determine your latitude. You are going for an existential experience to transcend self. According to Andrew Weil, author of *Eight Weeks to Optimum Health*, it is natural for humans to want to experience altered states of consciousness. Instead of turning to drugs and alcohol, why can't we turn to sex? Sex can be a life-giving force, but you must surrender to the experience.

My Way

When you truly know what you want, you may judge yourself, deciding that your needs are excessive. Trust me, you are bound to think that. A colleague, Colleen, wrote me from Houston:

> I may <u>"prove too much for the man"</u>. I fear that if I truly expect and ask for, long for, and search for what I really, really want from sex, then I will be too much. That's the scary part. The problem is he can't find a <u>home</u> with me if I'm too much. I'm so afraid of being too much. If I am too much, then I reexperience the wounding I had as a child when I was too much for my parents. I may have been too much for them, and now I'm too much

for him. I've always had those "terrible too's." I have gorgeous pools of large, luminous brown eyes. When I was a baby, they dominated my tiny face. I don't think my parents could tolerate my gazing at them. I was left alone a lot. Left with wet diapers, dirty face and those penetrating eyes. My parents had to look at me sideways or not at all. Now I seek to face my lover full frontal. If I can't make eye-and-soul contact with this man, why are we here? Does my way prove too much for him? Men have often liked the initial package. They've been flattered and amazed at how I remember everything they say, how I note nuances and inflections and intonations. My therapy clients appreciate that quality and keep coming back for more. With dates or lovers, it's not always so clear that they signed on for such a haul. Some may have just wanted to get laid or have some other good time. Many didn't want to be seen, and also didn't want to see me. As much as they liked my style, they left.

The kind of loving Colleen craved involved nuances of being eyeball-to-eyeball while also navel-to-navel. It involved truly tapping into untapped electric, erotic energies. Colleen is approaching the topic of selfish sex, being in a relationship to get needs met. Is it selfish to go for what you want? Maybe it's really a selfless gift to your partner. In her therapy practice, she gave. In her personal life, she was after something else. She knows that to really enjoy sex, she had to be selfish, a huntress. She wanted to be a human *being* instead of just a human *doing*.

This became her life's work. Could she be seen as fully as she saw others? Could there be a man strong enough, insightful enough, *there* enough? Would he want to take on that task, or could only a therapist show up that fully? She complained to me after a recent breakup, "I wasn't seeking someone who could hear litanies of past wounding traumas. I was looking for someone who could see exactly and fully the *totality* of me, as I show up in that moment. That would take a man who was genuinely interested in who I was. It requires someone who has grown into an adult himself." . . . She's still looking.

Prince Charming, Big Daddy

Looking for an adult does not mean you need a daddy and does not mean he has to stay forever. Once you find someone who seems attentive, especially if the sex is good, you might fear the same insatiability that you've known with food. If you are new to disciplining your food intake, and new to examining your feelings instead of eating over them, you may be seeking a love partner as therapist. I have tried to caution some AA women to tell less on their early dates, allowing instead for the man's projections to flower, allowing themselves to be viewed in a sexual way. So many want to tell their intimate problems when first becoming involved. That can change you from a love object to a worry object. What does that do to the relationship? Many a man has complained that when he understands his woman's woundings too much, it makes him incapable of loving her for fear of hurting her. So, he actually cares too much to sleep with her.

You may often feel weepy and blue, especially if you are a perimenopausal baby boomer. You may want a man to hear your pain and then jump your bones. Instead, listening to you makes him feel powerless to help and lowers his libido. He thinks you want to be left alone. He'd want the privacy. Instead, you want the intimacy.

Fallible Humans

Even Prince Charming is human and has his own agendas. People aren't as easy to control as food. You'd like to enter and stay in a blissful, visible place. Unfortunately, no one other person can be there for you all the time and in all the ways you would like. Food is always there when you need it. Your lover has to close shop sometimes so he can regroup for himself. Even when he closes down, you can stay open and available to life. You just have to focus and stay present in your body. Someday, this ability to focus will be so commonplace that all women will know this truth without so many explanations from therapists and healers. Women who lead my sweat lodges in the desert seem in touch with this part of themselves. They have a quality of self-forgetting. This does not come from a partner. It involves a quality these women bring from *within* themselves.

Now you are approaching what is so risky about this whole affair. Hindus believe that you and your lover were sent here from the spirit world as rough stones to smooth. You did some good rubbing and chafing with your parents, and that got rid of some of the rough edges. Now, you bring that flawed stone to a lover. You are somewhat a diamond in the rough. You can find a partner who encourages you to keep smoothing and polishing. That polishing process is what psychologists call *differentiation*. You keep working at it so that you soften and then meld easily to ultimately go to God and return to the spirit realm. When there is enough going for you in the relationship, you will stick with it. In other words, that relationship becomes your grinding stone, your life's work. Buddhists quip, "He who has a difficult wife has no need of the Buddha." That is your soul mate.

You have to decide if you are up for the task. Can you dare to be vulnerable and show yourself? Are you willing to have loved and lost? You must always enter into love expecting to lose. Don't fool yourself with promises. Let's face it, when 65 percent of marriages end in divorce, how can you hope for permanence? If nothing else, we all ultimately leave by dying. Can you be here for now?

Can you let yourself go with no guarantees? If you seek guarantees, it will limit your experience and, in a subtle way, it will make you hate the man you might love. While the man might be afraid of losing control, afraid of the power his lust has over him, you are also afraid of the tremendous power you wield, and you may turn that into a fear of losing his approval. Can you instead be brave enough to receive the unknown with no guarantees? Can you open yourself to be exposed? Can you reveal your fallibility, your vulnerability? If you are not putting those stakes on the table, then you may be hedging your bets and bargaining. That deadens your sexuality and doesn't let passion sweep you away.

If you don't wake up and grow up to this power, you inevitably will turn back to focus on controlling the body, limiting its juices. You will pretend your agenda is about weight and body image. You'll tell yourself, *Sure I'd like to have sex, but only when I get thin.* See how that will keep you fat? You will let your fat work *for* you, help you avoid the exciting though fearful prospect of growing into a sensual adult. If you are afraid of this unknown, you'll let your fears keep you fat. That's why you have to get started anyway, fat or thin.

No one could fault you for being fearful of this gift. You probably deeply sense how ominous this is and what delights as well as dangers are in store. You might be at best ambivalent about your sexuality, fearful of losing yourself in orgasm. Maybe you'll leave the planet and never return! Such fear is not necessarily unrealistic. Each time you couple consciously, you do lose a part of yourself. You will open to getting more out of life, but you also give up a dark yet protective coating, an ability to walk through life in a daze. In ecstasy, you lighten up, develop a bounce in your step and wildness in your eyes. You can almost feel the spaces between your cells.

In those spaces, a vibration starts. From those spaces, your soul or Self peers out. She wants to be seen. Your Self will change in relationship, in sexuality, in spirituality. If you are a growing, alive, sensitive organism as well as an ever evolving, passionate ball of energy, then it stands to reason that as *you* change, your sexuality will change, too. The two are interrelated. That is why you can go at your sexuality first and create the change there, and that can change your body and your Self. That is what makes this whole adventure so exciting and so precarious. In the past, you may have gone at the body first and thought the soul would follow. But, you may have been too full of your own self-doubt to trust *her* when she started to emerge. If you still distrust your own personal vibrations, you may regain weight and retreat into diagnosis. Instead, I invite you to begin a vulva vigil to welcome your soul.

Start by thinking of your lovemaking as a momentary act of prayer. In *Nature, Man and Woman*, Alan Watts wrote of such lovemaking: "Contemplative love, like contemplative meditation . . . has no specific aim; there is nothing particular that has to be made to happen (e.g., it does not purposely aim at orgasm). . . . In a relationship which has no goal other than itself, nothing is merely preliminary. . . ." In other words, enjoy the journey. At mealtimes, savor appetizers. At all times, attend to the first bite, the initial entry.

If you can hold this experience reverently and mystically, and cherish the tender mood, you will enter a state of grace you can carry along throughout the day. Some of my clients have described this truly connected orgasm the same way others describe meditation. They feel a sense of flow, relaxed concentration, and, with no effort, a beaming of the mind into alertness and concentration. They feel like they are hitting the wall with tremendous power, but like they could go on forever. They transcend themselves; they feel less self-involved, but totally at peace with themselves and others.

When I suggest prayer and meditation, my clients often argue, "What difference is that going to make?" I tell them, "Prayer does not change God. It changes the pray-er." By using your sexuality to go to a higher plane, both the doer and the act become sacred. E. M. Forster, in *Aspects of the Novel,* wrote, "When human beings love they try to get something. They also try to give something, and this double aim makes love more complicated than food or sleep. It is selfish and altruistic at the same time, and no amount of specialization in one direction quite atrophies the other." As much as your love-making can be a solitary quest for personal pleasure, there is also a mutuality with your partner, a heightened arousal you feel when you pick up on his arousal energy and he on yours. You desire his pleasure as well as your own. Eating, conversely, is done *by* yourself *to* yourself.

You may fear soulful sex, afraid you'll later feel more empty. After soulful, connected sex, you won't mind emptiness. If you have an addictive personality, this will be the hardest truth to bear. You've been fearing the void. Now you'll surrender to it. You actually *can* endure and survive emptiness. Just like drug addicts in recovery have to think of how to utilize all that excess time they used to spend copping a deal, you will have to find alternatives to the shopping, cooking, talking and salivating that are part and parcel of eating disorders. You'll grow to feel content without obsession.

I am so committed to teaching women about conscious coitus that at one time, I wanted to develop brothels for women within my treatment centers. I thought there should be a place where women could go to learn about focused sensuality with partners. In her novel *Butterfly*, Kathryn Harvey recounts activities in just such an establishment. The Mustang Ranch, a brothel outside Reno, Nevada, was going bankrupt and decided to open a women's wing to attract new business. Unfortunately, they didn't have enough time to advertise and help the concept catch on. I'm sure if we could have gotten the outing sanctioned by medical staff and insurance carriers, my patients would have brought them a thriving business!

I wanted to invite spiritually aware men into our facilities to teach patients to recognize how connection is or isn't made. It could resemble girls' night out at Chippendale's, but wouldn't be a group activity. My plan was to give our patients individual assignments, to use their sexuality to access spirituality. Even though I'd previously taken patients out on "flirt assignments," I now wanted to take them further into themselves, on a "Soul Search." They could turn on to soul to stay off of food.

In case you might feel offended at such a suggestion, you might compare this recommendation with many other more invasive and less pleasurable weight-loss alternatives administered to women by men in white lab coats. Intestinal bypass surgeries and liposuction are gross and commonplace. There have been many other treatments for this longing. In the early days of psychiatry, the response to women with excesses of weight or emotional energy was electric shock therapy to deaden sexual energy. Shocks were actually administered *to the genitals*. No matter what the complaint, the answer was hypnosis or electrotherapy to the genitals. In my early graduate training, I toured a prominent Los Angeles psychiatric hospital where stars' family members were secreted away. We were shown a convincing video of the benefits derived from shock treatments. Most memorable was a nurse's explanation that patients actually *wanted* this treatment, as it helped assuage guilt feelings; often it was masturbatory guilt. Such simple explanations for treating female libido abound. The last cliteroidectomy was performed in this country in 1945 on a five-year-old girl. The reason for it? . . . *Excessive masturbation*. By whose standards? Remember when Carl Jung visited our shores and saw suffragettes transferring sexual frustration into marches? He said that unless a woman is fulfilled, she will be a constant source of irritability and irritation. Modern medicine has replaced external shocks with internal chemicals all serving to sublimate that needy libido.

The Rules

There are no rules and no standards. You make them as you uncover, discover and discard. The first line of my first book is, "We're as fat as we are dishonest." To live and die as an authentic human requires attending to your own precious and volatile place of change. Your lover may say, "You're changing the rules!" Your reply is, "There are no rules. *I am changing!*"

You will hear addicts at Twelve-Step meetings talk about hating to be in "the hallways." No matter what dreaded outcome we might have to face, we'd rather know what lies ahead than wait for the answers. We don't do hallways. Well, to be human requires embracing your life and your loves *in the hallways*, in the uncertain, ever-changing, volatile present. At that flashpoint you will get to know yourself and your maker. Your lover can take you there.

You must stay in your fullness and wantonly insist and advertise that you want SEX. *E-e-e-w-w-w!* Does that bother you? Think about why. What are your hidden negative attitudes about sexuality? This project isn't as easy as it sounds. You aren't in it just to excite and titillate. It is easier to dress up from without than to change from within. It is much easier to buy lingerie than to touch your man. Buying activates your consumer instinct. Touching activates your heart and soul. Your vulva knows.

Doing It!

We live in a society that has worked overtime to paint sexuality as a dark and dirty endeavor, and especially to bar female sexuality and eroticism from the bedroom. Let's stop fearing it and look toward *doing it*. What does it mean to have sex? What do you give up? What do you get? We think about sex and death in the same secret ways. We are equally closed about both. We send flowers to weddings and funerals, but avoid discussion of the losses at either ceremony. Both events mark transitions where we transcend one state to go somewhere else. We are embarking on a soul's journey. As you become more mindful, you will be able to think about both sex and death more consciously. Both experiences create ecstasy, connecting you to the life force while you let go. If you have experienced the "little death" of orgasm, you can go more easily for the bigger letting go of your eventual physical demise. When you can practice and walk a path of total surrender, you will trust more and worry less. It needs no act of will.

We've been blessed with these resonant, pulsating bodies. We need to use them now to go to God. Sexual attraction creates energy in every cell. It is your job to keep the energy circulating and in open rotation. It is your job to pay attention. Too much has been laid on men to be responsible for the sex act. Many won't have the sensitivity to spiritual vibration that your body transmits.

Your body knows what you're waiting for. You are a ball of sexual energy and unless you come to terms with that fact and befriend it, know how to carry and use it, and stop fearing it, your sexuality will never be more than a dog wanting to scratch an itch. As a human being, your sexuality is more than relief from tension. Your sexual activity can be a natural tranquilizer or an energizer. We want to go deeper and higher to gain and trade energy.

Attention to Penetration

If you are just having sex to "get off," you are avoiding contact and remaining relatively alone. When you seek more than "sneezing sex," you will pay attention to penetration, paying attention to every single inch of the way. You will open up while still holding on to the perimeters. The trick is to become a semipermeable membrane, to let down boundaries and come back to center. All that flailing chatter out on the periphery was a way to protect too fragile a center.

You must pay exquisite attention to your own precious center. Each time you have sex without being mindful and attentive, you run the risk of eating over it. We all drift from time to time. When you leave the scene and move to automatic pilot, stop immediately and regroup until you are really there. Be grateful for the moments you notice. If you don't take these moments to regroup, you may start to hate sex. Imagine the horrific sex practiced in bygone days when men were instructed to delay ejaculation by thinking of baseball, and women were advised to grip the headboard and think of Mother England. No one was in the room.

If we were given this capacity for pleasure during sex, perhaps we're *supposed* to enjoy it! Can you believe that? Can you believe that pleasure can take you closer to Self? What if you could fill emptiness and find your way home by a new presence in your love life? You will probably judge yourself at first. You need to celebrate your seeker self and get her needs met. It is not selfish, but gracious. You are seeking amazing grace. The Indian teacher Osho tells us: "Unless you are overflowing with your own bliss, you are a danger to society, because a person who always sacrifices becomes a sadist."

YIMS
You're . . . in . . . My . . . Space

John Gray taught us in his runaway bestseller *Men Are from Mars, Women Are from Venus* that men need to go to their caves to be alone and think. Well, what about women? Remember, Virginia Woolf said one needs "a room of one's own." *You* also need space. When you transit out to the cosmos with your orgasm, you need time to regroup. You need time to be alone with yourself, being with your goddess and connecting with your own body. He took you there, he can lie beside you, but your cells are vibrating and you are resonating, and you don't need to be interactive on a personality level. You need to stay focused with yourself on a vibratory level. You are opened up to internal space.

In couples' counseling we often hear the woman complain that *he* has orgasm and then goes off into his own world. Well, after conscious coitus, you might be the same way. What if he goes off to an internal place where he doesn't invite you? Can you allow him a separate space and find your own? You may need to spend some quiet time going within to your goddess. One of the main reasons I created the "Hollis Hollow" retreats was because so many women didn't know how to access that goddess place. You long to go there, and a conscious lover can lead you there as well. While loving on this vibratory level, you will be more aware of the difference between internal and external spaces. When you let a man in, you are awakening your own drive to come out.

Ceil told me about always having great sex, but then feeling a little lonely afterward. "My feelings are so intense that I sometimes wonder if sex is worth the feelings of emptiness and pain that follow." After such an intense, involving experience, you also may feel a loss when you come back. You are flooded with intense connection and emotion, but ultimately have to come back to life as you know it. You might feel similarly about watching a sunset, walking in the desert, skiing in the mountains. In those moments of peace, you might be flooded with a glorious feeling of oneness and connection with natural beauty, yourself and your environment. As that fades, you face the reality that you are alone. Your partner brought you to a feeling of oneness, but you are two separate individuals. You are, in a sense, mourning leaving that cosmic home you've come to know. It is ever waiting there for your brief visitations, but it's not where you live. Allowing for the ebb and flow of feeling connection and then disconnection, whether with food or mate, lets you see the relationship between food, sex, life and death.

No Necrophilia!

So many of us are already deadened that the issue of death is best left unmentioned. It is sad when someone dies, but really a tragedy if they've never lived. They've never savored and sucked life dry. I want you to get megasatisfaction from all of life. If you are making love with a disconnected spirit, you may get more distortion, more sense of separation, more distance from your Self. This may leave you feeling so empty and alone that you may eventually have to leave. Instead of thinking about leaving, for now, learn how to pay full attention. Paying attention can help you stay. If solid bodies are a dance of molecules, then eating and dying are each reconfigurations of the dance. Death is just another passing moment. When you really and truly live each and every moment, you will not be afraid to die.

A young woman who called herself "Wanton Wanda" told of living with one man for more than a decade, all the while complaining to girlfriends about *his* low libido. Her friends responded with, "That's just how it is in long-term relationships." They'd accepted that guys just couldn't go the distance. They explained to "Wanda" that men seemed up for the chase and conquest, but not for the long haul. Wanda accepted this answer for a long time, but then her weight started creeping back on. She came to me saying, "Somehow there has to be more in life. Now that I don't use excess food to sedate me, I can't hang out in the dead zone. I hunger for life."

Wanda eventually left this man. She felt no life force within him. Her body unconsciously felt his death wish. Years later, he committed suicide. When she got the call, she gasped, "I knew it!"

Once you are turned on to this opening of internal space and using orgasm to go to God, you can no longer sleep with dead bodies. This may prove a loss and disruptive to your life. You can no longer make love with a disconnected soul. You can't love a ghost or a corpse. Once you discover how conscious coitus opens the cells, clears your vibration, excites and invites your spirit, you will find that sleeping with disengaged, unconnected men, instead of clearing you, will only give you more distortion, more density, more deadness. Maybe you've been struggling for years with certain men on a personality level, not paying attention to the vibratory incompatibility. If you do engage in this spiritual necrophilia, you will have to eat over it. Sex is for life. You can't use it in death.

Each day you'll have to choose life and energy over death and numbing. Some days you'll be ambivalent. Some days you'd rather hang out in the dead zone yourself. That is where food comes in. That's also why you may stay in deadened relationships. Unconscious sex and overeating let you stay numbed out, so you never have to face other appetites. So the next time you want to overeat, think of it as an act of slow suicide, and also an avoidance of your sensual, spiritual *life*.

You have to come to terms with your own death wish. Does your relationship encourage you to be more than you are or less? You may struggle within, trying to decide between merger or autonomy. You may long for space as well as merger. You may choose partners to help you play that out. If you are not comfortable with your own quest for apartness, you may blame your man. You will find that if you have your separate goddess self to touch and be touched by, you won't mind separations. Maybe you aren't meant to be either merged or separated, but instead to keep walking the halls.

Remember Carl Jung's idea that addiction is a longing in the depths of our beings, a spiritual emptiness, a "cosmic homesickness." We chose alcoholic spirits or other excesses to try to fill it. Going to God in orgasm could be like approaching that "cosmic home" to which Jung referred. You are capable of great ecstasy, and overeating or starving has kept you from going there.

You'll now be using sex to grow into spiritual adulthood. You may want to remain a child. You may have picked Peter Pans who wouldn't grow up so they wouldn't want your Tinker Bell to grow or change either. That may have seemed safe for a while, but true spiritual coupling happens between adults. You have to be old enough to know what you are doing and *who* is doing it.

Sexual, spiritual adulthood is not for sissies. It takes courage and commitment to look at yourself and change. You will have to ask yourself whether you want to love a child and be loved as a child, or become a full woman. If you are seeking cosmic home, you need to be a grown-up in your choice of mates. As Harold Kushner, author of *When Bad Things Happen to Good People*, wrote, "No matter how cute and charming a child might be, there is something incomplete about him."

As adults, we will try for completion. Falling in love is very serious business. We experience feelings similar to the fight-or-flight responses when physically threatened. We get weak knees, feel euphoria, the adrenal glands work overtime. We sweat, our hearts pound and our breath quickens. Our bodies know it's a matter of life or death.

Don't worry though; as you practice consciousness, you become more psychologically "at home," feeling a sense of safety. That safe feeling is something you create as a result of all the questions you've pondered in previous chapters. But, even with all that investigating, you can't know the taste of water until you drink it. Thirsty?

Drool Time

A blessed moment of connection and reverberation can quench the proper thirst. It can make you feel more alive than ever. That moment can happen if you've done the preparation first. You will have a meditative meltdown with your external environment. Along with conscious coitus, you need other conscious moments of letting go. You can take time alone watching cars pass, watching a tree in the breeze, watching kids play or a kite fly. These are moments of focus as well as intimate letting go that help you touch your cosmic home. That same sense of "home" can happen in moments of extreme terror and horror. It is a moment of self-forgetting. Touching home can also happen at a moment of merger with a sexual partner. Whether calm, excited or horrific, it is a moment of focus, a moment worth noting.

It is a moment of remembrance about how precious life is. Maybe we avoid it because it reminds us so much of impending death. Similar sensibilities are awakened in this life-giving art and in the dying act. If you've ever been scared in a near-death experience, you saw and experienced so much in such a brief time. You were challenging time and space. Life was elongated and highlighted. You were approaching that demarcation line into the spirit world.

The only other time you truly feel that merged is as a fetus inside the womb. At birth, you surely knew the atmosphere had changed. You moved from one way of being to another. Breathing in new air in this atmosphere changed your consciousness. Breathe now and think about this. When you were an infant, touching the bars on that crib, you had an early experience of alienation. Earlier in the womb, you had no sense of separation between outside and inside. Your internal world was the whole world. You floated around heaven all day. Once outside that world, you felt cold steel, or slightly warmer wood, but still "differentness." The whole world does not reside within you. You are lonely.

As you practice moments of eating or loving consciously, you will heal some of that loneliness. You will slow down to breathe often. You will experience your body filling. Imagine that your body is a happy puppy almost ready to wag its tail. There is stimulation, a vibration of energy traveling through you. Can you tolerate elongating those moments?

Sex Is the Way

The time is now. That moment of timelessness is what happens when the meal is right and when the loving is right. Hunting, eating, sex and death all create that timeless, momentous opportunity. It is a momentary opportunity for transcendence, when our bodies vibrate toward heaven, a little more willing to leave solid, secure ground. We are sensing and surrendering to our own personal vibration. That sense of cells vibrating creates a feeling of space and light within.

Religious prelates may speak of this as the transcendence into peace everlasting. Women after childbirth report a holy stillness—a "globed feeling." Participants at "Hollis Hollow" retreats speak of the same transcendence after the sweat lodge ceremonies. Before the late 1970s, only men participated in sweat lodges. The sweats were created for men to feel what childbirth was like. Female bodies had experienced searing transcendence during childbirth; they'd touched the cosmos. Obstetric staff speak about a peak "transition phase" in childbirth, just as the head is crowning. The mother experiences excruciating pain as well as exuberant joy. With uterine contractions, and all that expenditure of energy, it is often likened to orgasm. Sex therapist Betty Dodson was so bold as to suggest that fathers, at the moment of birth, stimulate the mother's clitoris as the baby's head is crowning. This would allow the mother to experience even more joy in childbirth and would give the infant its first sensual message.

Each moment you can truly savor your experience is training for the ultimate surrender and letting go into death. How much can you tolerate the *now?* There is a Hindu story about a man walking mindlessly along the edge of a cliff. He doesn't watch where he is going and stumbles off the edge. Miraculously, he grabs a berry bush laden with berries and hangs precariously, looking down on Bengal tigers circling below. His first thought is regret about the past. He looks up at the ridge and laments, "How stupid I was not to watch my path more closely." He clutches tighter to the bush and notices how luscious the berries look. Then his thoughts jump to fear of the future: "Yikes, I'm going to drop down and be gobbled up!" Instead of focusing on any past or future event, his teacher would encourage him to stay in the now, advising him to *"savor the berries."*

Surface Tension

There's a lot going on each and every moment in each and every cell. You are now walking that path between heaven and hell, trekking the earth, aspiring to the heavens. Angels are secure on high. They busy themselves with heavenly pursuits. Animals are secure below. They take their naps and don't worry much. Humans in the middle ground are fraught with neuroses. We are volatile, changeable, ever on the brink. It's that borderland where boundaries ebb and flow that causes difficulty. We live a life of constant change and negotiation.

We inhabit animal bodies—our temples. We invite others in to experience the flame of our sexual energy and our life force. Your sexuality is not owned or delivered by another. It is instead your own tool, the means by which you find your own path to a potential, powerful wholeness. You stand at the edge of the pool, afraid to dip a toe. You stand in your own shadow, but cannot turn around. Thank heaven for that sex drive! Eros forces you to grow. In turning toward the body, toward your man, toward eroticism, you loosen up and become ready to transform energy.

This is bound to make you tense. We actually face dying when we go toward life. It *is* a war.

Let's look at the war zone. In high school science classes, we learned about "surface tension" with a glass of water. The teacher filled a glass well to overflowing, then set it down quite still. With just a few more drops added, the top of the water rose in a mound, brimming *above* the top of the glass, but not a drop spilled over. How did that happen? It was explained that the water was held in by *surface tension*. It had to do with the molecules being so volatile and in transition that they created a holding energy field. The water molecules at the bottom of the glass, the grounded unchanging ones, had no problem with identity. They were pure H_2O—water. Their current was quiet, actually nonexistent. They didn't change. Above the glass was more action. Some molecules had evaporated out of the water, becoming more oxygen, less hydrogen. They existed as two parts oxygen: O_2. They were secure as air until they'd condense again to become water. But at the surface, at the top of the glass, there was a lot more going on. There was a lot of volatility and action, energy and power. Some water molecules were evaporating, jumping out to the air. Some air was condensing and falling back into the glass as water. The energy created by this activity held the water along the top of the glass, even though it looked like it should have spilled over. A single layer of molecules holds it all together. Conscious coitus helps you access that energy field at the boundary *between* two people. The tension and power at our boundaries, at the borderline of experience, is powerful and mysterious!

What does this have to do with sex and spirit? Well, when you decide to have your boundary penetrated, whether with food or another substance or person, you awaken in your molecules the concept of change. If you are conscious about what is really going on with these activities, you will be up for change, for melting, for remaking yourself each time anew. You won't expect to have sex and not be changed or affected in some way. You actually feel your own surface tension as you prepare to melt. A part of you is holding on, while the greater urge is to let go.

Be Still and Know That I Am God

Letting go may have nothing to do with romantic love. Romantic love is all projection, having more to do with greeting cards, roses and chocolates. Going for the connection I am proposing is going toward a goal of elevating your *own* vibration. You want *moments* that take you higher. We are all vibrating energies, and we want to raise the level of vibration and change our own energy field.

A tremolo is a phrase in music played as a quick vibration; it's a very rich tone. A good tremolo is not *on* the note evenly, but slightly ajar, in the space *between* notes. It is not "hooty." It is a trembling, fluttering reverberation. Psychologically it hearkens, echoes and calls to distant, long-gone days. A musician at the Metropolitan Opera told me that "a tremolo stretches the note to increase the passion."

Hello! This is the kind of stretch I want you to try in your loving. But to accomplish this, you must be vulnerable to that significant "other." Your knowing about connection at this vibratory level may explain why you have known some unlikely partners. You might choose a man for your bedroom whom you can't sit down with in the parlor. You may be vibrationally, though not socially, compatible. Often sex will be most erotic and satisfying with men you wouldn't take out in public. Some women report, "the sleazier, the better." Their mothers might hope they'd marry the Ashley Wilkeses of the world, but their bodies belong to Rhett Butler.

But it's really less about the man and more about *you*. Be careful not to let other people's agendas distract you. If you stay true to developing your own personal passion, a specific *you* will emerge. You are a specific woman, a specific energy to be penetrated. Be careful that you don't avoid your own self-growth on this level by becoming a rescuing nurse involved in other people's pain. That won't help you sort out who *you* are. You'll instead just learn who you are in relation to problems. That may not bring out your erotic self.

You might be a woman who has refused self-growth by getting involved in other people's problems and pain. You might be in a relationship that discourages your growth. In a way, you may be using those people as an avoidance technique. Child rearing is certainly an honorable excuse for such avoidance. Please remember, it will help your children if you have a better sex life.

Mystics defined eros as the "attraction of the soul upward to ideals." Tantric practitioners talk of sex as meditation and transformation. Sexual energy can be a powerful source for self-realization. If you take a look at Indian art, you will often see a woman teased by male energy. Shiva held tremendous sexual energy but was also the greatest ascetic. He was a tease. Truly sensual and erotic women don't want to play the game and don't want to be teased. Many of the "tango dancer" men were appealing because they kept women in that anxious, uncertain place. Women who were overweight during much of their dating lives are quite sensitive to the issue of teasing. Even when it is sexual and playful, offense is taken.

Both partners crave enlightenment, seeking more lightness in being. Most of us have been taught to live with a paradox and conflict between eroticism and asceticism. Sex, a natural function and drive, is to be denied, and so we practice religion to overcome our true natures. Religion teaches us renunciation and deprivation of the flesh. In most societies, women are given the bad rap as the holders of that lustful sensual energy.

Eve brought Adam the apple. The body resides in the dark side and must be controlled. The ultimate in religious devotion, the monastic life, teaches us to live in "deprivation." Could it be possible that true deification would allow a surrender to the Self, to your own true nature? How bad could she be?

You must use your Self to move beyond yourself. Religion teaches suppression with awareness. You need instead *indulgence* with awareness. You need to become friendly with your own sexual energy and then transform it. You can transform sex into meditation. In the ancient world, prostitutes were independent scholars performing vital functions and helping men go higher. If that's what sex is for, then we have to be ever more careful of our activities. What are you in it for? A date for dinner? You've been to dinner. . . . Since you know that this life is a transition, it becomes important to go one level below the surface to find connection on a deeper level. Your intimacy must have integrity.

Wisdom of the Organism

Again, the body doesn't lie. Can you trust it? Our bodies may know more than our minds can figure out. The 21 April 1997 *Time* magazine health report cited statistics that couldn't be explained. Young girls were approaching menarche early. Most physicians look for pubescence in girls by age eleven; but, by age eight, 48 percent of black girls and 15 percent of white girls begin puberty. Researchers could not explain the earlier onset. I'd venture to say it has something to do with permission and accessibility and cultural attitudes allowing and expecting certain behaviors. If we expect sex earlier, the body catches up with the psyche.

Your sexuality baffles medical science. While young girls awaken sooner than expected, older women carry on longer than previously known. I was speaking to a lively group at the Border's Book Store in Bailey's Crossroads, Virginia. A lovely redheaded woman drew my attention as she spoke up heatedly. She was irritated with my talk and kept asking me questions about my concern regarding excessive prescriptions of Prozac. Didn't I understand how it helped so many become more functional? Didn't I acknowledge that some in the population actually did need it? What is wrong with something that we *know* is "nonaddicting"? I gave her standard answers. Two percent of the population probably need prescribed drugs. Why was I seeing 85 percent of my hospital admissions bingeing and purging and *on* Prozac? Why was 78 percent of my typical audience on Prozac? I commented that I'd just come back from a therapists' convention where the exhibitor selling Paxil as a viable treatment plan was answering a therapist's question about "withdrawals." He was careful to reframe the term as "discontinuance disturbance." Did changing the name sweeten the smell? I explained that I just wanted more answers. The rose didn't smell sweet.

She kept the heat up. She asked those kinds of hostile questions that mask a powerful statement. However, she wouldn't come up with the statement. It was clear to me that she must be on some drug herself and that my lecture caused her to question things she preferred to keep hidden. She approached the podium last as others were filing out.

"I've been on Paxil a couple of months. The doctor told me 'no side effects,' but he never warned me about how it decreases libido. I've been so asexual. I'm fifty-eight and I have a new boyfriend and I really want to get it on." She smiled coyly.

"Then get off the Paxil," I answered matter-of-factly. She bristled.

"Just like that? But what about the doctor?"

"You want him, too?" I joked, going for an easy "lightness" to soften a difficult message.

She laughed.

I responded, "Look, these doctors don't necessarily know everything about sexually alive midlife women."

A big smile lit her face. "You know, you're right. I told him about the low libido, and I asked him what to do. He said, 'Try not taking the drug the day you want to have sex.'" She smiled. "The day? The *day!* He doesn't have a clue that I might want to get laid *every* day."

"Well, dear, that shows what he knows. Sometimes a younger male doctor just can't fathom an older woman *wanting* sex. I don't care what he's learned in medical school, emotionally he can't acknowledge that his mom has a sex life."

I looked at her and continued, "You are the one who will have to decide how important it is to *you*. You deserve to have an active sex life. You've met a man. Why can't you enjoy him? Maybe this is an ominous endeavor, a major transition. So you get nervous. . . . Paxil? Maybe the newness and excitement are hard to take. . . . Paxil? Maybe you need to go through this next stage of growth. . . . Paxil? You can be experiencing anxiety because it is such a powerful transition phase for you. If you take the drugs, you avoid the anxiety, the sense of loss as well as release, you learn nothing about transiting out. How important is it?"

She knew it was a very important question. She leaned over and said, "I love you," as she kissed me on the cheek. I wonder who's kissing her now. I wonder if and how she got off the Paxil.

How to Do It?

No matter how wise you become, sex takes constant practice. Does anyone really know how? This aspect of our lives is unpredictable, ever-changing, fraught with both peril and ecstasy, and largely unknown to most of us. No one really knows how. If you find someone who wants to outline your path, throw them aside and keep on trudgin'. You'll find the way.

Your own hand can lead you. Look down at your hand and view it as the objective tool it is. Think about how you use it, how it serves you; note its purpose. Don't bother evaluating whether you like its shape, veins or spots. We're looking at function, not form. Now close your eyes and think of that same hand. More precisely, *feel* that same hand. Feel the capillaries, corpuscles, energy vibrating out to your fingertips. You have a sense of your hand even though you don't see it. That vibratory level is the one on which you discharge as you surrender in orgasm.

Thinking of your capillaries, focusing on transmission of energies, should make you appreciate the aliveness of your senses. When you become aware of your own personal aliveness and can stay still holding the wonder of it, you begin to know your own pulse. You will seek men who are themselves alive and in touch with theirs. Those are the men who are in it for energy and connection, not for performance evaluations or power struggles. There will be those men who really want to make contact and seek sex as a spiritual, mystical, creative union that grows slowly, majestically, and develops into a third force, separate from the lovers and their organs. Once encountering such a man, your life will never be the same. You will attract such a man when you have done the necessary work.

He will be interested in sharing with you knowledge of *a way of being*. He may not have a bag of tricks, a textbook of techniques. He will know about being patient and paying attention. He will be able to wait with you to listen for the echo of your hollow, empty place. Your body's fluid responses will awaken the call to the other to come out. When that call vibrates between you, there's nothing to do but wait. As the AA Big Book says, "The answers will come when your own house is in order."

The Dance of Death

A fan asked Isadora Duncan if she could explain her dance. She replied, "My dear, if I could explain it, I wouldn't have to dance it." These matters call for expression in moving pictures. You might recall the old cartoons where large cats chased tiny birds endlessly across the screen. We squealed and delighted at the guile and dexterity of the bird outwitting the cat. In screen life, the bird escaped, but in real life, the bird bites the dust. I wonder how it would have affected our childhood sensibilities had the cartoonist captured the true passion of the end moment for the doomed bird.

Freud said we all have an ambivalent commitment to both life and death. Remember, the French call orgasm *la petite mort*, the little death. Humans, like no other animals, have awareness of our own impending death. This causes us to live differently. In his book *Why Zebras Don't Get Ulcers*, Robert Sapolsky describes zebras as peaceful because they live so much in the now and have no anticipation of their impending doom. As humans, we receive more information. Dying into the surrender of orgasm can be our way of experimenting, practicing, getting ready. We know we've got to go.

When the cat corners the bird, there is an exquisite moment of death when all running stops, but there is a vibrating communication going on between the two creatures. It is a moment of total stillness when all internal vibrations are at maximum frequency. It's just like the moment Elvis left the building. The cat and bird share an exquisite moment of intimacy that allows no others in. Those outside the dance often don't understand.

In that moment, looking death squarely in the face, both cat and bird are *one*. They have entered another dance. Both are part of a third place: a dance of death. Neither has the separate identity of predator or victim. They both exquisitely play out their roles. There is no differentiation between inside and outside. They are both in the middle. Their eyes lock, both are poised to spring and both are part of the same experience. Neither one is more or less noble than the other; neither one is more or less necessary to the ultimate end of the dance. They face off and they know on a deep level that they are part of the life force, the wisdom of the universe.

Often, the bird knows it's his last moment and the last thing he will see is the eyes of that cat. The bird is not thinking about the past or the future. All that exists are cat eyes. The bird surrenders to this moment as time everlasting.

Your surrender in sex holds some of the same elements. You surrender on a vibratory level to an inevitable resonance. As you watch two flamenco dancers poised in each other's faces, almost motionless, breathing into each other, feet tapping out a continuous buzz as castanets join in, you feel an electricity and urgency, and a willingness to die. The tension of opposites creates such a vibratory field that there is a momentous explosion.

In that moment, there is nowhere else either can ever be.

This drive to merge into oblivion and be carried away has everything to do with eating and sex and death. We long for it and run from it and have to keep doing the dance. It is a dance of death, a self-forgetting surrender of the ego. There is a difference between the sexual encounter and the loss of self into food. When you lose yourself to chocolate-chip ice cream, it is a slow melt with very little tension. When you lose yourself to crunchies like potato chips, you are expressing irritation, but getting no connection. Food is deadening while sex is enlivening. When you surrender during sex, you receive heightened awareness from keen vibrations transmitted at the moment of loss. When you dance into sex and love, you are vibrating and more alive, but definitely more at risk.

Dying may not seem such a mysterious or fearful fate if you've had some of these good little deaths throughout your life. All these moments can be holy. You can experience your own body with the same reverence and attention to vibration as the bird and the cat.

It's an animal, natural thing, having nothing to do with intellect. The barriers between inside and outside are melted. He comes in, you open up. Your body is a dance of molecules and atoms, and somehow the boundaries and separations of your thick hide, your egotistical self, melt. You are part of life. Like the hunter who steps into stillness before lunging that fatal spear into the bison, or the flamenco dancers who tease and breathe, waiting to pounce into lust, we are all standing at erect, exquisite attention. Nothing exists but our breathing and that vibration. That intense moment penetrates beyond opposites. In a thunderous moment of power, you feel a great stillness and silence. You go beyond all terror of annihilation and fall willingly into an inner ascent. All vibrations are magnified while all sense of boundaries is melted. In that moment come answers about active and passive, vulnerability and penetration, hunter and hunted, eater and eaten, love and death. A door opens and in an exquisite moment of seeming death, you actually begin to *be*. Life everlasting begins.

Afterword

As the final edits were completed for this book, the Starr Report was sent to Congress. The American public is now familiar with this document's graphic detail and full exposure of sexuality between President Clinton and a young woman who has had a lifelong struggle with weight. The kind of lurid details described in that report are not the same experiences I encourage. I want to elevate such activities to a higher plane of consciousness, and I encourage my readers to do the same.

Perhaps the Starr Report will sear out of our national consciousness any last vestiges of inhuman Puritanism. In addition, I hope it will instill within our national ethos a greater expectation from sexuality. Then, we can enter the millennium as adult sexual/spiritual beings.

I welcome any and all responses to this text, and I will try to answer your comments as best I can. With your permission, some letters may be paraphrased in my forthcoming book, *Vulva Voices*.

Please send your comments to:

HOLSEM, Inc./Hollis Seminars
2565 Broadway, Suite 711
New York, NY 10025

Works Cited and Suggested Reading List

Ackerman, Diane. *A Natural History of Love.* New York: Random House, 1995.

Al-Anon Family Groups. *One Day at a Time at Al-Anon.* Virginia Beach, Va.: Al-Anon Family Group Headquarters, Inc. 1968.

Alcoholics Anonymous World Services, Inc., staff, ed. *Big Book of Alcoholics Anonymous.* New York: Alcoholics Anonymous World Services, Inc., 1939, rev. 1990.

Anderson, Christopher. *An Affair to Remember: The Remarkable Love Story of Katharine Hepburn and Spencer Tracy* (abridged) Grand Haven, Mich.: Brilliance Corporation, 1997. Sound recording.

Anderson, Sherry Ruth, and Patricia Hopkins. *The Feminine Face of God: The Unfolding of the Sacred in Women.* New York: Bantam, 1995.

Avna, Joan, and Diana Waltz. *Celibate Wives: Breaking the Silence.* Los Angeles: Lowell House, 1994.

Bettelheim, Bruno. *The Uses of Enchantment: The Meaning and Importance of Fairy Tales.* New York: Random House, 1989.

Bloom, Amy. *Come to Me.* New York: HarperCollins, 1992.

Bloomfield, Harold, et al. *Lifemates: The Love Fitness Program for a Lasting Relationship.* New York: NAL-Dutton, 1992.

Brown, Peter. *The Body and Society: Men, Women and Sexual Renunciation in Early Christianity.* Ft. Collins, Colo.: Colorado University Press, 1990.

Bruch, Hilde. *Eating Disorders: Obesity, Anorexia Nerovsa, and the Person Within.* New York: Basic Books, 1973.

Campion, Jane. *The Piano.* 35 mm., 121 mins. Miramax, 1993.

Caplan, Paula J. *The Myth of Women's Masochism.* Toronto: University of Toronto Press, 1993.

Carter, Steven, and Julia Sokol. *What Really Happens in Bed? A Demystification of Sex.* New York: M. Evans & Co., 1989.

Cassell, Carol. *Swept Away: Why Women Fear Their Own Sexuality.* New York: Simon & Schuster Trade, 1984.

Chandler, Charlotte. *The Ultimate Seduction.* Garden City, N.Y.: Doubleday & Co., Inc., 1984.

Chapman, Arthur Harry. *The Treatment Techniques of Harry Stack Sullivan.* New York: Brunner-Mazel, 1978.

Chernin, Kim. *The Obsession.* New York: HarperCollins, 1994.

Cixous, Helene, and Catherine Clement. *Newly Born Woman.* Minneapolis, Minn.: University of Minnesota Press, 1986.

Covey, Stephen R. *The Seven Habits of Highly Effective People.* New York: Simon & Schuster Trade, 1989.

Crisp, Arthur H. "Some Aspects of the Relationship Between Body Weight and Sexual Behavior with Particular Reference to Massive Obesity and Anorexia Nervosa." Paper presented at the Association for the Study of Obesity meeting, Royal Society of Medicine, Academic Department of Psychiatry, St. George's Hospital Medical School, Tooting, London, S.W. #17, 9 December 1976.

Daniell, Rosemary. *Sleeping with Soldiers: In Search of the Macho Man.* New York: Holt, Rinehart & Winston, 1984.

Dodson, Betty. *Sex for One: The Joy of Selfloving.* New York: Crown Publishing Group, 1992.

Dworkin, Andrea. *Intercourse.* New York: New York Free Press, 1987.

Ehrenreich, Barbara. *The Hearts of Men: The American Dream and the Flight from Commitment.* New York: Doubleday, 1984.

Ehrenreich, Barbara, Elizabeth Hess, and Gloria Jacobs. *Re-Making Love: The Feminization of Sex.* New York: Doubleday, 1987.

Fisher, B. *Conversations with M. F. K. Fisher.* Jackson, Miss.: University of Mississippi Press, 1992.

Fisher, Helen. *Anatomy of Love: The Mysteries of Mating, Marriage and Why We Stray.* New York: Fawcett, 1994.

Forster, E. M. *Aspects of the Novel.* Orlando, Fla.: Harcourt Brace, 1956.

French, Marilyn. *The Women's Room.* New York: Ballantine, 1993.

Freud, Sigmund and Fritz Wittels. *Freud and the Child Woman: The Memoirs of Fritz Wittels.* Edited and with a preface by Edward Timms. New Haven: Yale University Press, 1995.

Friday, Nancy. *My Secret Garden.* Edited by Julie Rubinstein. New York: Simon & Schuster, Pocket Books, 1991.

————. *Women on Top.* New York: Simon & Schuster, Pocket Books, 1993.

Friedman, Manis, and Morris J. S. Friedman. *Doesn't Anyone Blush Anymore? Love, Intimacy and the Art of Marriage.* 4th edition. Bais Chana Press, 1997.

Glenmullen, Joseph. *The Pornographer's Grief: And Other Tales of Human Sexuality.* Edison, N. J.: Smithmark, 1993.

Gray, John. *Men Are from Mars, Women Are from Venus: A Practical Guide for Improving Communication and Getting What You Want in Your Relationships.* New York: HarperCollins, 1993.

Greer, Germaine. *The Change: Women, Aging and the Menopause.* New York: Fawcett, 1993.

Griscom, Chris. *Ecstasy Is a New Frequency: Teachings of the Light Institute.* Santa Fe, N.Mex.: Bear & Co., 1987.

Harvey, Kathryn. *Butterfly.* New York: Random House, 1988.

Heimel, Cynthia. *If You Can't Live Without Me, Why Aren't You Dead Yet?* New York: HarperCollins, 1992.

Hemingway, Ernest. *For Whom the Bell Tolls.* New York: Simon & Schuster, Scribner, 1940.

Hepburn, Katharine. *Me.* New York: Ballantine Books, 1996.

Heyn, Dalma. *The Erotic Silence of the American Wife.* New York: NAL-Dutton, 1997.

Hinshelwood, R. D. *A Dictionary of Kleinian Thought.* London: Free Association Books, 1989.

Hite, Shere. *The Hite Report.* New York: Knopf, 1987.

———. *Women and Love: A Cultural Revolution in Progress.* New York: Knopf, 1987.

Hogenson, George B. *Jung's Struggle with Freud,* rev. ed. Wilmette, Ill.: Chiron, 1994.

Hollis, Judi. *Divine Dine.* 60 mins., HOLSEM Productions, 1989, videocassette.

———. *Fat Is a Family Affair.* San Francisco: Harper San Francisco, and Center City, Minn.: Hazelden, 1985.

———. *Fat & Furious: Women and Food Obsession.* New York: Ballantine, 1995.

Horney, Karen. *Feminine Psychology.* Edited and with an introduction by Harold Kelman. New York: Norton, 1973.

Hwang, David Henry. *M. Butterfly.* New York: Penguin USA, 1994.

Ireland, Mardy S. *Reconceiving Women: Separating Motherhood from Female Identity.* New York: Guilford Press, 1993.

Jaglom, Henry. *Eating.* 35 mm., 110 mins. International Rainbow Pictures, 1990.

Janus, Samuel S., and Cynthia L. Janus. *The Janus Report on Sexual Behavior.* New York: John Wiley & Sons, Inc., 1993.

Jong, Erica. *Fear of Flying.* New York: Doubleday, 1994.

Kushner, Harold. *When Bad Things Happen to Good People.* New York: Avon, 1983.

Laing, R. D. *The Politics of Experience.* New York: Pantheon Books, 1967.

Langford, Laurie. *If It's Love You Want, Why Settle for Just Sex? Practical Steps to Avoid Having Sex Too Soon.* Rocklin, Calif.: Prima Publishing, 1996.

Lawrence, D. H. *Women in Love.* New York: Knopf, 1992.

———. *Lady Chatterley's Lover.* New York: Bantam, 1983.

Lisle, Laurie. *Without Child: Challenging the Stigma of Childlessness.* New York: Ballantine, 1996.

Marshall, Garry. *Pretty Woman.* 35mm., 119 mins. Touchstone Pictures, 1990.

Maurer, Harry. *Sex: Real People Talk About What They Really Do.* New York: Viking Penguin, 1995.

May, Rollo. *The Courage to Create,* 1st ed. New York: Norton, 1975.

Mayer, Ken. *Real Women Don't Diet!* New York: Kensington Publishing Corp., 1993.

Meadow, Rosalyn M., and Lillie Weiss. *Women's Conflicts About Eating and Sexuality: The Relationship Between Food and Sex.* New York: Harrington Park, 1992.

Meldman, Louis William. *Mystical Sex: Love, Ecstasy and the Mystical Experience.* Rockport, Mass.: Element Books, Inc., 1997.

Morris, Desmond. *Intimate Behavior.* New York: Kodansha America, Inc., 1997.

Nelson, Mariah. *The Stronger Women Get, the More Men Love Football.* New York: Avon, 1995.

Orbach, Susie. *Fat Is a Feminist Issue.* New York: Berkley Publishing, 1987.

Osho. *Tantra, Spirituality & Sex.* Edited by Swami D. Anutoshen. New York: Osho America, 1994.

Our Bodies, Ourselves: A Book by and for Women. 25th anniversary edition. Edited by Boston Women's Health Books' collective staff. New York: Simon & Schuster Trade, 1996.

Paglia, Camille. *Sexual Personae: Art and Decadence from Nefertiti to Emily Dickinson.* New York: Random House, 1991.

Rich, Adrienne. *On Lies, Secrets and Selected Prose 1966–1978.* New York: Norton, 1979.

Robinson, Phil Alden. *Field of Dreams.* 35 mm., 107 mins. Universal Studios, 1989.

Roiphe, Katie. *The Morning After: Sex, Fear and Feminism.* New York: Little, Brown, 1994.

Rossner, Judith. *August.* New York: Warner Books, 1989.

Sapolsky, Robert M. *Why Zebras Don't Get Ulcers: A Guide to Stress, Stress-Related Diseases and Coping.* New York: W. H. Freeman & Co., 1995.

Sartre, Jean-Paul. *Truth and Existence.* Edited and with an introduction by Ronald Aronson. Chicago: University of Chicago Press, 1992.

Scantling, Sandra R., and Sue Browder. *Ordinary Women, Extraordinary Sex: Releasing the Passion Within.* New York: NAL-Dutton, 1994.

Schnarch, David. *Constructing the Sexual Crucible.* New York: Norton, 1991.

——. *Passionate Marriage: Sex, Love and Intimacy in Emotionally Committed Relationships.* New York: Norton, 1997.

Sherman, Roger M. *Foodfright.* 16mm., 28 mins. Florentine Films, 1988.

Sherman, Vincent. *Mr. Skeffington.* 35 mm., 145 mins. Warner Bros., 1944.

Snowden, Lynn. *Nine Lives: From Stripper to Schoolteacher: My Year Long Odyssey in the Workplace.* New York: Norton, 1994.

Steinem, Gloria. *Revolution from Within: A Book of Self-Esteem.* New York: Little, Brown, 1992.

Stoltenberg, John. *What Makes Pornography "Sexy"?* Thistle Series of Chapbooks. Minneapolis: Milkweed Editions, 1994.

Strasberg, Susan. *Marilyn and Me: Sisters, Rituals, Friends.* New York: Warner Books, 1992.

Swift, Rachel. *How to Have an Orgasm . . . As Often As You Want.* New York: Carroll & Graf, 1993.

Thurber, James, and E. B. White. *Is Sex Necessary?* Cutchogue, N.Y.: Buccaneer Books, 1990.

Tisdale, Sallie. *Talk Dirty to Me: An Intimate Philosophy of Sex.* Anchor, N.Y.: Doubleday, 1995.

Truffaut, François. *Jules et Jim.* 35 mm., 110 mins. Les Films du Carosse, 1961.

Venus, Brenda. *Secrets of Seduction.* New York: NAL-Dutton, 1996.

Waal, Frans. *Bonobo: The Forgotten Ape.* Berkeley, Calif.: University of California Press, 1997.

Watts, Alan. *Nature, Man and Woman.* New York: Random House, 1991.

Weatherby, W. J. *Conversations with Marilyn.* New York: Little, Brown, 1992.

Weil, Andrew. *Eight Weeks to Optimum Health: A Proven Program for Taking Advantage of Your Body's Natural Healing Power.* New York: Knopf, 1997.

West, Morris. *The Joy of Writing Sex.* Cincinnati: Elizabeth Benedict's Story Press, 1996.

Westheimer, Ruth, and Jonathan Mark. *Heavenly Sex: Sex and the Jewish Tradition.* New York: New York University Press, 1995.

Willis, Ellen. *No More Nice Girls: Countercultural Essays.* Hanover, N.H.: University of New England Press, 1992.

Wolf, Naomi. *The Beauty Myth: How Images of Beauty Are Used Against Women.* New York: Doubleday, 1992.

———. *Promiscuities: The Secret Struggle for Womanhood.* New York: Random House, 1997.

Wood, Beatrice. *I Shock Myself: The Autobiography of Beatrice Wood.* Edited by Lindsay Smith. San Francisco: Chronicle Books, 1985.

Woolf, Virginia. *A Room of One's Own.* Orlando, Fla.: Harcourt Brace, 1989.

Wyse, Lois. *Women Make the Best Friends.* Thorndike, Maine: Thorndike Press, 1996.

Index

About the Author

r. Judi Hollis has been counseling addicted families since 1967, when she helped open New York City's Phoenix House Programs. Since that time, she has been training counselors internationally, as well as opening addiction treatment centers around the country, most notably her own HOPE Institutes, which were the first Twelve-Step eating-disorder units.

She holds graduate degrees in rehabilitation counseling and psychology from the University of Southern California (USC) and is a licensed marriage and family counselor. She has taught at USC, Goddard College, Chapman College and the University of California at Los Angeles (UCLA). She has also led community groups and served on hospital staffs around the world.

Her bestselling *Fat Is a Family Affair* was a groundbreaking treatise in the treatment field. It was followed by *Fat & Furious* and many workbooks, and video- and audiotapes. She currently maintains personal consulting practices on both coasts, dividing her time between New York City and Palm Springs.

With her radio show, *Dr. Jude's Ladies' Locker Room*, she developed an audience for the material in this book. She appears often on television with Oprah, Sally, Maury, Leeza and others, and her work has been featured in *Shape, Teen, Glamour, Self, Cosmopolitan* and *Elle* magazines.

Dr. Hollis can be reached by calling toll-free:

800-8-E-N-O-U-G-H

Other Materials by Dr. Judi Hollis

*J*udi Hollis has devoted the last thirty years to educating recovering individuals and their families. Thousands have benefited from her residential and inpatient treatment programs and nationwide seminars. The following resource list is provided to assist you in your further exploration of the ideas presented in this book.

Also by Dr. Judi Hollis:

BOOKS

Fat & Furious (Ballantine)
Fat Is a Family Affair (Harper San Francisco and Hazelden)
It's Not a Dress Rehearsal (HOLSEM Productions)
Let Them Eat Cake (HOLSEM Productions)

PAMPHLETS

(All published by HOLSEM Productions)
"Accepting Powerlessness"
"Humility vs. Humiliation"
"I'm Not Ready Yet"
"Relapse for Eating Disorder Sufferers"
"Resisting Recovery"

"Transferring Obsessions"
"When AAs Go to OA"

VIDEOTAPES

Dark Secrets, Bright Victory (Hazelden Foundation/Dick
   Young Productions, New York City)
Divine Dine (HOLSEM Productions)
Family Matters (Hazelden Foundation/Dick Young
   Productions, New York City)
Hot & Heavy (HOLSEM Productions)
Live to Eat—Eat to Live (HOLSEM Productions)
Starving for Perfection (HOLSEM Productions)

AUDIOTAPES

Codependent Compulsions (HOLSEM Productions)
Fat & Furious (HOLSEM Productions)
Fat Is a Family Affair (Hazelden)
Going Deep (HOLSEM Productions)
Hope for Compulsive Overeaters, vols. 1 & 2 (Hazelden)
Hot & Heavy (HOLSEM Productions)
Let's Talk Radio (HOLSEM Productions)
Y 2 OA? (HOLSEM Productions)

For more information about video- and audiotapes, books
and seminars, please call toll-free:

800-8-E-N-O-U-G-H